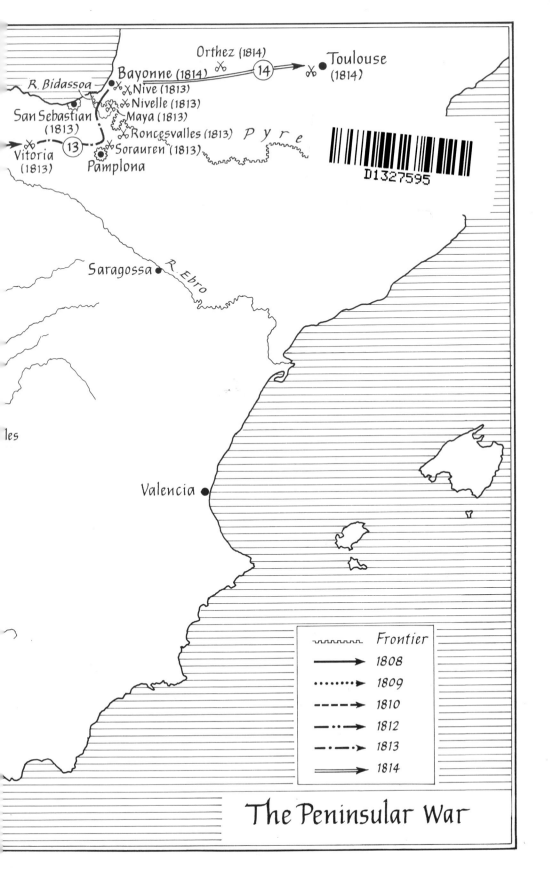

The Peninsular War

Wellington's Peninsular War

WELLINGTON'S PENINSULAR WAR

Battles and Battlefields

Julian Paget

LEO COOPER
LONDON

First published in 1990

This edition updated and published in 1996,
reprinted 1997 by
LEO COOPER
an imprint of Pen & Sword Books Ltd,
47 Church Street,
Barnsley, South Yorkshire S70 2AS

Copyright © Julian Paget 1990, 1996, 1997

ISBN 0 85052 603 5

A CIP record for this book is available from the British Library

Printed in Great Britain by
Redwood Books, Trowbridge, Wiltshire

Contents

Appendices

List of Maps

Foreword

by The Duke of Wellington, LVO, OBE, MC, DL

Many years ago when I was Defence Attaché at the British Embassy in Madrid I had the opportunity to visit and walk over most of the battlefields of the Peninsular war. It is something I would thoroughly recommend to all who are interested in military history; but one's appreciation of a field of battle of the past is enormously heightened if reference can be made to an account of the battle which not only details the sequence of events but gives an up-to-date picture of what one is looking for. Over the centuries features change and modern developments radically alter the topography. Today the ridge of Busaco for instance is covered by trees and Vitoria and Talavera are bisected by motorways. I was lucky enough on my walks over those historic fields to have in my hand Jac Weller's recently published *Wellington in the Peninsula* which enabled me to re-create vividly in my mind those scenes of long ago.

The pace of change in Spain and Portugal has increased rapidly in the last twenty-five years and an up-to-date picture of those great campaigns in the Peninsular is long overdue. In Julian Paget's book we have that picture, greatly enhanced by the author's own distinguished career in the Army. He approaches the problems faced by my ancestor with the sort of military perception which will benefit his readers when they visit the battlefields and of which I hope to take advantage in the years ahead.

Acknowledgements

I am very grateful to a number of people for the help they have given me over this book. I owe much in the first place to Serena Fass and the staff of Serenissima Travel for setting me on the path of studying the battlefields of the Peninsular War. I am also indebted to Stephen Drake-Jones, Chairman of the Wellington Society of Spain for checking many facts, figures and references for me; Michael Stilwell and Robert Bremner for help over the campaigning in Portugal; Lord Nicholas Gordon-Lennox, British Ambassador in Madrid, and his staff for their help and support; Lt-Colonel Bill Watson for supplying some of the maps and Neil Hyslop for drawing them so effectively; also Mrs Gibbon for typing the manuscript. I am also most grateful to Colonel Henry Radice who provided many of the photographs of the battlefields which appear in the book.

Preface

There have been many books written about the Peninsular War, and I hesitate to add yet another to the list. But, having led several battlefield tours to the Peninsula, it seems to me that there is a need for one, simple account of the campaign.

Some of the histories are classics, but out of date. Some cover particular aspects, such as Michael Glover's excellent *Wellington's Army*. Some are very involved; some are biased one way or another. The only one that deals with the actual battlefields is Jac Weller's *Wellington in the Peninsula*, but that was written 20 years ago and is now out of print.

My aim in this book is to provide a short, simple but complete account of the whole war, including details of the battlefields as they are today, and how to go and look at them. This account is written primarily from a British viewpoint, but I have tried to present a balanced picture of the whole campaign, giving due credit to the Spanish and Portuguese war efforts, without which victory would not have been possible.

The book is written in various sections, giving varying degrees of detail. It starts with a broad-brush review of the whole war and the background to it, for those who want to grasp the outline story and the historical setting in just one chapter. Then there is an account of the war year by year, outlining events in more detail: these seven chapters give a complete and chronological account of the whole campaign.

Finally, there is a chapter on each of the major battles in which the Peninsular Army was involved. These include a detailed account of the battle, maps of the battlefields, orders of battle, and instructions on how to find the battlefield today and what to see there. The maps show the ground as it was at the time of the Peninsular War, but also include enough modern features such as roads, railways and landmarks, to enable readers to identify the ground where the fighting took place.

In addition, there are several Appendices giving basic information about the rival armies, the commanders involved and the British regiments which saw service in the war.

It is hoped that this approach will be of interest to a wide range of people, including the general reader, the professional historian, the harassed young officer seeking a quick answer and tourists who want to look at history and stand where Wellington stood.

There is something very dramatic and impressive, to my mind, about standing today where Wellington stood, and being able to look at the same ground as he did. Most of the battlefields of the Peninsular War are still identifiable, and are not built over, though there are unfortunately motorways across both Talavera and Vitoria.

In most cases, it is not difficult to envisage the battle, and I hope my book may help readers to do just that. Salamanca, Talavera and Vitoria can be clearly imagined. The Crossing of the Douro took place near the modern road bridge (and temptingly near the port 'lodges' of Vila Nova!). The Lines of Torres Vedras can be seen on many hilltops. One can still stand on Cadoux's Bridge across the Bidassoa or on the Tres Puentes Bridge at Vitoria. There is a modern motorway along much of the Retreat to Corunna, but it is still possible to follow the old road, and one can easily still imagine the horrors and hardships of that mid-winter nightmare.

Studying the Peninsular War, I have been constantly struck by the number of comparisons that can be made with the Second World War, and it is one of the themes of the book. To give just two examples: the importance to British strategy of sea-power is dominant throughout both wars, and on a smaller scale, the parallels between Corunna in 1809 and Dunkirk in 1940 are obvious.

The Peninsular War is a fascinating piece of history, and I hope that this book will help a few more people to understand it, and to obtain pleasure from reading about it, as well as perhaps looking at some of the battlefields.

Chronology

1807

18 October	French troops cross Spanish frontier.
30 November	Junot captures Lisbon.

1808

23 March	French occupy Madrid.
2 May	Madrid uprising.
15 June – 13 August	First Siege of **Saragossa**.
14 July	Bessières defeats Cuesta at **Medina del Rio Seco**.
22 July	French under Dupont surrender at **Baylen**.
1 August	British force under Wellesley lands in Portugal.
17 August	Wellesley defeats Delaborde at **Rolica**.
21 August	Wellesley defeats Junot at **Vimiero**.
30 August	Convention of Cintra.
30 October	French evacuate Portugal.
8 November	Napoleon enters Spain with 200,000 men.
23 November	French victory over Spanish at **Tudela**.
4 December	Napoleon occupies Madrid.
10 December	Moore advances from Salamanca.
20 December - 20 February	Second Siege of **Saragossa**.
21 December	Cavalry action at **Sahagun**.
25 December	Retreat to Corunna begins.

1809

1–14 Januaray	**Retreat to Corunna.**

13 January	Victor defeats Venegas at **Ucles**.
16 January	Moore defeats Soult at **Corunna**, but is killed.
28 March	Victor defeats Cuesta at **Medellin**.
28 March	Soult captures Oporto.
22 April	Wellesley returns to Portugal.
12 May	Wellesley crosses **Douro** and drives Soult out of Oporto.
24 May – **11 December**	Siege of **Gerona**.
28 July	Wellesley defeats Joseph at **Talavera**, and is created Viscount Wellington.
18 October	Spanish success at **Tamames**.
20 October	Work starts on Lines of Torres Vedras.
19 November	Mortier defeats Spanish at **Ocana**.

1810

5 February	Victor begins two-year siege of **Cadiz**.
10 July	Massena captures **Ciudad Rodrigo**.
24 July	Ney defeats Craufurd on **River Coa**.
28 July	**Almeida** surrenders.
27 September	Wellington defeats Massena at **Busaco**.
10 October	Wellington occupies **Lines of Torres Vedras**.
14 October	Massena halted by **Lines of Torres Vedras**.
17 November	Massena withdraws to Santarem.

1811

21 January	Soult captures **Olivenza**.
19 February	Soult defeats Spanish at **Gebora River**.
5 March	Graham defeats Victor at **Barrosa**.
10 March	Soult captures **Badajoz**.
15 March	Massena withdraws from Santarem to Spain.
22 March	Beresford defeats Latour-Maubourg at **Campo Major**.
3–5 May	Wellington defeats Massena at **Fuentes de Onoro**.
6–15 May	Beresford starts First Siege at Badajoz.
16 May	Beresford defeats Soult at **Albuera**.
19 May–17 June	Second Siege of Badajoz.

June–September	Manoeuvring along Rivers Caia and Coa.

1812

19 January	Wellington captures **Ciudad Rodrigo**.
7 April	Wellington captures **Badajoz**.
24 June	Napoleon invades Russia.
22 July	Wellington defeats Marmont at **Salamanca**.
12 August	Allies occupy **Madrid**.
19 September	Wellington besieges **Burgos**.
22 October	Wellington abandons siege of **Burgos**.
2 November	French re-take Madrid.
19 November	Allied army returns to Ciudad Rodrigo.

1813

22 May	Wellington starts final offensive.
21 June	Wellington defeats Joseph at **Vitoria**.
28 June – 31 August	Siege of **San Sebastian**.
25 July	Soult counter-attacks through the Pyrenees. Actions at **Maya** and **Roncesvalles**.
28–30 July	Wellington defeats Soult at **Sorauren**.
31 August	Graham captures **San Sebastian**. Wellington repulses Soult at **San Marcial**.
8 September	Citadel of San Sebastian surrenders.
7 October	Wellington crosses the **Bidassoa**.
25 October	Pamplona surrenders.
10 November	Wellington defeats Soult on the **Nivelle**.
9–10 December	Wellington defeats Soult on the **Nive**.
13 December	Hill repulses Soult at **St Pierre**.

1814

27 February	Wellington defeats Soult at **Orthez**.
20 March	Action at **Tarbes**.
6 April	Napoleon abdicates.
10 April	Wellington defeats Soult at **Toulouse**.
14 April	French makes **Sortie from Bayonne**.
17 April	Soult capitulates.
27 April	Bayonne surrenders.
30 April	Treaty of Paris.

The War in Perspective

CHAPTER ONE

The Peninsular War (1808–1814)

Introduction

It is essential to look at the Peninsular War as a whole, in order to understand and fully appreciate individual events.

The war lasted six years (1808–14), but it was only a small part of the struggle against Napoleon Bonaparte that lasted for 20 years (1795–1815) and was known until 1914 as 'The Great War'. It involved campaigns not only in Europe, but also in the Middle East, Russia, the West Indies, South America and South Africa.

One of the most intriguing features is the number of close parallels that can be drawn between the Napoleonic Wars and the Second World War of 1939 to 1945, and this is an inescapable theme throughout this book.

The first obvious similarity is that the Peninsular War was above all a matter of sea power. Britain, with its superb navy, controlled the seas, and from the start this enabled the Army to keep attacking Napoleon's outlying territories. At the same time, the Navy thwarted every French effort to starve Britain into submission by cutting off her trade and her food supplies. There were no U-boats then, but the principle was the same as in the 1940's.

In 1800, as in 1940, a defiant Britain stood virtually alone, inspired to fight on by the rhetoric of William Pitt, just as we were by that of Winston Churchill 140 years later.

Napoleon, like Hitler, set out to conquer the Middle East, and like Hitler, he was stopped in Egypt. But he still ruled supreme throughout Europe; Britain alone remained in the fight and inevitably had to remain on the defensive in order to survive.

From 1803 to 1805 (just as in 1940–41), we faced the threat of invasion, when Boney assembled a Grand Army of 160,000 troops and a fleet of 2,100 barges, determined to crush the only country that still thwarted his ambitions.

"Let us be masters of the Channel for six hours," he demanded angrily of his admirals, "and we shall be masters of the world."

But Admiral Villeneuve could no more grant him that than could Admiral Raeder and Field-Marshal Goering grant it to Hitler 137 years later.

In 1803, it was 'those far-distant, storm-beaten ships, on which the Grand Army never looked, (that) stood between him and domination of the world.' In 1940 the only difference was that there were a few Spitfires as well.

"I do not say the French cannot come," growled Lord St Vincent, the First Sea Lord in Nelson's day. "All I say is that they cannot come by sea."

It was a spirit, and a fact, that Napoleon could in no way overcome. After two years of frustration, he finally gave up, turned the Grand Army about and vented his fury on Austria, Russia and Prussia, all of whose armies he resoundingly defeated. But still Britain fought on.

Origins of the War

In 1806 Napoleon, thwarted over invasion, decided to try to starve Britain into submission, just as Hitler did with his U-boat warfare; to this end he issued the Berlin Decrees, forbidding any country in Europe from trading with England. But Portugal, a great maritime nation who did almost half their business with England, refused to comply, whereupon Napoleon sent 30,000 men under General Junot through Spain to occupy Portugal.

They reached Lisbon on **30 November, 1807** – just 24 hours after the Navy had evacuated the Portuguese royal family to Brazil (shades of Holland in 1940).

Not content with that, Napoleon invaded Spain in the **spring of 1808** and put his brother, Joseph Bonaparte, on the throne. It was in fact a major error, for both Spain and Portugal rose up against the invaders, and appealed to Britain for help. It was given, and the Peninsular War had begun.

The Spanish Ulcer

On **2 May, 1808**, the famous 'Dos de Mayo', the Spanish people rose in revolt against the French, and for the next six years they waged a ruthless, unremitting struggle against them – a Resistance Movement that was to be as decisive as in 1940–45. It became known as 'The Spanish Ulcer', a running sore from which France would ultimately bleed to death.

The Spanish Army was erratic and unreliable, but brave and full of spirit. They met with many defeats, but their great contribution was that for six years they tied down so many of the 250,000 Imperial troops in Spain that France never succeeded in concentrating enough men to defeat Wellington's 50,000[1]. Napoleon sent some 600,000 men over the Pyrenees altogether, a drain on his resources that he could ill afford and which would achieve little.

Alongside the Spanish Army were the 'guerrillas',[2] who operated with relish, courage and skill throughout the Peninsula, and were a constant threat to the invaders. Convoys were ambushed and messengers waylaid, so that it eventually reached the stage where it took 200 cavalry to ensure that a message got through, and up to 1,000 men to enable a French general to travel round the country and survive.

The whole population in both countries fought the enemy relentlessly, be it as soldiers or guerrillas, and it was a major factor in the war. Wellington, to use a modern phrase, had 'the hearts and minds' of the people, and it was a significant advantage to him. At the end of six years of occupation and oppression the Spanish people were undefeated, and they could justifiably speak of having fought *La Guerra de la Independencia*.

Wellington's Strategy

To understand the campaign in the Peninsula properly, we need to know something of the strategy that was followed by the British Government, based on the appreciations made by Wellington.

Again, one is struck by the similarities to the Second World War. In 1808, as in 1940, Europe was dominated by a ruthless and powerful dictator with an apparently invincible army that had overrun virtually the whole Continent. Only Resistance Movements survived in most of the occupied countries, and only Britain fought resolutely on, hoping others would join her one day.

The situation in 1808 gave the British Government an opportunity to use their sea-power, for the Peninsula was ideal for sea-borne operations from north, south, east and west, and it was on Napoleon's doorstep. Sea-power enabled England to send an expeditionary force to Portugal in **August, 1808**, withdraw it from Corunna **five months later**, and then send another to Portugal in **April, 1809**.

It seemed a remarkably bold venture to despatch this second force under Sir Arthur Wellesley, but the decision was based on his own Appreciation of the Situation[3] in which he set out the strategy that was to be followed throughout the Peninsular War.

Wellesley maintained that Portugal could be defended by quite a small expeditionary force, provided that four requirements were met:

a. The Spanish must continue to resist and must support England.
b. England must retain her sea-power.
c. The expeditionary force must not suffer defeat or undue losses.
d. The French must be prevented from concentrating 100,000 men against them.

It was on the strength of this far-sighted assessment that England's main army landed in Portugal in 1809. Wellesley's strategy throughout was to ensure that it survived, which was why he remained so firmly on the defensive for the first three years and took few risks. He fought when the odds were favourable, and won, and prevented the French from ever concentrating enough men to defeat him.

Then in **1812**, the tide turned. Napoleon, like Hitler, invaded Russia, and immediately faced the problems of a war on two fronts, as well as a vast coast-line to defend against Allied sea-power. In 1812, as in 1942, the Allies were at last in a position to take the offensive. Eighteen months later, the war was won.

How Was It Done?

It is of value to outline at this stage the ingredients of Wellington's success, because one can then see how they apply to each of the battles.

The over-riding factor of sea-power has already been mentioned. As Sir Arthur Bryant put it in his ringing phrases: "The British people put a ring of sea-water round the tyrant's dominion, slowly tightened it, and then greatly daring, sent in their armies to assail his inner fortress." He was writing that in 1944, and he added: "The events of the past four years have made this story strangely familiar."

The resistance of the Spanish and Portuguese people was another vital element without which the war could not have been won. It meant that Wellington always had first-class information[4] – an advantage that usually comes to any liberating power. He usually knew more of the French plans, strengths and dispositions than did either Napoleon or indeed the Marshals of Spain themselves. It is intriguing that he was regularly breaking the French codes, just as we did through 'Ultra' in World War Two.

Wellington was much better than the French at providing supplies and seeing that they reached his troops. He organized his Commissariat extremely well, and he also always insisted on paying for what he took from the Spanish and Portuguese. The French, on the other hand, tried to 'live off the land', which inevitably led to plundering and was difficult in a country that was already living largely at subsistence levels, and was made even less hospitable by Wellington's 'scorched earth' policy.

Sea-power, the support of the people, and supplies all contributed to victory in the Peninsula. But above all, it was Wellington himself who was primarily responsible. First, his strategy was far-sighted and effective. Second, his tactical skill was such that he out-manoeuvred every Marshal sent against him and never lost a battle. Most of the battles were between armies of around 50,000 each, and it was a matter of command and control, at both of which Wellington was a true master.

Finally, he organized, trained and inspired with confidence not only a raw British army, more accustomed to defeat than victory, but also did the same with a Portuguese army, to the point where it fought with distinction alongside his own and finally out-numbered it. As in World War Two, the British Soldier, properly trained, was a battle-winning factor.

Wellington dominated the scene, incidentally spending the entire six years in the Peninsula without leave, and it is an interesting thought as to what might have happened if he had been a casualty at any time. He came very close to disaster on six occasions, being almost captured three times, and being three times struck by bullets, but fortunately without any serious injury. As there was no one of equal calibre to take over, the war might well have taken a very different course, and Napoleon might well have stayed on the throne of France.

Notes

1   The Peninsular War proved the truth of the old saying that, 'In Spain a small army is beaten and a large one starves.'

2   This is the origin of the word we know today. Strictly, 'guerrilla' means 'a small war', and the person who fights it is a 'guerrillero', but the fighter today has become a 'guerrilla'.

3   Written in March, 1809.

4   At Waterloo the position was completely reversed, and it was Wellington who was forced to declare, "Humbugged, by God".

The War
Year by Year

CHAPTER TWO

1808 – Triumph and Disaster

General Situation

1808 was a year of dramatic changes of fortune for the Allies in the Peninsula. New Year's Day saw Napoleon dominant in Europe, and as in 1940, only England still stood defiant. In May he invaded Spain, who appealed to England for help. As a result a British expeditionary force was landed in Portugal in August, and within a month it had, under Sir Arthur Wellesley, forced the French to evacuate that country. It seemed at that moment that they might soon be driven out of Spain as well, yet on New Year's Day 1809 the British army was in full retreat to Corunna. Again as in 1940, they just escaped to fight on to final victory, but complete disaster was very close.

The Peninsular War may be said to have started on **14 June 1808** when Wellesley was appointed to command the expeditionary force of 9,500 men.[1] His instructions from Lord Castlereagh, the Minister of War, were to support Portugal and Spain in 'throwing off the yoke of France, and the final and absolute evacuation of the Peninsula by the troops of France.' He discussed his task with his old friend, John Croker, who, noticing that Wellesley was unusually silent, asked him what he was thinking.

The general replied "Why, to say the truth, I am thinking of the French that I am going to fight. I have not seen them since the campaign in Flanders, when they were capital soldiers, and a dozen years of victory under Bonaparte must have made them better still . . . My die is cast; they may overwhelm me, but I don't think they will out-manoeuvre me. First, because I am not afraid of them, as everybody else seems to be; and secondly, because if what I hear of their system of manoeuvre is true, I think it is a false one against steady troops. I suspect all the continental armies were more than half-beaten before the battle was begun. I, at least, will not be frightened before-hand."

It was a remarkable forecast of the way in which the Peninsular Army would over the next six years frustrate and defeat the seemingly invincible *Grande Armée* of France.

The Spanish Ulcer

While the British expeditionary force was being assembled, the Spanish inflicted a series of unprecedented setbacks on the French. The besieged garrison of Saragossa, under the inspiring leadership of 28-year-old José Palafox, inflicted 3,500 casualties on the invaders, twice forcing them to abandon the siege. Gerona likewise defied 6,000 French troops during July, and 13,000 in August. Valencia too forced Marshal Moncey's 9,000 men to retreat in disorder.

The only bright spot for France was their victory over the Spanish at Medina de Rio Seco, just north of Valladolid, on **14 July, 1808**. Then a mere five days later came an unbelievable blow to the pride of the Imperial forces in Spain. General Dupont had been sent to suppress an uprising in Andalusia and, when the Spanish under General Castanos advanced against him, he manoeuvred so incompetently that on **22 July**[2] over 18,000 troops of the Imperial Army were ignominiously forced to surrender at Baylen to a greatly inferior Spanish army.

Napoleon was furious. "There has never been anything so stupid, so foolish and so cowardly since the world began," he raged. It was indeed a shameful defeat, and it was enough to make King Joseph and most of the French troops evacuate Madrid and withdraw north of the Ebro.

By the end of the summer in 1808 the Spanish people had driven the invaders out of three-quarters of their country, inflicting on them some 40,000 casualties – almost as many as the Peninsular Army would inflict in the course of the six-year-war that lay ahead.[3] The contribution of the whole Spanish nation to the struggle against Napoleon should never be underestimated or overlooked. The Spanish Ulcer was already beginning to drain away the life-blood of the French Empire.

British Landing in Portugal, August, 1808

The expeditionary force sailed from Cork on 13 July, with Wellesley going ahead in the fast frigate *Crocodile*. They landed unopposed[4] on

1 **August** at Figuiera da Foz at the mouth of the Mondego River, 80 miles north of Lisbon, and on **the 5th** Wellesley's 9,500 were joined by 5,000 from Cadiz under Major-General Sir Brent Spencer.

Once ashore, Wellesley divided his force into six small brigades, each with three guns; he was very short of horses, having only enough to mount 240 of his 390 light dragoons and to pull three of his five batteries of guns. But he immediately started to build up his supply system, which would soon give him such a marked advantage over the French.

On **10 August** he moved off south towards Lisbon, following the coast road, so that he remained in close touch with the Navy. About this time, he received news that his force was to be increased by a further 15,000 men, but that, as a result, command would have to go to someone more senior. The 39-year-old Wellesley would therefore be superseded not only by General Sir Hew Dalrymple, Governor of Gibraltar, aged 58, who had only once in his career seen active service, but also beneath him by Lieutenant-General Sir Harry Burrard, aged 53, who had not seen action for 10 years.

Realising that this was primarily a political move, Wellesley accepted the inevitable and set about seeing how he could defeat the French before his senile seniors arrived on the scene.

The Battle of Rolica (See Chapter 9)

When the French commander in Portugal, General Junot, heard of Wellesley's landing, he sent his ablest commander, General Delaborde, to delay him until reinforcements could arrive from Abrantes.

On **15 August** the first encounter of the Peninsular War for the British Army occurred when there was a brief skirmish at Alcobaca. On **the 16th** Wellesley occupied Obidos, and the **next morning** he observed that Delaborde had taken up a defensive position just north of the village of Rolica, some four miles beyond Obidos.

Knowing that he out-numbered the French, but that reinforcements for them were only half a day's march away, he decided to attack without delay. He divided his force into three and tried to outflank the French; but Delaborde saw through the manoeuvre and withdrew skilfully to a much stronger position on a steep ridge a mile south of Rolica.

Wellesley repeated his pincer movement, but the plan went wrong when one battalion attacked the enemy centre prematurely, and he was forced to launch a full attack to support them. The French were finally overrun, and by 1600 were in retreat southwards, having lost 600 men and 3 guns against 479 British casualties.

Rolica was not a major battle, but it was significant simply because it was a victory. For 16 years the French had seldom been defeated in battle, even against superior odds, whereas the British troops had known little but defeat. So it was most encouraging for them to start off a campaign with a success for a change, and it did much for the morale of both the Army and the country.

The French may have concluded, as a result of Rolica, that Wellesley was not a particularly good offensive commander; but, if so, they would soon learn otherwise at Oporto, Salamanca and elsewhere.

The Battle of Vimiero (See Chapter 10)

Wellesley moved south the **next day** to Vimiero[5] at the mouth of the Maceira River to cover the landing of two brigades (Acland and Anstruther) which had just arrived from England. This brought his strength up to 17,000 and 18 guns, and he now planned to advance on Lisbon.

But on the evening of **20 August** Sir Harry Burrard arrived, and to Wellesley's dismay, ordered him to do nothing until Sir John Moore's 10,000 men had joined him from Corunna. Angrily, Wellesley cancelled his orders for an advance, but then at midnight came the unexpected but most welcome news that the French under Junot were advancing from the south. Wellesley was still in command, as Sir Harry had stayed aboard ship, so he now cheerfully prepared for battle.

He took up positions facing south, but when the French appeared at about 0900 on **21 August**, it was from the east. He rapidly re-aligned his brigades, placing two on Vimiero Hill and four along the Eastern Ridge, which ran north-east from Vimiero village.

The first French attacks were against Vimiero Hill, but their columns were four times repulsed by the deadly volleys of the British infantry in line. By 1100 they had given up.

Junot now launched two attacks against the Eastern Ridge, but they too failed, and by noon the battle was over. The French had lost 1,000 men and 14 of their 23 guns, and they were incapable of any further attacks. The British casualties were only 720, and their morale could not have been higher. The road to Torres Vedras and Lisbon lay open.

Well pleased, Wellesley galloped up to Sir Harry Burrard, who had now come ashore, and raised his hat to him.[6] In a voice loud enough to be audible to his staff, he declared, "Sir Harry, now is your chance. The French are completely beaten. Let us move on to Torres Vedras . . . We shall be in Lisbon in three days."[7]

As if to reinforce the point, a message arrived from one of his brigade commanders that he had 2,000 Frenchmen trapped in a ravine, and wanted leave to attack them.

But Sir Harry again said "No", and could not be budged. He insisted that everything must wait until Moore arrived. Angrily, Wellesley turned and remarked in disgust to his officers that they might as well go off and shoot some red-legged partridges.

So Junot was left to withdraw his demoralised army unhindered.

The significance of the Battle of Vimiero was that veteran French troops, following Napoleonic tactics that had brought them victory throughout Europe, had been utterly defeated. From the highest to the lowest, they could not really believe it, and indeed, they continued to follow the same tactics for many more years, although the result was one defeat after another.

The Convention of Cintra

The next morning, **23 August**, Sir Hew Dalrymple arrived as C-in-C, and immediately endorsed Burrard's decision to remain on the defensive.

But that same afternoon Wellesley was fully vindicated when General Junot sent General Kellerman to negotiate terms for a surrender. Within two days it was agreed that the French would evacuate Portugal, and would be returned to France. The armistice, which was later incorporated into the famous, or infamous, Convention of Cintra, was signed on **31 August**.

But when the terms of the Convention became known in England, there was universal outrage over two of its clauses. These were, first, that the French were to be returned home aboard British men-of-war, and second, that they would be allowed to include in their 'personal belongings' the loot that they had plundered from the Portuguese.

The generals concerned, including Wellesley, were accused of ineptitude, and were all recalled for a Court of Inquiry. Dalrymple was relieved of his command, and Burrard was retired. Happily for the country, Wellesley was cleared of blame, but was not for the moment given any further command. He therefore resumed his political appointment as Chief Secretary of Ireland.

Sir John Moore's Campaign

When Wellesley returned to England on **4 October, 1808**, Lieutenant-General Sir John Moore was left in command of the 30,000
troops still in Portugal, and was ordered to advance into Spain with
20,000 of them to help the Spanish drive the French back across the
Pyrenees.

It was an optimistic order, for, although there were around 80,000
Spanish troops in the field, they had no coordinated plan and no
recognised C-in-C with whom Moore could collaborate.

Moore decided to advance on Burgos, where he could link up not
only with the Spanish armies facing the French across the Ebro, but
also with a force of 10,000 being sent out from England to Corunna
under Major-General Sir David Baird. He set off on 18 October, but
unfortunately sent his artillery and cavalry on an enormous loop south
via Badajoz and Madrid to join him at Salamanca, because he was
advised (wrongly, it turned out) that the direct route through Ciudad
Rodrigo was impassable for guns.

What Moore did not know also was that Napoleon had himself
crossed into Spain on **8 November** with 200,000 troops, determined
to settle the Spanish trouble once and for all. "The hideous leopard,"
the Emperor told his soldiers, "contaminates by its presence the
peninsula of Spain and Portugal. Let us carry our victorious Eagles to
the Pillars of Hercules."[8]

By **13 November**[9] Napoleon had reached Valladolid, half-way to
Madrid, and Moore was at Salamanca, waiting for Baird and Hope to
join him.

It was **26 November** before Moore heard that the Spanish armies
he was supposed to support had disintegrated under Napoleon's
'blitzkrieg'. He immediately realized that he must abandon his plan to
advance on Burgos, and he issued orders instead for a withdrawal. This
decision met, however, with the strongest condemnation not only from
the Spanish and from the British Ambassador in Madrid, but also from
his own commanders and troops, who were eager for a fight.

On **4 December** Hope arrived at Salamanca at last with the cavalry
and guns, but Baird was still at Astorga. The pressures on Moore to
stay and fight were now immense, and on **6 December** he took the
momentous decision to countermand his orders for a withdrawal, and
to advance again on Burgos.

"I was aware that I was risking infinitely too much," he wrote, "but something must be risked for the honour of the Service, and to make it apparent that we stuck to the Spaniards long after they had given up their cause for lost."[10]

To Baird he wrote, "If the bubble bursts and Madrid falls, we shall have to make a run for it."[11]

In fact the risks were far greater than Moore realised. First, Madrid had already fallen on **4 December**. Second, he thought he was faced by only 80,000 French in Spain, whereas Napoleon now had 250,000. Finally, he did not know that Napoleon was even now advancing against him with 80,000 men, determined to cut off and finally destroy this impertinent British army.

On **11 December, 1808**, Moore marched north with 20,000 men, and on the **20th** joined Baird's 10,000 at Mayorga. He now had his army complete at last, and on **Christmas Eve** they were heading cheerfully towards Carrion, to attack Soult, who was there with only 16,000. But soon after midnight came the order to withdraw. It was received with angry frustration, and when the 42nd learned of it "nothing could be heard on every side but the clang of firelocks thrown down in despair".

But they were not to know, as their general now did from a captured despatch, that the jaws of a powerful trap were just about to close on them, with Soult to the north and Napoleon to the south. "The bubble had burst" indeed, and they would "have to make a run for it".

The retreat to Corunna was about to begin.

Retreat to Corunna (See Chapter 11)

On **Christmas Day, 1808**, Moore's army of 30,000, including over 4,000 cavalry, crossed the Esla at Castrogonzalo, and climbed westward into the grim snow-covered mountains of Galicia.

For the next three weeks they struggled through appalling conditions with almost no food, fuel or shelter; sick or wounded had to be abandoned, and strong men collapsed and died by the roadside.

Morale sank and discipline faltered. Yet whenever the pursuing French closed in, they turned and fought, and to the end, they never lost a Colour or a gun. As Fortescue put it: "When the sound of the French trumpets was borne on the wind, the pallid British scarecrows would instinctively face about."

The brunt of the fighting fell on the Rearguard under the command initially of Brigadier-General Craufurd, but from Astorga, Major-General Edward Paget took over. The cavalry was commanded by

Lord Henry Paget (later Earl of Uxbridge and Marquess of Anglesey), and the two brothers effectively kept the French at bay to the bitter end.

On **30 December** Moore and his army reached Astorga, and three crucial decisions were made there. First, Napoleon realized that there was now little chance of cutting off the British army, as he had hoped; so he handed over the pursuit to Soult, and returned to France, having received news of political intrigue in Paris in his absence.

Second, Moore had to decide whether or not to stand and fight at Astorga. It was a possible defensive position, and a success would enable him to withdraw under less pressure. His troops were, as one of them wrote, "exasperated to retreat before an enemy they despised," and he had about equal numbers to the French.

But he was still 200 miles from Corunna, and he thought he was still opposed by Napoleon himself. Above all, he could not forget that his army was virtually the only one that England possessed; a victory would achieve little, and a defeat would lose him all. "A battle was the game of Bonaparte," he commented, "not of the British."

He decided against a fight, but his decision was met with fierce resentment; his generals openly challenged it, while the morale of the soldiers sank even lower.

Moore had been criticized for this and also for the decision he now made to split his force, and send two brigades (Craufurd's Light Brigade and Alten's K.G.L.) south to Vigo. They totalled 3,500 men and, although this eased his administrative problems, it deprived him of that number of good troops both for the rearguard and for the final battle at Corunna.

So Moore drove his demoralised troops relentlessly on, until, on **10 January, 1809,** they emerged at long last from the mountains and staggered into Corunna – only to find that the transports had not yet arrived.

The Battle of Corunna (See Chapter 12)

Moore could muster 15,000 men and 12 guns to cover the final embarkation and to fight, if necessary, but it was not really enough. Soult had some 20,000 men, with as many again closing up behind, but fortunately he did not launch his assault until **16 January.**

He then made holding attacks against the Allied centre round Mount Mero, and made his main effort against Moore's right flank, hoping to break through to Corunna itself. But Moore anticipated this, and placed two-thirds of his force well back where they could block such a thrust. Not only did they halt the French, but they then drove them back almost to their own lines.

Victory was in sight, but at that moment a round struck Moore and he was mortally wounded. Command now devolved on Sir John Hope, but it took some time for him to take over, and, as dusk fell, the fighting petered out.

Embarkation continued that night and all next day, and on the night of **19 January** 19,000 of Moore's army sailed for home. They left behind 800 dead, including Sir John Moore, to whom Soult generously erected a monument in Corunna.

Summary

Moore's campaign had been a disaster for England. Far from driving the French out of Spain as had been expected, the British army had itself been ignominiously bundled out of the Peninsula, with the loss of 6,000 of its 30,000 trained men and much of its arms and equipment.

The whole of Spain and most of Portugal had been left in the hands of the vengeful French armies, and England could now expect little affection or support from the people of these countries. It seemed that the newly-born spirit of revolt must now surely die, and that was a cause of grave concern.

There was also cause for much concern at the Army's Headquarters in Horse Guards. The discipline of the troops had, with notable exceptions, been "infamous beyond belief", to quote its commander. The administration had proved totally inadequate, and it was clearly going to be a difficult and costly task to rebuild the shattered remnants into an effective fighting force again.

All this was, moreover, a great political embarrassment to the Government, who had encouraged Moore in his bold venture, and it inevitably made them reluctant to initiate any further such operations in the future.

But that was to look at one side of the coin only. Napoleon too had suffered setbacks. He had failed to destroy the British Army, as he had hoped, and his programme for the re-conquest of Spain and Portugal had been seriously disrupted. The Imperial eagles no longer flew over Lisbon, and his armies had not yet subdued southern Spain. That would all have to wait now until the summer.

So it could be said with some justification that Moore had, by his bold advance from Salamanca in December, 1808, prevented Napoleon from making himself master of the whole of Spain by the end of that year. Had the Emperor achieved this, unhindered by the British, it is likely that the flame of resistance in the Peninsula might have been extinguished completely and never been re-lit, as it would soon now be in 1809.

Notes

1   It was a controversial appointment as Wellesley was, at 39, the youngest Lieutenant General in the Army and would pass over Sir John Moore, aged 47. But Moore generously accepted that it was in the national interest, and so the matter was settled.

2   The actual battle was on 19 July.

3   Fortescue, VI, 177–8.
Liddell Hart, *Decisive Wars of History*, 105–6.

4   Students at Coimbra Unversity helped by seizing the fort and holding until Wellesley's marines could take over – a feat commemorated by a plaque on the main gateway.

5   The common English spelling is 'Vimiero', but the Battle Honour is 'Vimiera', and the Portuguese spelling is 'Vimieiro'.

6   Rifleman Harris happened to be watching, and he wrote, 21 years later, "Methinks it is something to have seen that wonderful man even do so commonplace a thing as lift his hat to another officer in the battlefield."

7   Fortescue, VI, 231.

8   Correspondence, Vol XVIII, No 14445, p.39.

9   It was also Moore's birthday.

10 *Sir John Moore*, Carola Oman, p.559.

11 Letter of 6 December, 1809. *A Narrative of the Campaigns of the British Army in Spain*, James Moore, 1809, p.149.

CHAPTER THREE

1809 – Return To The Peninsula

General Situation

1809 could hardly have begun worse for England. Moore's army had been ignominiously driven out of Spain and Napoleon again ruled supreme in Europe; it was even harder now to see how he could be challenged. Only 16,000 British troops remained in the Peninsula, and they were committed to the defence of Lisbon.

The brunt of the Allied resistance to Napoleon rested with the 135,000 Spanish troops under arms, and the year began badly for them too. On 13 **January** they were defeated at Ucles, and then on **20 February** the gallant garrison of Saragossa finally surrendered after their resistance of eight months. They had inflicted 10,000 casualties on the French, but had lost a horrifying 54,000 themselves. In **March** the Spanish armies met with a further two defeats (Ciudad Real on the **27th**, and Medellin on the **28th**), but they fought on, together with the nationwide guerrilla movement.

To their credit, the British Government and Lord Castlereagh refused to be discouraged by these setbacks and remained resolute that the struggle must be carried on.

It is impossible not to compare 1809 with 1940. In each case a courageous C-in-C (be he called Moore or Gort) saved Britain's main army. In each case it meant suffering an ignominious retreat (be it at Corunna or Dunkirk), and abandoning our allies for the moment; but at least the dictator dominating Europe was deprived of final victory. In each case England still retained three vital assets; first, her sea-power; second, a strong Government under an inspiring leader; and finally, the invincible spirit of the people. Thus armed, it was possible to fight on – and the country did.

Wellesley's Strategy

Early in 1809 Sir Arthur Wellesley argued that Portugal could, and should, be held by a British army.[1]

He was promptly told to carry out his own plan, and on **22 April, 1809** he landed in Lisbon – just three months after the withdrawal from Corunna.

The Allies controlled only the southern half of the country, for Marshal Soult, with 20,000 men, had on **29 March** re-occupied Oporto, and now controlled as far south as Coimbra. As Wellesley and Soult confronted each other in the summer of 1809, it was the start of a six-year duel between the two great commanders that would end with Soult's surrender at Toulouse in April, 1814.

Wellesley moved with astonishing speed, and within 36 hours had decided on his plan. "Seldom had a general conceived so detailed a plan in so short a time," wrote Jac Weller.[2]

Moreover, before he launched any operations, he rapidly reorganized his army to improve its mobility and fighting efficiency. Four changes in particular were put into effect immediately.

First, he improved the administration to ensure that the army could "move far and fast".

Second, he formed the various brigades into self-contained "divisions" operating under their own commanders and staffs, thus achieving greater flexibility in many directions.

Third, he added a "light company" to each infantry brigade, thus substantially increasing the proportion of light troops and strengthening his line of skirmishers.

Finally, he built up the Portuguese Army under British officers, and placed a Portuguese battalion in each of his British brigades. This was the start of a highly successful collaboration that was to develop throughout the campaign, so that by 1813 half the Peninsular Army would be Portuguese, and they would be a thoroughly effective fighting force.

Only two weeks after his arrival, Wellesley was ready to move. He had to face not only Marshal Soult in the north, but also General Lapisse round Ciudad Rodrigo, and Marshal Victor in the south at Talavera. Both the latter armies were well placed to invade Portugal and, if all three combined, they would out-number the Allies by 2 to 1.

The French armies were, however, widely separated by difficult country, and Wellesley was confident that he could, from his central position, defeat them individually before they could unite against him. He decided to start with Soult, drive him from Portugal and then turn against Victor in the south.

He divided his army into three separate groups, each with its own task. General Mackenzie was left, with 12,000 men[3] to protect Lisbon. Beresford, with a force of 6,000,[4] was sent towards Amarante to cut off Soult's line of retreat eastwards.

Wellesley himself took command of the main body, consisting of 16,000 British and 2,400 Portuguese, with 24 guns, and on **8 May** he set off for Oporto.

The Crossing of the Douro (See Chapter 13)

As he advanced north, Wellesley made full use of his sea-power to carry out a series of flanking attacks from the sea against the French as they withdrew. Early on **12 May** he closed up to the Douro, having driven the French back into Oporto; he found that Soult had destroyed the only bridge across the river and had taken every boat across to the north bank. That done, the Marshal felt confident that the British could not attack him across the river; he expected the attack, if it came, to be from the west, using the Navy, and all his defences were facing in that direction.

Within a matter of hours, Soult was disillusioned. In one of the boldest operations of his career, Wellesley successfully launched an assault crossing, using a mere four wine barges that he found, and which held only 30 men each. He took the French completely by surprise and was able to seize an unoccupied building, the Seminary, with 600 men before the enemy realized what was happening.

By then it was too late, and all their desperate counter-attacks failed. Another Allied crossing further upstream at Avintas cut their lines of withdrawal, and by the afternoon, Soult and his 11,000 men were in full retreat. Their direct escape route to the east being blocked by Beresford, they were forced to abandon most of their transport and head into the mountains to the north.

The Crossing of the Douro was a brilliant, opportunist operation, executed with amazing speed and skill, and Oman called it "one of Wellesley's strongest titles to fame".[5] It led to the French being driven out of Portugal for the second time, with severe losses in men and equipment. It proved that Wellesley was not a purely defensive commander, though it took the French a remarkably long time to appreciate this fact. It was another severe setback to the morale of the French Army of Portugal, and a great boost to that of the British and Portuguese.

Now, after a lightning campaign of a mere two weeks, Wellesley was ready to move south against Victor at Talavera.

Cooperation with the Spanish

The campaign now entered a new phase, involving cooperation with the Spanish armies. This was beset with many problems, for there was still no central authority in Spain with whom to coordinate a central strategy. Each general tended to follow his own plans in his own theatre, and was reluctant to collaborate with anyone else, either Spanish or British.

Wellesley had so far been able to operate independently, and he was now unlucky to come up against one of the most awkward Spanish commanders.

Don Gregorio de la Cuesta, Captain General of the Estramadura, was aged 70,[6] cantankerous, obstinate and incompetent. He was described by Rifleman Costello[7] as "that deformed-looking lump of pride, ignorance and treachery", while Colonel John Colborne[8] referred to him as "a perverse, stupid, old blockhead".

Cuesta deeply resented having to take advice from Wellesley, 30 years his junior. He also thoroughly distrusted him, to the point where he would only talk to him through his (Cuesta's) Spanish Chief of Staff, who had the intriguing name of O'Donoju.

Wellesley had to contend not only with the perverseness of Cuesta, but also with the incompetence of the Spanish Junta, who had promised to supply his army with food and transport in Spain, but failed to produce either.

On 9 July Wellesley concentrated his army of 20,000 at Plasencia, and set off the **next day** to make a joint plan with Cuesta, who had 35,000 troops. He was full of confidence, declaring, "The ball is at my feet, and I hope I shall have strength enough to give it a good kick."[9]

Relations between the two commanders got off to a bad start, however, when Wellesley arrived five hours late, due to the Spanish guides getting lost, and he had as a result to review the Spanish army, drawn up in his honour, by torchlight.

The Allied Plan

Despite the personality problems, a plan was finally worked out whereby their combined armies totalling 55,000 would join up at Oropesa and advance against the French at Talavera, where Victor had only 22,000 men. But it was known that General Sebastiani was south of Madrid with another 22,000, while King Joseph had 12,000 in Madrid, and that these three armies could concentrate within two days.

A Spanish army of almost 30,000 under General Venagas was, however, located south of Madrid at Sierra Morena, and it was now ordered by Cuesta to move north and threaten the capital, so as to prevent Sebastiani from reinforcing Victor at Talavera. A force of 3,500 Portuguese under Sir Robert Wilson was also sent as a flank guard to the north, where they threatened Madrid from the west.

The British and Spanish armies duly met up at Oropesa on **21 July**, and the Spanish advanced against Victor, who was defending the line of the River Alberche; the British remained in reserve.

Wellesley planned a joint attack for the **23rd**, in which Cuesta promised to take part. But at dawn, with the British troops all in position, there was no sign of the Spanish. Three hours later Wellesley found Cuesta sound asleep, and, when aroused, he declared that his men were too tired to fight that day!

It was a great opportunity lost and Wellesley was furious. When the French withdrew that night, he refused to follow them deep into enemy territory, particularly as he was now so short of supplies that his men had been on half-rations for two days.

Cuesta, however, now became perversely bold,[10] and declared that he would pursue the French by himself. He set off on the **24th** for Madrid, but duly came up against 46,000 Frenchmen at Alcabon, 22 miles short of Toledo, and was driven back in great disorder on the **25th** to the Alberche, pursued by the French.

Wellesley had to act swiftly to resolve a critical situation, for it was now the Allies who were out-numbered and threatened. Cuesta withdrew from the Alberche and Wellesley set about establishing a defensive position along a much stronger line running for some three miles north from Talavera de la Reina, and centred on a feature called the Cerro de Medellin.

The Battle of Talavera (See Chapter 14)

Although Wellesley had some 55,000 men 'on paper', 35,000 of these were Cuesta's Spanish, in whom he had little confidence, and he was soon proved right, for 2,000 of them fled early in the battle. This meant that he had in effect to face King Joseph's 46,000 veterans and 86 guns with only 17,000 British and 3,000 King's German Legion, supported by 36 guns.

The French began with a night attack late on **27 July** against the Cerro de Medellin, a key feature on the left of the Allied line. When this was repulsed, they attacked the British line throughout the **28th**. In Wellesley's own words, "Never was there such a murderous battle", but at the end of the day it was the French who withdrew, despite their superiority in numbers.

As at Rolica and Vimiero, the disciplined fire-power of the British line broke the massed French columns time and time again. But it was costly, for, although Wellesley lost 5,365 against the French 7,268, it represented 25% of his strength and only 18% of theirs.

Although the French had been decisively defeated, it had been "a near run thing", to use one of Wellesley's favourite phrases. What began on the 23rd with the Allies in a position to attack with a 2 to 1 superiority ended in a desperate defensive battle, outnumbered 2 to 1.

The battle proved beyond doubt the effectiveness of Wellesley's new tactics. His skirmishers thwarted the French *tirailleurs* as at Vimiero. He again posted his men behind the crest, which protected them from the artillery fire. Above all, the English line again defeated the French column. Finally, he demonstrated again his close, personal control of the battle at all times – an ability that would continue to prove decisive right up to Waterloo.

It was a great victory that was greeted with tremendous enthusiasm back in England and Sir Arthur Wellesley was created Baron Douro of Wellesley and Viscount Wellington of Talavera.[11]

He was himself somewhat at a loss what title to choose, and he sought the help of his elder brother, who replied:[12]

"After ransacking the Peerage and examining the map, I at last determined upon Viscount Wellington of Talavera and Baron Douro of Welleslie in Somerset – Wellington is a town not far from Welleslie ... I trust you will not think there is anything unpleasant or trifling in the name of Wellington."

His brother's research had apparently revealed that some of Wellesley's ancestors had in mediaeval times owned land round the village of Wellington in Somerset, and he therefore suggested this as a title, which Sir Arthur accepted as a good solution to the problem.

Back to Portugal

The French had suffered a severe setback at Talavera, but they still remained a very real threat. Wellington now withdrew his troops to Oropesa, but learned on **3 August** that Soult was advancing south from Salamanca with 50,000 men and threatening to cut off the Peninsular Army from Portugal.

He immediately withdrew across the Tagus to Arzobisco and on **20 August**, with his troops half starved for lack of supplies, he retreated again, this time to Badajoz, where he could guard the approach to Lisbon. He would have preferred to cross the frontier into Portugal, but, for the sake of good relations with Spain, he agreed to stay on Spanish soil.

The Lines of Torres Vedras (See Chapter 15)

As always, he was looking far ahead and he now began to think about "the worst case", which might be a successful French invasion of Portugal by a force large enough to overwhelm the allied army. The answer that he found led him, in **October, 1809**, to ride back to the Lisbon area to plan and reconnoitre a series of fortifications north and west of the capital that would become known as the Lines of Torres Vedras.

Accompanied by his Chief Engineer, Colonel Richard Fletcher, he rode personally over the whole length of the three defensive lines that he had in mind, some 50 miles in length altogether. Work began immediately and the Lines took a year to complete. They were built entirely by Portuguese labour, with the greatest possible secrecy, and this was so successful that the French never learned of the existence of the fortifications until they came face to face with them a year later.

For the remainder of 1809, and indeed until February, 1810, Wellington firmly refused to undertake any operations that involved cooperation with the Spanish. He could not forget, or forgive, their failures at Talavera, and he was not prepared to risk his own army again.

His attitude put a considerable strain on Anglo-Spanish relations, but he was adamant. "Till the evils of which I think I have reason to complain are remedied . . . I cannot enter into any system of co-operation with the Spanish Army."[3]

The Spaniards carried on the fight, nevertheless, and on 18 **October** General del Parque defeated the French at Tamames, the most noteworthy Spanish victory since Baylen on 19 July, 1808.

But on 19 **November** the Spanish suffered a severe reverse at Ocana, losing 18,000 men, 50 guns and 30 Colours. Ten days later, on the **29th**, they were beaten again at Alba des Tormes, suffering 3,000 casualties, while the French lost only 300.

These French successes increased the threat to Portugal, and on 9 **December** Wellington finally withdrew back across the frontier and settled into winter quarters in Portugal.

Summary

Wellington could look back with some satisfaction on 1809. His small, largely untried army had driven the French out of Portugal for the second time, and had then defeated them at Talavera. The French had won no victories against him and had not as yet invaded Portugal; they might well do so in 1810, but he was as well prepared for that as could be.

He had growing confidence in his Peninsular Army, as did every man in it, and the Portuguese troops were coming on well too. The Spanish nation was still fighting proudly against the invaders, despite Corunna and the setbacks to their own armies. The flame of resistance still glowed in the Peninsula, despite an occupying army that numbered quarter of a million.

As in 1940, the Allied strategy had to be one of survival at this stage, with offensive blows being struck where and when any opportunity arose. And, as in 1940, there was no thought of surrender.

Notes

1   See also page 6.
2   *Wellington in the Peninsula*, p.71.
3   4,500 British, 7,000 Portuguese and 500 administrative troops.
4   1,875 British and 4,125 Portuguese.
5   Oman, II, p.363.
6   He had been ridden over by his own cavalry three months before, and so now travelled in a coach drawn by nine mules.

7   *Memoirs of Edward Costello of the Rifle Brigade*, p.23.
8   *Life and Letters of Lord Seaton*, G. C. Moore-Smith.
9   It is intriguing to compare this with Field-Marshal Montgomery's remarks in a similar vein!
10 Wellesley called it 'whimsical perverseness'.
11 A plaque was erected by the Wellington Society in the Parador at Oropesa in 1984 to commemorate the 175th anniversary.
12 Raglan MSS, No 93, 22 Aug, 1809, from W. Wellesley-Pole.
13 Despatches, V, 213.

CHAPTER FOUR

1810 – 'Non Ultra'

The Defence of Portugal

1810 was a comparatively uneventful year, with little activity by either side until the autumn, when the French invaded Portugal for the third time.

Wellington was forced to remain on the defensive, being heavily outnumbered by the French. He was responsible for the defence of Portugal, and the only troops that he felt he could rely on were the British and to a lesser extent Beresford's Portuguese, who had not as yet been tried in battle. He still had no confidence in the Spanish armies.

The first nine months of 1810 were extremely difficult for him. The Spanish Government were being very uncooperative, and he was also being strongly criticized in London as well as Madrid for his inactivity. It was to his credit that he resolutely maintained his long-term strategy in the face of such pressures.

Another French invasion of Portugal seemed inevitable, and there were three possible routes by which the French might advance. This meant covering a front of 150 miles, which strained his limited resources to the utmost.

The least likely approach, in his view, was in the centre down the Tagus, and he left this to Beresford and his Portuguese troops, centred on Abrantes.

The southern corridor ran through Badajoz[1] and Elvas, and was the most direct route to Lisbon. He covered this with 20,000 men (7,000 British and 13,000 Portuguese) under Sir Rowland Hill, whom he trusted more than most of his generals in an independent command.

He considered that the French would most probably use the northern corridor, which ran through Ciudad Rodrigo[2] and Almeida, both of which fortresses were in Allied hands. He took control of this sector himself, with his headquarters at Celerico, and put the remainder of his army in that area.

This sector was about 40 miles wide and he gave the Light Division[3] the task of providing a screen in front of it, a role that they carried out brilliantly under their outstanding commander, Major-General Robert Craufurd. So well trained were they that it took only seven minutes to get the whole division under arms by night and 15 minutes to get them into order of battle, with baggage loaded. They not only kept the French at bay for five months, but also effectively prevented them from finding out much about the Allied dispositions. They held a line along the River Agueda, which was aptly described as being like a web that quivered at the lightest touch.

Wellington meanwhile reorganized and trained his army, and also reconnoitred possible lines of defence. He quickly picked on the dominating 10-mile-long ridge at Busaco, that has been described as "one of the finest defensive positions in Europe". It was ideal for his purpose, which was to fight a defensive battle on his own terms. He planned his positions and, with his usual foresight, built a lateral road just behind the ridge, so that he could move his troops unseen from one part of the line to another, just as he also did behind the Lines of Torres Vedras.

At the same time he set about implementing every possible measure to frustrate the French, should they succeed in invading the country.

He built up the Portuguese Army under Beresford, with British officers being transferred into most units, and he was soon able to put a complete Portuguese brigade into most of the British divisions.[4] He strengthened the Ordenanza, the Portuguese 'Home Guard', so that they could (as did our Home Guard in 1940–41) relieve the regular troops of many static duties.

He also planned and obtained Portuguese agreement to a "scorched earth" policy, should the French actually enter the country. It seemed hard to demand that the impoverished peasants should destroy or remove their precious crops, mills, equipment and transport, but they would lose them in any case to the marauding French, and they had done it before against other invading armies.

Meanwhile, work continued apace on the construction of the Lines of Torres Vedras, and so good was the security that most of the British Army did not even know of their existence, while the French certainly did not.

As one more weapon in his armoury, Wellington also built up a remarkable intelligence system, so that he was always extremely well-informed about what was happening on "the other side of the hill". Indeed, he often knew more of the French plans and dispositions than did most of their commanders, who found it virtually impossible, due to the activities of the guerrillas, to keep in touch with each other, let alone with the Emperor in Paris.

In addition to the intelligence-gathering activities of the Light Division, he had a number of daring officers, such as Major Colquhoun Grant and Major The Hon Charles Cocks, who operated far behind the enemy lines with 5 or 6 men, watching the enemy and reporting back.

He also had a network of "agents" and "correspondents", who kept him supplied with valuable information from all over the Peninsula. They included loyal Spaniards, merchants, officials, priests and many others from all walks of life.[5] Some acted purely out of patriotism, others were paid promptly and in cash.

The French Advance

By the Spring of 1810 the threat to Portugal was very real, for Napoleon, having forced Austria to make peace, was able to send a further 100,000 men to the Peninsula, making a total there of around 325,000. He even considered taking over command himself again, to finish off this tiresome campaign once and for all. But he was involved in divorcing the barren Josephine and marrying Marie Louise of Austria, and so he decided against it.

Instead, in **April, 1810**, he sent Marshal Massena to the Peninsula with instructions to "drive the British leopards into the sea". But he still refused to give Massena, or any other Marshal, overall command in the Peninsula, and insisted that they must still take their orders from Paris – even though they usually took a month to arrive and were then hopelessly out-of-date.

Massena was a fine commander, and was regarded by Wellington as "the ablest general after Napoleon".[6] But he was not very enthusiastic about his new command; he had been campaigning now for 20 years, and was, at 52, Napoleon's senior Marshal. He would have preferred to retire and settle down with his exciting new mistress, Madame Lebrerton;[7] but he had no choice, and the only consolation was that Madame did accompany him, fetchingly dressed in the uniform of a Captain of Hussars!

The campaign of 1810 began on the Portuguese front when Massena advanced in **May** and laid siege to the fortress of Ciudad Rodrigo, which was defended by a garrison of 5,500 Spanish troops under a 70-year-old, but very resolute Spanish general, Andres Herrasti.

They held out most gallantly and Wellington was under considerable pressure both from the Spanish Government and from his own troops to go to their support, but he firmly refused to risk his own army in an attempt to relieve the city, which he knew would be to play into Massena's hands. On **10 July** the garrison was finally forced to surrender.

The French now advanced and, on **24 July**, Ney, with 24,000 men, very nearly caught the Light Division on the wrong side of the River Coa. It was Craufurd's fault, for he had not followed his orders, but Wellington forgave him with the memorable words:

"If I am to be hanged for it, I cannot accuse a man who I believe has meant well, and whose error was one of judgement, not of intention . . . although my errors, and those of others also, are visited heavily upon me, that is not the way in which any, let alone a British army, can be commanded."[8] That, surely, is the judgement of a truly great commander.

Wellington had hoped that the equally strong fortress of Almeida would hold out as long as Ciudad Rodrigo had done, and it might have, but for a most unfortunate accident. It came under French artillery fire at the **end of July**, and on **26 August** a trail of gunpowder from a leaking barrel was set alight by a shell. The entire magazine blew up, killing 500 of the garrison and forcing the commander to surrender **two days later**.

Nothing had gone right for Wellington so far in 1810, but now his luck changed. Massena did not renew his advance westwards until **15 September**, and then he took just the road that Wellington had hoped that he might – across the Busaco Ridge.

"There are many bad roads in Portugal," Wellington wrote with some relief,[9] "but the enemy has taken decidedly the worst in the whole kingdom."

The Battle of Busaco (See Chapter 15)

Once he knew the enemy's intentions, Wellington took up his positions on the Busaco Ridge, and at the same time sent for Hill to join him with 20,000 men. The Allied Army was now 52,000 strong, half British and half Portuguese, and Wellington reckoned that that would be enough, even though the French had 65,000. After 14 months on the defensive, he was now ready to fight – provided that it was on his terms, as he reckoned it would be.

"I have enough men to defeat Massena," he declared. "If he attacks me here, I shall beat him."[10]

Wellington's prediction proved to be absolutely correct. On **27 September, 1810** Massena launched a series of frontal attacks against the Busaco Ridge and was soundly defeated.

Wellington might well have pursued the French, but this was not part of his long-term strategy. He was satisfied to have inflicted a sharp defeat on the enemy at minimum cost to his own army, and now he had no hesitation in completing the next phase of his plan by withdrawing to the completed Lines of Torres Vedras.[11]

Massena followed, confident that he could still drive the British into the sea. Hurrying after Wellington, he left 4,000 wounded in Coimbra, inadequately guarded, whereupon Colonel Trant with 4,000 Portuguese Militia carried out a brilliant raid and captured 4,500 French troops.

The Lines of Torres Vedras (See Chapter 16)

The Peninsular Army now withdrew according to plan, laying waste the countryside as they went, and by **10 October** they were all settled in behind the Lines.

Massena was close behind them and he saw the Lines for the first time on 10 October. He immediately realized what a formidable barrier they were and, when a probing attack on the **14th** was repulsed with heavy loss, he accepted that he had no hope of breaking through and made no further assaults.

Wellington had expected that his "scorched earth" tactics would force the French to withdraw within a week or so due to starvation, but somehow they held on until **15 November**, when Massena slipped away to Santarem.

Wellington followed cautiously, and refused to attack, declaring, "I could lick these fellows any day, but it would cost me 10,000 lives, and as this is the last army that England has got, we must take care of it."[12]

It was a policy that made sense, for the French lost 25,000 men that winter from starvation and disease, more than the casualties in most major battles.

So, the Lines of Torres Vedras served their purpose in full measure.[13] They brought the French invasion of Portugal to a complete and permanent halt, and from now on, although there was still a long, hard road ahead, there was little chance that Napoleon's Marshals would ever succeed in driving the British "leopards" into the sea, as they had done two years before at Corunna.

Notes

1 and 2   Badajoz and Ciudad Rodrigo, being in Spain, were garrisoned by Spanish troops.

3   The Light Brigade became the Light Division on 1 March, 1810. It included a regiment of K.G.L. cavalry and Ross's Battery of the Royal Horse Artillery. Both the 14th and 16th Light Dragoons were placed "under command".

4   1st Division did not have one, nor did 2nd Division; they were closely associated with the only all-Portuguese Division. Craufurd's Light Division had British and Portuguese battalions in each brigade.

There were usually 5 or 6 British officers in each Portuguese battalion, and they received two steps in rank. Most but not all Portuguese brigades were commanded by British officers.

5   The artist, Goya, was one who used to glean useful gossip from the French commanders whom he painted, and then passed it back to Wellington.

6   Letter to Stanhope.

7   The wife of a Captain on his staff and sister of a former mistress.

8   Letter to Wellesley, 31 July, 1810.

9   Despatches, VI, 454.

10   Napier, II, p.115.

11   He was asked later what he considered to be the greatest attribute of a commander, and replied, "To know when to retreat, and to have the courage to do it."

12   Fortescue, VII, 555.

13   The Monument at Alhandra to Colonel Fletcher, Wellington's Chief Engineer, who constructed the Lines, is inscribed 'Non Ultra', or 'No Further.'

CHAPTER FIVE

1811 – 'A Near-Run Thing'

1811 began with the Peninsular Army established in comparative comfort behind the Lines of Torres Vedras, while Massena and his starving soldiers struggled to survive at Santarem. To the east Soult was besieging Badajoz without much success, but the French did inflict two defeats on the Spanish armies – first, at Olivenza where the garrison finally surrendered on **22 January**, and second, on the Gebora River on **19 February**.

The Battle of Barrosa (See Chapter 17)

In **March, 1811** came the welcome news of a fine British victory at Barrosa. An Allied garrison of around 26,000 had been besieged in Cadiz since January, 1810, but this was accepted by Wellington as part of his strategy, because they tied down an equal number of French troops who would otherwise be free to fight the Peninsular Army.

In February, 1811, plans were made for an Anglo-Spanish force of 13,000 to make a sortie from Cadiz by sea and land behind the investing French army. But the Spanish commander, General La Pena, proved so incompetent that on **5 March** the British element of 5,000 found itself isolated at Barrosa and under attack by 9,000 French under Marshal Victor. The British commander, Sir Thomas Graham, decided that his only hope lay in a bold counter-attack and, very much against the odds, he won the day.

On the same day Massena finally began to withdraw his demoralized army from Santarem. He had been thwarted ever since his retreat from the Lines by Wellington's firm refusal to fight; he was constantly harassed by guerrillas, and his men could no longer live off the land in the face of Wellington's "scorched earth" policy. He now retired back into Spain, and Wellington pursued him closely, covering 300 miles in

28 days, and might have trapped him at Sabugal on 3 **April**, but for blunders by General Erskine, commanding the 5th Division.

On 11 **April** Massena was back in Salamanca, having abandoned most of his transport and lost at least 25,000 men out of his original 65,000, mostly from starvation and sickness.[1] It was convincing proof of the success of the Allied strategy, and also of the value of the Spanish and Portuguese guerrillas.

Wellington had now driven the French out of Portugal for the third time, but he still faced serious problems. Badajoz had been captured by Soult on 10 **March**, and so both the "keys to Spain" were now in enemy hands. If Massena and Soult were to unite, they would have at least 70,000 men against his 58,000. Worse still, he was obliged, in order to defend Portugal, to divide his army between Ciudad Rodrigo and Badajoz, 120 miles apart. This made control extremely difficult, for his lines of communication in the north were 200 miles long and he had little choice but to remain on the defensive.

He set up his own headquarters at Frenada in the north, with 38,000 men, and put General Beresford in command in the south with 20,000.[2]

On 25 **March** Beresford drove back the French at Campo Mayor, but the success was marred by the British cavalry, who charged, lost all control and suffered severe casualties.

On 16 **April** Wellington rode south to see Beresford,[3] and ordered him to invest Badajoz, even though his chances of taking it were small, as he had no siege train and very inadequate artillery. He also advised Beresford that, if attacked by Soult, a possible defensive position might be around the village of Albuera, 14 miles south-east of Badajoz.

By the **28th** he was back in his headquarters, much to everyone's relief, as they had little confidence in his deputy, Sir Brent Spencer, and news had just come in that the French were advancing in the north.

The Battle of Fuentes de Onoro (See Chapter 18)

On 3 **May** Massena advanced westwards from Ciudad Rodrigo with an army of 48,000, determined to avenge his defeats at Busaco and the Lines of Torres Vedras. His plan was to break through and relieve the besieged fortress of Almeida, the only French garrison remaining in Portugal.

Although he had only 38,000 infantry, Wellington was prepared to fight if he could find a suitable defensive position. He had no Busaco

Ridge available this time, but he saw a possible line centred on the village of Fuentes de Onoro, astride the road into Portugal. He occupied it, hoping that Massena would oblige by attacking frontally, as he had at Busaco.

On the afternoon of 3 May Massena did indeed oblige, with a massive frontal assault against Fuentes de Onoro, which was repulsed. There was a pause on the 4th and he attacked again on the 5th, this time from the south and came near to outflanking the Allied position. But Wellington managed to hold on, thanks to his usual close control of the battle and to a fine fighting withdrawal by the Light Division, supported by the cavalry, who on this occasion excelled themselves.

The battle was, in Wellington's words, "the most difficult one I was ever concerned in and against the greatest odds." He also said that "If Boney had been there we should have been beat."[4] But he might have added that, if Boney had been there, he would probably not have fought the French at all at such unfavourable odds. In the event, it was a classic defensive battle.

The French finally withdrew, and Massena was, not surprisingly, replaced shortly afterwards – by Marshal Marmont, a capable, ambitious man who took immediate steps to restore the morale and fighting efficiency of his army.[5]

It was a moment of triumph for the Allies, but was followed by a week of setbacks. On the night of 10/11 May 900 of the 1,300 French garrison of Almeida escaped, due to gross negligence by General Erskine, who was commanding the investing troops. Wellington angrily described it as "the most disgraceful military event".[6]

The Battle of Albuera (See Chapter 19)

Only a day later, on 12 May, Beresford was forced to abandon his siege of Badajoz, because Soult was advancing against him from the south with 25,000 men, including 4,400 cavalry and 50 guns. Beresford had 35,000 men and 38 guns, and took up a position round Albuera, as Wellington had advised.

Soult attacked on 16 May, not frontally as expected, but against the Allied right, which was held by the Spaniards.

A grim slogging match followed, with heavy losses on both sides from volleys at close range. It was very much "a soldiers' battle", with Beresford exercising little control over events. The day was saved by Sir Lowry Cole, who at a crucial moment counter-attacked on his own initiative with his 4th Division, and it was the French who eventually withdrew first.

But it was another "near-run thing", and the British infantry suffered around 50% casualties. Beresford has been much criticized for his handling of the battle, and Wellington sent him shortly afterwards to take command of the expanding Portuguese Army, a task that he carried out extremely well. He was replaced by Sir Rowland Hill, who had just returned from sick leave.

Wellington now renewed the siege of Badajoz, but it resisted all his efforts, and on **19 June** news came that Soult and Marmont had joined forces and were advancing against Badajoz with 58,000 men. Wellington promptly withdrew behind the Guadiana, but surprisingly the French did not attack – evidence of the new respect they now had for Wellington as a commander and for the fighting qualities of his Peninsular Army.

At the **end of June** both sides returned to their original positions, and Wellington began besieging Ciudad Rodrigo. He was not optimistic, as he still had no siege train and, when the French again concentrated against him, he abandoned the blockade on **20 September** and withdrew.

There was an anxious moment on **25–28 September** when Picton's 3rd Division was nearly trapped at El Bodon, and on the 25th Wellington himself narrowly escaped capture, when he mistook some French Chasseurs for his own Hussars.[7] But he got his army safely back into Portugal and there was no more campaigning that year.

Notes

1   There were only 8,000 battle casualties and 2,000 prisoners.
2   Including 3,000 British and 15,000 Spanish.
3   He covered 70 miles a day, wearing out two horses and losing two dragoons from his escort in flooded streams. He also nearly got himself captured while reconnoitring Badajoz.
4   Supplementary Despatches, VII, p.117.
5   To look after his own morale he brought with him from Illyria 12 cooks and a large staff of liveried servants to ease the discomforts of campaigning in the Peninsula.
6   He said he would not, however, sack Erskine, as he might well be sent someone even worse from the Horse Guards. He regarded it as a case of "better the devil you know".
7   The Hussars had just been issued with new caps which were dangerously like those of the French cavalry.

CHAPTER SIX

1812 – The Tide Turns

General Situation

1812 saw the tide beginning to turn in favour of the Allies, and it was a year of considerable activity. The campaigning began and ended at Ciudad Rodrigo, but much happened in between.

Napoleon was already in the New Year planning his invasion of Russia, set for June 1812, and he therefore at last handed over control of the five French armies in Spain[1] to the men on the spot. He placed King Joseph[2] in overall command, with Marshal Jourdan as his Chief of Staff; it was a wise move, but it came too late for them to be able to form any effective, unified strategy. He also ordered 27,000 troops to be sent back to France from Spain, which in turn meant that Marmont had to send 10,000 men from his Army of Portugal to reinforce Suchet in Valencia.

Wellington soon heard of this, and immediately planned to take advantage of it by capturing Ciudad Rodrigo, which he considered he could do before either Marmont or Soult could intervene.

The Capture of Ciudad Rodrigo (See Chapter 20)

Determined to waste no time, Wellington invested the fortress on **8th January**, and pressed ahead with the siege, despite severe winter conditions. On **19th January** he issued one of his typically laconic orders. "Ciudad Rodrigo must be stormed tonight." It duly was, with only 500 casualties – a feat described by Sir Arthur Bryant as "one of the greatest of the whole war".[3] The success was marred, however, by the death of General Craufurd, the brilliant commander of the Light Division, and also by the undisciplined behaviour of the troops after the assault.

The Capture of Badajoz (See Chapter 21)

Within five days Wellington was planning to capture Badajoz, and by **16 March** he had already surreptitiously moved the bulk of his army south and was investing the town. The outlying Fort Picurina was taken by storm on the **24th**, but progress was slow and, when Wellington heard that Soult was advancing from the south and that Marmont was threatening Ciudad Rodrigo, he ordered an all-out assault for **6 April**, even though preparations were not quite complete.

The main effort against the south-east corner of the fortress failed, with severe losses, but two subsidiary attacks unexpectedly met with success and the garrison surrendered.

Badajoz had fallen, but at the very high cost of 4,924 casualties, and it is said to be one of the two occasions when Wellington broke down and wept on reading the list of names.[4] He wrote to Lord Liverpool: "The capture of Badajoz affords as strong an instance of the gallantry of our troops as has ever been displayed. But I greatly hope that I shall never again be the instrument of putting them to such a test as they were put to last night."

The horrors of that desperate night affected the troops too, and the survivors went on a rampage that brought shame on the Peninsular Army.

Wellington's Plan

Wellington was now better placed to take the offensive than ever before. He held the initiative and could advance into Spain by either of two routes. Weighing the odds, he decided that the time was ripe for a bold thrust into central Spain, which would divide the French armies in the south from those in the north, and would at the same time threaten Madrid, a valuable prize politically. More than that, if he could also seize Burgos, he would cut the enemy forces off from their bases in France – an ambitious but worthwhile target.

Leaving Hill with 18,000 to hold the south as in 1810, he moved north to attack Marmont. But first he set about isolating him, through organized actions by Spanish troops and guerrillas throughout Spain, and by seaborne landings on both the Biscay and Mediterranean coasts. As a result, the French never managed to concentrate enough men to outnumber him. Hill contributed with a raid against Almarez and the destruction of the bridge there, which virtually cut Marmont's army off from that of Soult.

On 13 **June** Wellington advanced towards Salamanca, which he entered on the **17th**, making it the first Spanish city to be liberated in three years. He had some 48,000 troops, while Marmont had 40,000, and both therefore wanted to fight only on favourable terms. For the next month they marched and counter-marched, manoeuvring like two boxers sparring for an opening and a knock-out blow.

There was an anxious moment on 18 **July** when both Wellington and Beresford were intercepted by French cavalry while on reconnaissance and only just managed to fight their way out with drawn swords.

The Battle of Salamanca (See Chapter 22)

On 20 **July** Wellington and his army were back in Salamanca, with the French some 10 miles to the east round Huerta. He was looking for a fight now, because he knew (though Marmont did not!) that King Joseph had sent 13,000 men from Madrid to reinforce Marmont's army.

On the night of the **21st** a violent thunderstorm broke over both sides – an event that would be recalled by the British troops three years later as an omen of victory on the night before Waterloo.

On 22 **July** the armies were only about a mile apart, marching on parallel courses near the village of Los Arapiles, some five miles south of Salamanca. At about 1400 Wellington, who had been watching the enemy closely, noticed that Marmont had so extended his line of march that it was vulnerable to a flank attack against its centre.

With the famous remark "By God! That will do," he launched one of the greatest opportunist battles in history. It was the moment when "40,000 Frenchmen were defeated in 40 minutes"; it was also the moment when Wellington established himself beyond doubt as a brilliant attacking general rather than as a primarily defensive one.

By dusk Marmont had been wounded and his army was in full retreat, having lost 13,000 men, 2 Eagles and 6 Colours, and suffered a most humiliating defeat.

With the French now thoroughly demoralized, Wellington advanced on Madrid, which was liberated on 12 **August**, amid scenes of tremendous rejoicings.

The Peninsular Army was allowed to relax there for a month, but then they were marched north to Burgos, which was invested on **19 September**, five days before Napoleon entered the smouldering ruins of Moscow.

The Siege of Burgos (See Chapter 23)

For the next five weeks Wellington besieged the fortress of Burgos, but he had under-estimated the task and his assaults all failed. Hearing that the French were closing in on him, he abandoned the siege on **21 October**, glad to be away from what he now called "this damned place".[5] **Three days later** Napoleon began his Retreat from Moscow.

Wellington fared better on his retreat back to Portugal than did the Emperor, but he described it later as "the worst scrape I was ever in".[6] He had 35,000 men, but was being closely pursued by 60,000; supplies went astray, the weather was atrocious, and he lost 6,000 men, including General Sir Edward Paget, who was captured. He also had to recall Hill and abandon Madrid on **30 October**. But he managed to get most of his army safely back to Ciudad Rodrigo by **20 November** and the French abandoned their pursuit. He now settled in for the winter and prepared for a full-scale offensive in 1813.

Summary of 1812

Although the year ended on an unhappy note for Wellington, much had been achieved. He had captured both Ciudad Rodrigo and Badajoz, had soundly defeated the French at Salamanca, and had liberated Madrid, albeit temporarily. He had taken 20,000 French prisoners and 300 guns, and had freed the whole of southern Spain.

The failure to seize Burgos was a setback, but a temporary failure only; the losses at Badajoz had been grievous, but the siege had ended in success. Morale was high in the Peninsular Army, for everyone now felt confident that they were better, man for man, than the enemy, and that under the leadership of "Old Nosey" they would lick them as they had at Salamanca. The French, on the other hand, had little of which to be proud in 1812, and little hope of better things ahead.

On the wider strategic scene, the picture was encouraging too. Napoleon's Retreat from Moscow had been a disaster, and from now on his star was on the wane. The tide had turned inexorably against him, and the surrender of the Imperial Armies, unthinkable a year ago, was now only 16 months away.

Notes

1 Suchet	East Coast	60,000
Dorsenne	Army of the North	48,000
Marmont	Army of Portugal	52,000
Soult	Army of the South	54,000
Joseph	Madrid	18,500
		232,500

2 Joseph was no military genius, but he was a sound ruler, and even the Spaniards called him 'Tio Pepe' or 'Uncle Joe.'

3 *Years of Victory*, p. 466.

4 The other occasion was after Waterloo.

5 Despatches, IX, 446, 5 October.

6 Despatch, 31 October, 1812.

CHAPTER SEVEN

1813 – On The Offensive

The Strategy of 1813

1813 was the year when the Allies finally went on to the offensive in the Peninsula after five frustrating years when the odds made it impossible. The crucial question was whether or not Napoleon would as a result withdraw his armies from Spain in order to defend France against the Allied attacks from the east. He, like Hitler, was reluctant to abandon one inch of territory, but he did order Joseph to withdraw from Madrid and take up a new defensive line along the River Douro.

The parallels with 1944 are striking, for Napoleon was now committed to a war on two fronts, and the tide had turned against him. As in 1944, confident, well-trained Allied armies were liberating Occupied Europe and advancing towards the enemy's homeland.

It was mobile warfare, remarkably similar to the 1944–45 campaign in North-West Europe, with Soult's massive offensive across the Pyrenees in July, 1813, closely resembling von Runstedt's Ardennes offensive of December, 1944. But for Napoleon, like Hitler, it was a losing battle, and by April, 1814, he would be forced to abdicate.

Wellington's Plan

Wellington spent the **winter months of 1813** preparing his army for his Spring offensive. Discipline was tightened, 5,000 new drafts were absorbed, and the authorities at Horse Guards were, with some difficulty, persuaded to let him remove several of his worst commanders.[1]

He was on 2 October at last made C-in-C of the Spanish armies, but it only added to his problems, for he now had to control an additional 160,000 troops, poorly organized and spread throughout Spain.

The Peninsular Army was 81,000 strong, together with 25,000 Spanish actually under command, but the French, now under the supreme command of King Joseph, could muster 200,000, and they were mostly located in northern Spain, and therefore well placed to concentrate against Wellington's forces.

The French were holding the line of the River Douro between Zamorra and Valladolid and expected Wellington to advance against them from the south.

But he, as usual, intended to attack where he was *not* expected, and his plan was to make a wide sweep to the north which would outflank the French not only on the Douro, but the whole way back to France. It was a bold and imaginative plan, which had been discounted by the French because they thought it was impossible to supply any large force in that area from Portugal. But Wellington was proposing to do just that by moving his supply base forward from Lisbon to Santander, thus greatly reducing his lines of communication.

He also planned several diversions to prevent the French from concentrating against him. He activated the guerrillas in northern Spain, and also arranged a sea-borne assault against Tarragona by 18,000 troops under Sir John Murray. It was not a successful operation, but it achieved Wellington's purpose.

He sent Hill with 30,000 men and six brigades of cavalry to Salamanca to make the enemy think that this was the main line of advance of the Allied Army, and he himself joined Hill initially, to make it look more convincing.

The main thrust, however, was to be to the north under Graham, with six out of his eight veteran divisions, a total of 60,000 men. His objective was Zamorra, and D Day was set for **22 May**.

As he crossed the frontier with Hill, Wellington is supposed to have exclaimed, "Farewell, Portugal. I shall never see you again." It was accurate, as always, but uncharacteristically theatrical.

Events now moved swiftly. On **26 May**, Hill captured Salamanca and the **next day** the French abandoned Madrid for the third time.

On the 29th Wellington rejoined Graham,[2] who on **2 June** captured Zamorra.

The French had been taken completely by surprise and their right flank was now constantly threatened. They retreated to Burgos, but this time Wellington by-passed it to the north; on **13 June**, Joseph withdrew again, having blown up the Castle.

The next possible line of defence was the Ebro, but this too was turned by Graham, and Joseph was forced to retreat yet again, this time to the communications centre of Vitoria, which he reached on **19 June**.

1. British and French Commanders in the Peninsular War

1. Sir Thomas Picton; 2. General Crawfurd; 3. Sir Thomas Graham; 4. Sir Henry
Clinton; 5. Sir Rowland Hill; 6. Sir John Moore; 7. Marshal Lord Beresford;
8. Napoleon; 9. Wellington;
10. Marshal Soult; 11. Marshal Massena; 12. Marshal Ney;
13. Marshal Marmont; 14. Marshal Junot; 15. Marshal Victor; 16. Marshal Suchet.

2. **Rolica.** The Memorial to Colonel Lake in the centre of the French position. The hill in the far background is the left of the French line. "In the desperate fighting Colonel Lake was killed and only 4 officers and 30 men survived unwounded". (p.62)

3. **Vimiero.** The Monument on Vimiero Hill, looking east with the village to the left and the Eastern Ridge in the background. It "marks the area of fierce fighting by Fane's and Anstruther's brigades". (p.71)

Wellington was close behind, and, knowing that reinforcements might reach Joseph on the 22nd, he decided to attack on the 21st.

The Battle of Vitoria (See Chapter 24)

Joseph expected Wellington to attack from the west, and he took up a strong position with 66,000 men in three lines between Vitoria and the Arinez feature, using the Zadorra River and the mountains to the north and south to protect his flanks.

But when Wellington attacked on **21 June, 1813**, it was not from the west. He had 79,000 men and he used his superior numbers to make thrusts from four different directions.

After feints from the south and west, he launched his main effort from the north. Dalhousie and Picton, with 10,000 men, attacked the French right flank from the direction of Mendoza, while another column under Graham, 20,000 strong, swung even further east, and cut the enemy's escape routes north-east from Vitoria.

All went well and the French were completely out-manoeuvred. By 1700, their defences had collapsed, and they fled eastwards, abandoning a vast baggage train of loot and losing 151 out of 153 guns, as well as 8,000 casualties.

It was a crushing defeat and the Allies had now driven the French from the whole of Spain except for a few garrisons including San Sebastian and Pamplona. Above all the victory had immense propaganda value, for Napoleon had just won two impressive victories at Lutzen and Bautzen and was in a position to negotiate on his own terms; but Vitoria changed all that. Wellington was now appointed Field-Marshal and recognized as the leading Allied commander.

The Battles of the Pyrenees (See Chapters 26–28)

Wellington now had to decide whether or not to advance into France. It was tempting to follow up the demoralized enemy, but the problems and risks were considerable. He had advanced 400 miles in 40 days, and, like Montgomery in 1944, had major administrative worries. His 25,000 Spanish troops would become a liability if he entered enemy territory, for they would inevitably seek revenge for six years of occupation, and he could not afford that when he had to win the hearts and minds of the French people. He therefore made the difficult decision to leave all but the most reliable Spanish troops in Spain.

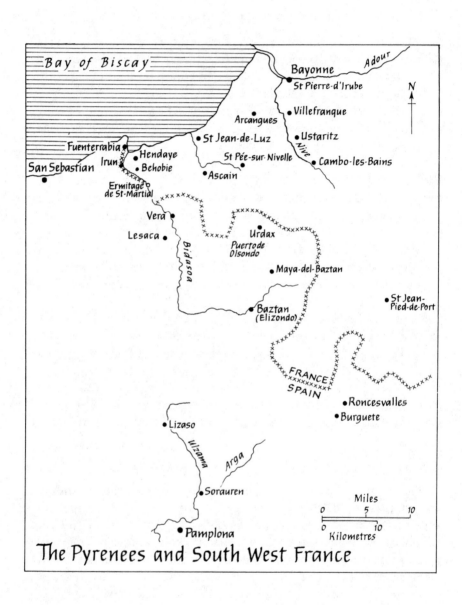

Bay of Biscay

Adour

Bayonne
St Pierre-d'Irube

N

Arcangues

Villefranque

St Jean-de-Luz

Ustaritz

Nive

Fuenterrabia

St Pée-sur-Nivelle

Cambo-les-Bains

Irun

Hendaye

San Sebastian

Behobie

Ascain

Ermitage
de St-Martial

Vera

Bidasoa

Urdax

Lesaca

Puerto de
Olsondo

Maya-del-Baztan

St Jean-
Pied-de-Port

Baztan
(Elizondo)

FRANCE
SPAIN

Roncesvalles

Burguete

Lizaso

Ulzama

Arga

Sorauren

Miles
0   5   10

0   10
Kilometres

Pamplona

The Pyrenees and South West France

He still faced 200,000 French troops, fighting in and for their homeland, and it was always possible that Napoleon himself, after his victories in the east, would turn in full strength against the Peninsular Army. Reluctantly, Wellington decided not to advance, but to hold the line of the Pyrenees until he had captured San Sebastian and Pamplona.

There were only three passable roads through the Pyrenees – the coast road at Irun, the Pass of Maya and the Pass of Roncesvalles. There were, however, 70 small passes that could be infiltrated by infantry, and Wellington had only 60,000 troops to hold a 50-mile front. He therefore adopted the same tactics as in 1811 on the Lines of Torres Vedras, i.e. holding the front line in minimum strength and keeping the bulk of his army in reserve, ready to deal with any breakthrough.[3]

Expecting Soult to attack along the coast to relieve San Sebastian, he placed seven out of his ten divisions covering that sector.[4] He was stretching his resources to the utmost by trying to capture two fortresses as well as defending the frontier, and he confessed later that this "daring scheme" was "one of the greatest faults he ever committed in war".

Soult used the respite granted to him to reorganize the remnants of the four armies now under his command into one Army of Spain, 80,000 strong. He knew that Wellington was over-extended, and also that he expected any French attack to be along the coast. For a moment Soult held the initiative and he used it to launch a brilliant counter-offensive.

At dawn on **25 July, 1813,** 21,000 men under D'Erlon attacked the Pass of Maya, but were checked after heavy fighting (see Chapter 26). At the same time 40,000 under Soult himself attacked and captured the Pass of Roncesvalles 20 miles to the south (see Chapter 27). Soult's grand plan was to relieve Pamplona and then turn north to relieve San Sebastian, which would at the same time cut off all Wellington's forces in the northern sector.

It was a remarkably bold venture, and remarkably similar to the German Ardennes Offensive of 1944. It achieved complete surprise, but finally failed in the face of skilful Allied counter-moves.

Wellington was at San Sebastian on the morning of the **25th** when Soult attacked and it was not until 0400 on the morning of the **26th** that he heard at his headquarters at Lesaca that Stewart had been driven back from the Pass of Maya. He immediately rode to Elizondo and consulted with him. He then rode south to Almandoz, where he heard at 2000 for the first time of Cole's unauthorized withdrawal from Roncesralles the night before.

At dawn on **27 July** Wellington headed south again and found Cole at last at Sorauren, 5 miles north of Pamplona, where he had taken up a defensive position, with the French close behind him. Wellington took over command and the **next day** defeated a strong attack by Soult at the Battle of Sorauren (see Chapter 28).

This effectively checked the French advance on Pamplona, and Soult was now in trouble, for he had been relying on obtaining fresh supplies from Pamplona. But he knew that politically it would be disastrous for the French to be driven ignominiously out of Spain again, and he therefore planned a last desperate throw, although the odds were heavily against him. Three French divisions under D'Erlon thrust westwards on **30 July** and drove Hill back to Lizaso. But the same day Wellington launched his own counter-attack at Sorauren and soon drove the French there back into the Pyrenees in disorder.

Soult's position was now hopeless and he ordered a withdrawal. The Allies, however, held the escape routes at Maya and Roncesvalles, and the remnants of his army had to straggle north to Vera to reach France again. By **31 July** they had all been driven back across the frontier, having lost 13,500 men out of 61,000. They were now in no position to withstand the strong Allied offensive that was to follow.

Capture of San Sebastian (See Chapter 25)

Following the unsuccessful assault on **25 July** Graham waited until **31 August** before trying again. This time the fortress was taken, but at the cost of 2,376 casualties.

The Battle of the Bidassoa (See Chapter 29)

On the **same day** that San Sebastian fell Soult attacked again, this time westwards across the Bidassoa. One thrust by Clausel at Irun against the Spanish troops on the San Marcial feature was repulsed and another attack at Vera also failed.

It was Soult's last attempt to defend the frontiers of France and for the next six months he would be fighting a series of rearguard actions, as he was driven steadily back to Toulouse.

The Crossing of the Bidassoa (See Chapter 30)

September, 1813, saw a pause in the campaign, while both sides reorganized. The strategic situation improved steadily for the Allies, with Russia, Prussia and Austria all joining the Alliance against Napoleon. The familiar arguments in favour of a Second Front began to be heard, as in 1942–44, and it was agreed that an invasion of France by the Peninsular Army would increase the pressure on Napoleon.

On **7 October** Wellington carried out a brilliant operation, in which he successfully crossed the Bidassoa both at Irun near the coast and five miles inland at Vera, where he captured the key feature of the Greater Rhune. He was now through the Pyrenees and on French soil at last.

The Battle of the Nivelle (See Chapter 31)

Pamplona finally surrendered on **23 October** and Wellington now felt in a position to advance deeper into France; on **10 November** the Allies broke through the strong French line along the River Nivelle.

Soult had expected Wellington to attack along the coast, but the main thrust came against his centre, threatening to cut off his troops near the coast. He was forced to withdraw once more, taking up a defensive line along the River Nive from Cambo-les-Bains through Bayonne to the sea.

The Battle of the Nive (See Chapter 32)

On **9 December** the Allied army advanced again, and closed in on Bayonne, as well as driving the French from their positions along the Nive.

But Soult now had the advantage of interior lines, i.e. being on the inside of the circle, and he used this to deliver two well-planned counter-attacks against the Allied forces encircling Bayonne.

On **10 December** he attacked Sir John Hope's force near the coast, taking them by surprise and driving them back three miles before being checked.

Then on **13 December** he switched to attack Hill, who was isolated east of the Nive at St Pierre (see Chapter 33). He outnumbered Hill's force by more than 2 to 1, and he came very close to inflicting a severe defeat. But allied reinforcements arrived just in time, and eventually it was the French who withdrew.

So, by the **end of 1813** Wellington was firmly established deep in France, investing Bayonne, and already he was planning the final blows to be struck early in 1814.

Summary

The achievements of Wellington and his Peninsular Army in 1813 are impressive. They advanced 500 miles, starting from Portugal and ending deep in France. They defeated the French consistently and with growing confidence, and were now poised for final victory.

The Allies did not have any overwhelming numerical superiority, but they did have three decisive advantages, which they used effectively. The first was the strategy that Wellington adopted and implemented. The second was the Peninsular Army itself, which was now a highly-trained and very confident fighting force, that had achieved a marked psychological supremacy over the demoralized French.

The third and most significant factor of all was Wellington himself as a commander. He dominated every moment of the year's campaigning, consistently and confidently out-manoeuvring the French at every turn.

Notes

1 He rid himself of five cavalry and ten infantry generals, but did *not* ask for replacements as he feared that he would probably be sent someone even worse.
2 He rode 50 miles in two days, crossing the Douro at Miranda, where he was winched across in a wicker basket.
3 It is interesting to compare this again with British plans in 1940 and German plans in 1944.
4 *Northern Sector*
 Headquarters   Lesaca
 1st Division
 3rd Division
 4th Division
 6th Division
 7th Division
 Light Division
 Longa (Spanish)
 Passes of Maya and Roncesvalles (Hill)
 2nd Division
 Silviera (Portuguese)
 San Sebastian (Graham)
 5th Division

CHAPTER EIGHT

1814 – Victory At Last

The Political Factor

As happens towards the end of any war, 1814 saw political factors becoming increasingly significant. Napoleon was negotiating with the Allies, and there was a possibility that he might be allowed to remain on the throne, but with his Empire reduced to pre-Revolutionary boundaries. He realized by now that his only hope probably lay in splitting the Alliance, and he was trying to achieve this.

But, by the Treaty of Chaumont, signed on 1 March, 1814, the four Allies, England, Russia, Prussia and Austria, agreed that they would fight on until Napoleon was overthrown. Already, armies of the last three were advancing westwards towards Paris on a broad front, but in February they suffered a series of setbacks at the hands of Napoleon. It is intriguing that Wellington expressed his disapproval of this policy, advocating instead one concentrated drive on Paris, just as Field-Marshal Montgomery pressed for one major thrust on Berlin in late 1944.

Now that the Peninsular Army was operating in France itself, Wellington was very concerned to win the "hearts and minds" of the French people. To this end he enforced a policy of no retribution and no plundering, and also insisted that all supplies and equipment acquired locally must always be paid for.[1] As Soult's army never paid, the civilian population soon came to prefer the British troops to their own army, and their cooperation was reckoned to be worth up to two divisions to Wellington, because he could have fewer troops on guard duties.

The Spanish troops were another problem.[2] As Wellington himself wrote, "They are in so miserable a state, that it is hardly fair to expect that they will refrain from plundering . . . without pay and food, they must plunder, and if they plunder, they will ruin us all."[3]

Wellington's Plan

Wellington now had 63,000 men, apart from the Spaniards, and he intended to maintain his offensive. His plan for 1814 was to manoeuvre Soult eastwards away from Bayonne, and so split the French army. He intended to do this by a series of outflanking attacks, such as had worked so well against Joseph in Spain in 1813, but this time from the south.

Soult had 54,500 men, having had 10,000 men and 35 guns removed from him by Napoleon in January, 1814. Roughly half his army of seven divisions were north of the Adour defending Bayonne, and the other half were facing west across the Joyeuse, some 10 miles east of the Nive, which was held by the Allies.

Wellington ordered Hope, with 31,000 men, to besiege Bayonne from the south and to cross the Adour when he could. Hill, with his corps of 13,000 men, was to thrust eastwards between the Pyrenees and the river Gave de Pau. A reserve of four divisions remained with Wellington on the Nive, as a pivot between the two operations.

On **14 February, 1814,** Hill crossed the Joyeuse,[4] and by the **17th** had advanced 20 miles and isolated St Jean-Pied-de-Port. This made Soult do just what Wellington wanted, which was to withdraw two divisions from Bayonne.

Wellington now ordered Hope to cross the Adour west of Bayonne, which he did in a very successful operation on **23 February**. A small force of five companies of the Guards was ferried across by boat, and managed to secure a foothold, helped perhaps by a salvo of Congreve rockets which, to everyone's surprise, landed on target with demoralizing effects.[5]

With the help of the Navy a bridge of boats was built across the Adour at a point where the estuary was only 300 yards wide, and by the **26th** Hope had 15,000 troops north of the river. Bayonne, with its garrison of 17,000, including one field division, was now surrounded and isolated from the rest of Soult's army.

The Battle of Orthez (See Chapter 34)

Hill meanwhile continued to advance eastwards, and by **25 February** had pushed the French back to Orthez on the Gave de Pau. On the morning of the **27th** Wellington closed in on Orthez from the west, with 31,000 men to add to Hill's 13,000.

Soult had 36,000 and 48 guns and took up a strong position on a ridge to the west of the town. He repulsed Wellington's first attack, but when Hill attacked from the east of the town, in support of Wellington's second assault in the west, Soult withdrew, to avoid being cut off.

On **4 March** Wellington was contacted by the loyalist mayor of Bordeaux,[6] who offered to hand over the city to the Allies; a column under Beresford was promptly sent off and Bordeaux was liberated on **12 March**, 7th Division remaining there as the garrison.

Soult continued to retreat and, following a sharp rearguard action at Tarbes on **20 March**, he withdrew on the **24th** into Toulouse.

The Battle of Toulouse (See Chapter 35)

The Allied armies of Russia and Prussia entered Paris on **30 March**, 1814, and Napoleon abdicated on **4 April**.

But the news from Paris did not reach either Wellington or Soult until the 12th and on **10 April** Wellington attacked Toulouse. It was a difficult operation, as the city was protected by two rivers, the Garonne to the west and the Ers to the east, and Soult had dug in his 42,000 men on the Calvinet Ridge just east of the city.

Wellington's chosen line of attack was against the southern end of the ridge, but this meant a three-mile approach march under fire between the Ers and the eastern side of the ridge. Nevertheless Beresford was ordered to do this with 4th and 6th Divisions, while feint attacks were made from the north and west.

It was a tricky manoeuvre and things went wrong. Picton attacked, contrary to orders, and the Spaniards attacked prematurely and suffered heavily. There was hard fighting all day, but the attack from the south was eventually successful, helped by a gallant second assault by the Spaniards.

After 12 hours fighting, the French gave way, and Soult abandoned the city **next day**.

Wellington entered Toulouse in triumph on **12 April**, and that night heard the news of Napoleon's abdication. He informed Soult, who refused to believe it, but did agree to an armistice.

The Sortie from Bayonne (See Chapter 36)

But sadly Toulouse was not the last engagement of the war. Bayonne was still under siege, and on the night of **14 April** the French

Governor, General Thouvenot, launched a desperate sortie from the Citadel. It is uncertain whether he was ignorant of the armistice, or whether he acted out of anger, but either way, the result was 905 French and 838 British casualties to no purpose.

On **17 April, 1814**, Soult finally accepted defeat and, after six long years, the Peninsular War was at an end.

Finale

Although the French garrison of Bayonne held out until **26 April, 1814**, the Peninsular War can be said to have ended on **17 April 1814**, when Marshal Soult finally surrendered to his old opponent, the Duke of Wellington.

The French Army was disbanded and Napoleon's Marshals had to decide whether to support the Emperor or to switch their loyalties to the Bourbons. Soult chose the latter course.

Wellington was appointed British Ambassador in Paris, and the Allied leaders assembled in Vienna to dismember Napoleon's Empire and divide the spoils.

Wellington's magnificent Peninsular Army was also disbanded. Some of the Regiments were demobilized, while others were sent to Canada to fight the Americans, who had declared war on Britain in 1812.

So it was that at the Battle of Waterloo, just over a year later, victory was won by a "scratch force", collected together in great haste, and angrily described by Wellington as "an infamous army" compared to his Peninsular veterans.

Wellington was extremely proud of his Peninsular Army, as they were of him, and they had considerable confidence in each other. They had fought together against Europe's finest troops for six hard years, and as the Field-Marshal himself declared, they had achieved everything he had asked of them. They had fought their way from Lisbon to Toulouse, and they had never been defeated.

Notes

1 Wellington was, however, very short of cash with which to pay for goods, particularly as the French peasants refused to accept Spanish or Portuguese coins. He asked Commanding Officers confidentially whether anyone perhaps had a counterfeiter among his men. He found 40, and soon had his own mint turning Spanish dollars into forged 5-franc Napoleonic pieces.

2 They had behaved particularly badly after the Crossing of the Nivelle in November, 1813, plundering the town of Ascain.

3 Despatches, IX, 306–7.

4 The first of four rivers that Hill had to cross; the others being the Bidouse, the Saison and the Gave d'Oloron.

5 A specimen of the Congreve Rocket can be seen in the Military Museum in Madrid.

6 He had the intriguing name of Lynch, being descended from an Irishman who had emigrated in 1688.

The Battles
and Battlefields

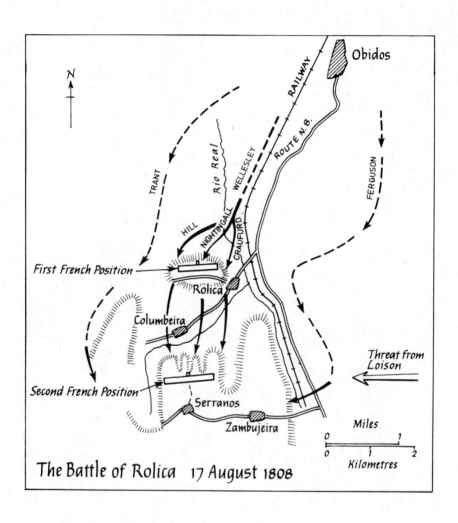

N

Obidos

RAILWAY

ROUTE N.8.

TRANT

Rio Real

WELLESLEY

FERGUSON

HILL

NIGHTINGALL

CRAUFURD

First French Position

Rolica

Columbeira

Threat from
Loison

Second French Position

Serranos

Zambujeira

Miles

0   1

0   1   2

Kilometres

The Battle of Rolica   17 August 1808

CHAPTER NINE

The Battle of Rolica

Wellesley's Plan

Wellesley landed in Portugal at the mouth of the Mondego River on 1st August 1808, and advanced south to Obidos, which he reached on the 16th without opposition.

On the morning of 17th he carried out his customary thorough reconnaissance, and observed that the French, under General Delaborde, had taken up a defensive position some four miles to the south just in front of the village of Rolica.

Wellesley knew that he had a 3 to 1 superiority in numbers,[1] and he therefore decided to divide his force into three columns in order to encircle the enemy with a pincer attack.

Rolica lay in the centre of a horseshoe of steep hills about one mile wide and two miles long, with the open end facing Obidos. He sent Colonel Trant[2] with 1,350 Portuguese round behind the hills to the west, while to the east he deployed 4,500 British infantry and 6 guns under Major General Ferguson; he made this force rather stronger because 9,000 French under Loison were near Abrantes and so threatened that flank. Fane's Brigade filled the gap between Ferguson and the centre column which was under Wellesley's command. This was 9,000 strong and consisted of three British brigades (Craufurd. C., Nightingall and Hill), a weak battalion of Portuguese 'Cacadores' and 12 guns. Soon after dawn, they formed up with impressive precision opposite the centre of the French position, and then advanced steadily across the open plain towards Rolica.

Had Delaborde thought that this was the main attack, he would have fallen into Wellesley's trap, but he was too experienced to be so easily tricked. He had a detachment well out to the east watching for Loison, and they duly reported Ferguson's line of advance. Calmly Delaborde waited until the pincer movement was almost complete, and then withdrew skilfully back to an even stronger position about a mile south of Rolica. This was on a steep ridge, divided by four narrow gullies, and it could only be attacked frontally.

Wellesley's plan now was to repeat his original manoeuvre, but this time to let the two flanks close in on the French before he launched his main attack in the centre. Unfortunately there now occurred one of those courageous blunders which have happened periodically in the history of the British Army.

Colonel Lake, commanding the 1/29th (Worcesters), who were one of four battalions in the centre column, should have limited his action to skirmishing, while the flanking columns closed in. But instead, he led four companies straight up one of the gullies into the centre of the French position where they soon found themselves cut off. In desperate fighting Colonel Lake was killed, and only 4 officers and 30 men survived unwounded.

To save a dangerous situation Hill brought the 1/9th (East Norfolk) to their rescue, while Wellesley ordered a general attack without waiting for the flanking columns to close in. But the steep, broken ground prevented the British from using their superior numbers fully, and three assaults on the ridge were repulsed. The French fought doggedly, hoping that reinforcements under Loison would appear in time to save the day.

Finally, about 1600, Wellesley's infantry fought their way to the crest, just as Ferguson's column appeared. Delaborde now realized that he could hold on no longer, and he withdrew successfully through Zambujeira behind a screen of cavalry. For the loss of 600 men and 3 guns, he had inflicted 479 casualties on the British (half of them in 1/29th).

Wellesley did not press the pursuit, first because the French cavalry were still strong and effective, while he had very few, and second, because he had heard that Loison was now only five miles away. He also heard that two brigades from England were waiting to land, so he pressed on south to Vimiero, a village at the mouth of the Maceira River, whose estuary offered a suitable landing place.

THE BATTLEFIELD OF ROLICA

Where To Go

The best place to start is the beautiful Moorish walled town of Obidos, on the N.8 between Coimbra and Torres Vedras.

Rolica battlefield is some 3 miles further south along the N.8, about a mile west of the main road, and is signposted.

It is possible to drive still further south along the N.8 and turn off right to the village of Serranos, from where you can visit the second French position.

What To See

OBIDOS

From the northern ramparts you can see the scene of the skirmish on 16 August that preceded the Battle of Rolica. From the southern ramparts you can look towards Rolica, and see the French positions as Wellesley did on the morning of the battle. Within the town is the small square palace in the main street where Wellesley spent the night before the battle.

There is a Parador in the old Castle in Obidos, which is a picturesque town, apart from its military interest.

ROLICA

Turn off the N.8 towards the village of Rolica, and, just after crossing the railway, take the first turning right. After about a mile, stop on the crest of the ridge. (Viewpoint A)

You are now on the first French position, looking north, as they did, towards Obidos from where the British advanced across flat, open country.

To the east and west are the two ridges that form the horseshoe of which Rolica is the centre, and behind which Wellesley sent his two wide outflanking forces.

To the south is the village of Rolica, and beyond it can be seen the ridge that formed the second French position.

COLUMBEIRA

Drive back into Rolica, turn right and continue for ½ mile to the next village, Columbeira. Stop where there is a clear view to the south, (Viewpoint B) and you can see, about a mile away, the second French position.

Four spurs project northwards towards you, and the right-hand gully was the scene of the premature attack by the 29th. The whole position is a strong one, and you can see why three British attacks were repulsed.

SERRANOS

If you leave your vehicle on the high ground north of the village, you can walk along a track to a Monument to Colonel Lake placed at the head of the gully up which he led the 29th. **(Viewpoint C)**

From the same area you can see the battle from the French viewpoint.

Notes

1 16,000 men and 18 guns against 4,400 French with 5 guns.
2 Wellesley later described him as "A very good officer, but as drunken a dog as ever lived."

The Battle of Rolica

Order of Battle: Rolica – 17 August, 1808

ALLIES				FRENCH	
Brigades	*Commander*	*Strength*	*Position*	*Brigades*	*Strength*
1st	Hill		*Centre:*	Infantry	4,000
3rd	Nightingall		12 guns	Cavalry	300
5th	Craufurd C.		400 cavalry		
		9,000			
2nd	Ferguson		*Left*		
4th	Bowes		6 guns		
6th	Fane				
		4,500			
Portuguese	Trant	1,350	*Right*		
	Cavalry:				
	British	240			
	Portuguese	230			
Commander		Wellesley		Delaborde	
Strength		16,000		4,400	
Cavalry		470		300	
Guns		18		5	
Casualties		479		600 (plus 3 guns)	

65

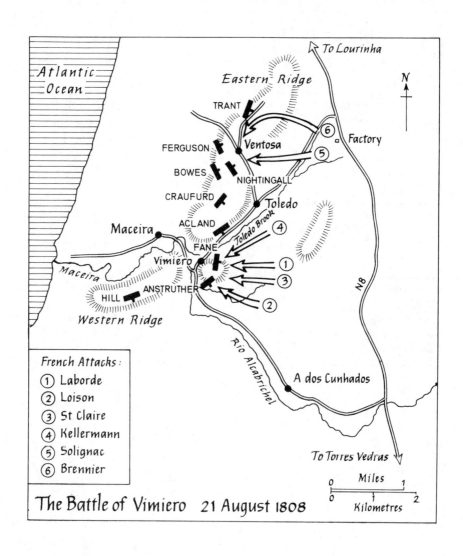

Atlantic
Ocean

Eastern Ridge

To Lourinha

N

TRANT

Ventosa

FERGUSON

⑥ Factory

⑤

BOWES

NIGHTINGALL

CRAUFURD

Toledo

ACLAND

④

Toledo Brook

Maceira

FANE

Vimiero

①

Maceira

③

N8

HILL ANSTRUTHER

②

Western Ridge

Rio Alcabrichel

French Attacks:
① Laborde
② Loison
③ St Claire
④ Kellermann
⑤ Solignac
⑥ Brennier

A dos Cunhados

To Torres Vedras

Miles
0   1
0   1   2
Kilometres

The Battle of Vimiero   21 August 1808

CHAPTER TEN

The Battle of Vimiero

Wellesley's Plan

Having driven back the French at Rolica on **17 August**, Wellesley moved on south to Vimiero at the mouth of the Maceira River, to cover the landing there of two brigades (Acland and Anstruther) that had just arrived from England.

He expected the main French force to advance against him from the south, and he therefore took up positions round Vimiero facing in that direction. A steep ridge runs north-east from the mouth of the river for some four miles to Ventosa. About one mile from the sea the river cuts a gorge through this ridge, dividing it into the East Ridge and the West Ridge, with the village of Vimiero lying just south of the gorge. On the south-east edge of the village is Vimiero Hill, a rounded feature, about 800 yards across, with dominating views to the south and east.

Wellesley initially made Vimiero Hill the key to his position holding the West Ridge strongly and putting only one brigade on the East Ridge. But when the French closed in on the morning of **21 August** he saw that they were advancing further to the east, and were therefore threatening to turn his left flank. He immediately changed the whole direction of his position, leaving only one brigade (Hill) to hold the West Ridge, and moving three brigades (Ferguson, Nightingall and Bowes) to the area of Ventosa on the East Ridge, facing south-east. He left two brigades (Fane and Anstruther) on Vimiero Hill, and put Acland's Brigade to fill the gap between them and Ventosa. Trant's Portuguese Brigade and Craufurd's Brigade were positioned north of Ventosa to protect his extreme left flank.

In accordance with the new tactics that he had worked out to defeat the French, he placed his troops out of sight as far as possible on the reverse slopes, and ordered them to lie down, so as to avoid casualties from the French artillery fire. He also pushed forward an exceptionally strong line of skirmishers to frustrate the French *tirailleurs*.

The French Plan

General Junot, marching north from Lisbon, planned to attack Wellesley without delay before he could land any more reinforcements. Having joined up with Loison and Delaborde, he had around 13,000 men and 23 guns against Wellesley's 17,000 with 18 guns, but this did not worry him.

He meant to attack at dawn on **21 August**, but his leading troops got lost and it was 0800 before he arrived within sight of Vimiero. His reconnaissance was perfunctory, and he concluded, quite wrongly, that Vimiero Hill was the centre of the British position.

He planned therefore to launch his main attack against the hill, while at the same time sending two brigades (Brennier followed by Solignac) to create a diversion by attacking Ventosa.

The Battle

Wellesley controlled the battle from the Eastern ridge, and soon appreciated that the main French effort was against Vimiero Hill. He could see the white-jacketed columns advancing, 30 men wide and 42 deep. In front were the usual *tirailleurs*, but they were making slower progress than usual, because of the skilful tactics of the British skirmishers.

The French also found decidedly disconcerting a new and lethal shell that was being fired at them. It had been invented by a Major Shrapnell[1] and burst in the air, scattering a deadly hail of grapeshot downwards on to the tightly-packed ranks.

Delaborde's troops advanced nevertheless in two columns about 400 yards apart, and at about 0900 they struck Fane's Brigade on the north face of Vimiero Hill. They came up against the 1st/50th[2] in a two-deep line just over the crest. At a range of about 100 yards, the British line fired their first volley, while the artillery tore great gaps in the French columns.

The British could bring to bear every one of their 900 muskets, whereas the French could use only 200 of their 1,200; with each volley, at precise 15-second intervals, the enemy ranks withered. When Fane's men charged with the bayonet, the French broke and fell back down the slope.

At the southern end of the hill Loison's column met a similar fate against Anstruther's Brigade, and 7 French guns were captured.

At this point Sir Harry Burrard appeared, but declined to take over command, saying that Wellesley was to finish off the battle he had begun.

Undeterred by his initial failure, Junot now launched a brigade of grenadiers against the same objective. One column was stopped by Fane's brigade, while the other advanced against the village of Vimiero, but halted in the face of devastating musketry and artillery fire from three sides as Acland's Brigade joined in from the north.

Four French attacks had now been shattered and every gun supporting them captured. There seemed to be an opportunity for a counter-stroke, and Wellesley launched his cavalry.

"Now, Twentieth, now is the time."[3]

Led by Colonel Taylor, the 20th Light Dragoons rode forward, but unfortunately lost all control and the Commanding Officer and half his men were killed, wounded or captured. It was a foretaste of what would happen all too often to Wellesley's cavalry during the campaign.

The fighting in front of Vimiero was over by 1100, with the French incapable of further attacks. But to the north the battle continued.

General Solignac, with some 3,000 infantry, 600 cavalry and 3 guns, marched north behind Brennier, then turned west and attacked Ventosa. Here he came up against nearly 6,000 British infantry under Ferguson, again concealed on the reverse slope.

It took only two minutes and some 10 volleys before the French withdrew, leaving their guns behind. Solignac himself was seriously wounded, and his brigade was driven northward, cutting it off from the rest of the French force.

Now came the sixth and last of Junot's disastrous, uncoordinated attacks. Brennier had reached a point north of the whole British position when he heard the volleys against Solignac, and swung south to join in the fighting. Attacking with cavalry and four battalions against two British battalions (1/71st and 1/82nd)[4] he had some success at first, and even recaptured Solignac's guns.

But, yet again, the French columns could not stand against the disciplined musketry of the British line, and before long they too withdrew, leaving behind 6 guns and General Brennier, who had been wounded.

It was still only noon, and the French had lost 1,800 men and 14 out of 23 guns. It was an impressive victory for the Peninsular Army.

Summary

Admittedly Junot had been out-numbered and had made mistakes, but there were three other reasons why the French were so soundly defeated at Vimiero, and, as they would continue to apply throughout the Peninsular campaign, it is worthwhile setting them out in some detail.

The first was Wellesley's outstanding tactical skill. He was exceptionally good at guessing what was happening, and was likely to happen on 'the other side of the hill'. He also excelled at reacting calmly and swiftly to any enemy moves, and in such a way that he ended up the winner. Had this not been the case, he might well have lost at Vimiero.

The second and even more significant feature of Vimiero was the defeat of the previously all-conquering French column by the two-deep British line. It was well-known that infantry in line had a marked advantage over an advancing column in terms of effective muskets; but Napoleon had till now neutralized this with his screen of *tirailleurs* backed by a barrage of artillery fire, so that by the time his columns closed up to the enemy infantry, the latter were too demoralized and harassed to do them much damage. Once the two sides were at close quarters, the shock effect of the columns usually overwhelmed the thin line and brought victory.

The third reason was that Wellesley's new line of skirmishers frustrated the *tirailleurs*, while his practice of concealing his men behind reverse slopes not only protected them from the *tirailleurs* and enemy artillery fire, but it also prevented enemy commanders from accurately locating the Allied positions.

Thus, the Battle of Vimiero was very much a landmark. It was a decisive victory, and it also proved the effectiveness of Wellesley's tactics. Above all, it was a great boost to the morale of the small but dedicated Peninsular Army.

THE BATTLEFIELD OF VIMIERO

Where to go

Take the N 8-2 from Torres Vedras north-west towards Lourinha. Turn left after 4 miles on the road to A. dos Cunhados. It is then 5 miles to Vimiero, approaching it from the south-east.

In the centre of the village is a sign to "The Monument", and this stands on the top of Vimiero Hill, on the south edge of the village. This is **Viewpoint A** and is an excellent point from which to identify the landmarks of the battlefield.

The French view can be seen by driving along the road running north-east from Vimiero, through Toledo, to the junction with the N 8-2. (**Viewpoint B**)

It is interesting then to drive to Ventosa, where there was heavy fighting, and to see the line of attack by Brennier and Solignac. (**Viewpoint C**)

What to see

Vimiero is an easy and interesting battlefield to see, as all the features are identifiable, and the land is undeveloped, though the village is much enlarged.

Viewpoint A. The Monument on Vimiero Hill is in honour of the battle and marks the area of fierce fighting by Fane's and Anstruther's Brigades. The open, undulating ground to the east was the line of advance of Delaborde, Loison and St Clair in their unsuccessful attacks on the hill.

To the west and north is Vimiero itself, and, beyond it, running away to the north-east, is the Eastern Ridge, with Ventosa visible at the far end. To the west of Vimiero is the Western Ridge, ending in the gorge through which runs the Maceira River.

Along the near side of the Eastern Ridge runs the road to Toledo and a small stream, and this was the line of advance of Kellerman's grenadiers.

At the far end of this valley a distinctive, modern factory can be seen on the skyline, and this is on the N. 8-2 at about the point where Solignac started his attack on Ventosa.

Viewpoint B is just to the left of the factory, as seen from Vimiero Hill, and from here, as at **Viewpoint C**, you can see how strong Wellesley's positions were on Vimiero Hill and along the Eastern Ridge, and what a clear view he had of every French move.

Notes

1 This later became "Shrapnel".
2 West Kent Regiment.
3 Compare this with his orders to Major-General Maitland at Waterloo: "Now, Maitland, now's your time," – the order that launched the First Guards into the decisive charge of the battle.
4 The Glasgow Highlanders and The Prince of Wales's Volunteers.

Order of Battle: Vimiero – 21 August, 1808

ALLIES					FRENCH	
Brigades	*Commander*	*Strength*	*Position*		*Brigades*	*Strength*
2nd	Ferguson	2,450	*Ventosa*		Solignac	2,800
3rd	Nightingall	1,520	3 guns		Brennier	3,000
4th	Bowes	1,813				
		5,783				5,800
8th	Acland		*North of Vimiero* 2 guns		Kellerman (Two Grenadier brigades)	2,100
		1,332				
6th	Fane	2,005	*Vimiero Hill*		Thomière	1,400
7th	Anstruther	2,703	12 guns		Charlot	1,100
		4,708				2,500
1st	Hill	2,658	*Western Ridge* 2 guns			
5th	Craufurd C.	1,832	*Left Flank*			
Portuguese	Trant	1,750				
		3,582				
	Cavalry:				*Cavalry*	2,000
	British	240				
	Portuguese	260				
Commander		Wellesley			Junot	
Strength		18,000			14,000	
Cavalry		500			2,000	
Guns		18			23	
Casualties		120			2,000 (and 14 guns)	

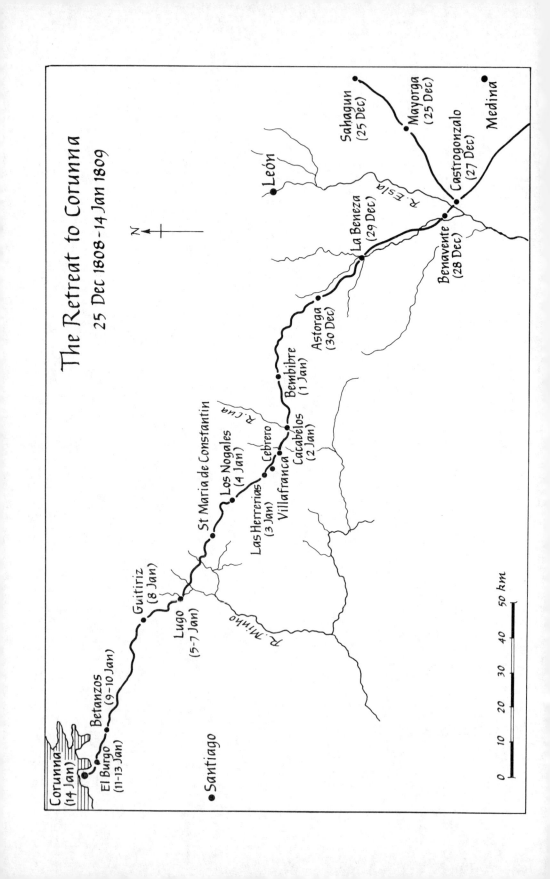

The Retreat to Corunna
25 Dec 1808 – 14 Jan 1809

Medina

Mayorga
(25 Dec)

Sahagun
(25 Dec)

Castrogonzalo
(27 Dec)

León

Benavente
(28 Dec)

La Beneza
(29 Dec)

R. Esla

Astorga
(30 Dec)

Bembibre
(1 Jan)

Cacabelos
(2 Jan)

Villafranca

Cebrero
(3 Jan)

R. Cúa

Las Herrerias
(3 Jan)

Los Nogales
(4 Jan)

St Maria de Constantin

Lugo
(5–7 Jan)

R. Minho

Guitiriz
(8 Jan)

Santiago

Betanzos
(9–10 Jan)

El Burgo
(11–13 Jan)

Corunna
(14 Jan)

N

0   10   20   30   40   50 km

CHAPTER ELEVEN

The Retreat to Corunna (25th December 1808 – 10th January 1809)

On **Christmas Eve 1808** General Moore was leading his army of 30,000 northwards towards Sahagun to attack Marshal Soult who was there with only 16,000 men.

But that night Moore learned that Napoleon himself with 80,000 men was closing in on him from the south, and the British army was thus in imminent danger of being trapped between the two French forces. He realised that the only hope now of saving his army from destruction was to withdraw immediately before the jaws of the trap closed.

The Retreat began therefore on **Christmas Day,** when his force crossed the River Esla at Castrogonzalo, and headed westward through the Galician mountains towards Corunna. Sullen and angry that they had had no chance to fight, the troops stumbled along tracks knee-deep in mud that pulled mens' shoes off their feet, so that some of them hobbled the 312 miles[1] to Corunna barefoot.

Fortunately for them, Napoleon paused for 24 hours at Tordesillas to re-group; his information was that Moore was still at Sahagun, and he saw an opportunity to trap him there.

"Should the British pass today in their positions," he declared, "they are lost."

But they had already slipped away, and when the French advanced on the **27th,** they found that their prey was safely across the now flooded Esla, with the bridge blown behind them.

Moore had escaped the trap, but his troops did not like retreating, and at Benavente they looted and pillaged,[2] venting their resentment against the local Spaniards, many of whom refused to help with food or shelter.

On the **29th** Napoleon set up his headquarters at Valderas on the east bank of the Esla and sent forward 600 Chasseurs of his Imperial

Guard, under Lt-Colonel LeFebvre-Desnouettes, across the river to harass the British rearguard at Benavente. They drove in the British picquets, but were then themselves attacked by the 10th Hussars and the 3rd Hussars of the King's German Legion (K.G.L.) and trapped against the river. Nearly 200 were killed or captured, including their commander;[3] the Riflemen of the Rearguard cheered at the sight, while Napoleon is said to have watched in fury on the opposite bank.

On **30 January** the main body reached Astorga, where it was joined by 9,500 disorganized remnants of La Romana's Spanish army from Leon. They had virtually no supplies or equipment, following their recent defeat at Mansilla, and they were thoroughly demoralized. Their presence did little to strengthen Moore's fighting power, and it added considerably to his already formidable administrative difficulties.

It was at Astorga that Moore made two crucial decisions; first, not to stand and fight there, and second, to send two brigades (Craufurd and Alten) by a different route to Vigo. (See Page 18)

On the **last day of 1808** Moore's army reached the village of Bembibre and, on finding some wine vaults there, they broke into them and many drank themselves into a stupor. The next morning, the rearguard rounded up those who could still walk and drove them westwards, but 1,000 or more, together with exhausted women and children, had to be left and were cut down the next day by the pursuing French cavalry.

The **first day of 1809** brought nothing but desperation for the retreating army, as they struggled through snow and ice over the barren mountain passes, with no food, no shelter, no fuel, stumbling famished and frozen against the piercing winds.

"We suffered misery without a glimpse of comfort," wrote a private of the 71st.[4]

At Villafranca del Bierzo was a depot with 14 days' supplies, but the starving soldiers were not prepared to wait for them to be issued; they ransacked the stores and everything was gone in two hours. The horrors and excesses of Bembibre were repeated, and order was only restored when Moore himself took control[5] and marched the remnants out of the village towards Lugo, driving them relentlessly for 36 hours non-stop through the worst conditions yet.

The drunkards and the laggards had dropped out long since, and now even the tough old soldiers were collapsing and dying by the roadside. Sick and wounded, women and children had to be abandoned,

when the carts could not move through the deep drifts on Monte
Cebrero; most of the baggage train was lost, and £25,000 in silver
dollars was tipped over a precipice.

The Rearguard[6], however, who were in constant contact with the
enemy, maintained their discipline and fighting spirit; under the
command of Major-General Edward Paget, they kept the French at
bay.

But at Cacabelos on **3 January** the General found a party
plundering. After a drum-head court martial, he ordered some to be
flogged and others to be hanged. As the last two were being prepared
for the noose, the French launched a surprise attack. Telling the
offenders that they would be pardoned if they fought well, he galloped
off to deal with the enemy; they were soon repulsed and the soldiers
were spared.

The fight put up by the Rearguard made the 'Duke of Damnation',[7]
as the British troops called Marshal Soult, unusually cautious, and he
did not press the pursuit as hard as he might have.

On the **6th** Moore halted at Lugo and prepared to fight. Morale rose
instantly, for the angry soldiers longed to vent their bitterness on
someone, and who better than those who had brought them to this
intolerable, endless misery.

But Soult held back, and, after waiting for two anxious days, Moore
decided that he must move on again.

The night of the **8th** was one of the worst of the whole retreat. A
thick mist came down, combined with freezing rain, and several
regiments lost their way completely. The French cavalry closed in and
seized 500 more prisoners, while the survivors staggered on.

But relief came at long last. On the **10th** they emerged from the
merciless mountains and saw ahead the coastal plain with villages and
fruit trees, and the Atlantic sparkling in sunshine such as they had not
glimpsed for two nightmare weeks. On the **11th** they straggled into
Corunna – only to find that the ships had not yet arrived.

As Sir John Moore watched the survivors of his ragged and
demoralized army plod down the slope towards the town, there
occurred one of those incidents that establishes an everlasting
tradition. It cannot be better described than in the words of Sir John
Fortescue himself:

"A brigade caught the General's eye, for they were marching like
soldiers.

" 'Those must be the Guards,' he said, and presently the two battalions of the First Guards,[8] each of them still 800 strong, strode by in column of sections, with drums beating, the drum major twirling his staff at their head, and the men keeping step as if in their own barrack yard . . . The senior regiment of the British infantry had set an example to the whole army."[9] It was a tradition that would be proudly recalled, and repeated, during the Retreat to Mons in 1914 and on the beaches of Dunkirk in 1940.

The army had plodded over 300 miles, under appalling conditions, and according to their Commander-in-Chief, only three bodies had maintained their discipline and morale throughout – the Light Brigade, the Guards and the men of the Rearguard, who had fulfilled their task magnificently.

Fortescue wrote of them:

"They had done harder work, they had endured harder marches and they had undergone greater privations than the rest of the army; and they had been more frequently engaged in petty actions with the enemy. Yet there were relatively fewer men missing from their ranks than from any other Division, for, like the Guards, they had faced the high ordeal of the march like disciplined men."

THE RETREAT TO CORUNNA

Where to go and what to see

Ideally, one should start, as Moore's army did, at Castrogonzalo and follow the road to Corunna, but it is almost as good to do it in reverse. The modern highway, the N.VI, runs all the way through the Galician mountains, and it is an easy day's drive of just over 300 miles. It does not follow the twisting muddy tracks along which Moore's troops stumbled, but one can still imagine what they must have suffered, particularly if one travels in mid-winter.

At Castrogonzalo, the original Roman Bridge over the Esla still stands alongside the modern road bridge.

There is a good Parador at Benavente, and the country from there to Astorga is open and flat; Astorga does not seem a particularly good defensive position, as it could be out-flanked.

There is another Parador at Villafranca, where the mountains start and continue until some 20 miles short of Corunna. The scenery is most impressive, but it is grim and barren country.

4. **Corunna.** The old bridge, destroyed by Moore in 1809, at El Burgo, alongside the new road bridge across the Rio Mero.

5. **Corunna.** Monte Mero from the French positions on the Heights of Penasquedo, with Corunna Bay in the background behind the modern city, which did not exist in 1809. "The key feature of Monte Mero in the centre was held by Baird's 1st Division". (p.81)

6. **Oporto.** The site of Wellesley's Crossing of the Douro at Oporto as it was in 1809. On the left is the town, with Wellesley's pontoon bridge in the centre at the spot where Sherbrooke crossed. The Seminary is visible on the cliff in the background, and to the right is the Convent Serra do Pillar used by Wellesley as an observation post. (*National Army Museum, London*)

7. **Oporto.** The same scene in 1988. (*Jeremy Bull*)

The Retreat to Corunna

Just short of Corunna is the village of El Burgo, which was the scene of the last rearguard action. The original bridge is still there alongside a new one, and it still has the gap in it blown up by Moore's engineers.

Notes

1 Opinions vary as to the distance, and this figure is based on the evidence of the Royal Greenjackets detachment who, starting on 1 January, 1984, followed on foot the exact route of the Rearguard and calculated it as exactly 300 km or 312 miles.

2 Among other places they looted the Palace of the Duquesa de Osuna, now a Parador.

3 He was taken in front of Moore and complained that his sword had been taken from him when he was captured, whereupon Moore magnanimously presented him with his own general's sword.

4 *Journal of a Soldier*, p 58–9.

5 He ordered a drum-head court-martial, and had one soldier shot. The army were then made to march past the corpse.

6 The composition of the Rearguard varied, but it included at various times: *Cavalry* (under Lord Paget): 7th, 10th, 15th and 18th Hussars; 3rd Hussars (KGL). *General Edward Paget's Reserve Division*: 1/20th; 2/28th; 1/52nd; 1/91st; 1/95th.

7 He was the Duke of Dalmatia.

8 1st and 3rd Battalions.

9 *History of the British Army*; Vol IV, page 375.

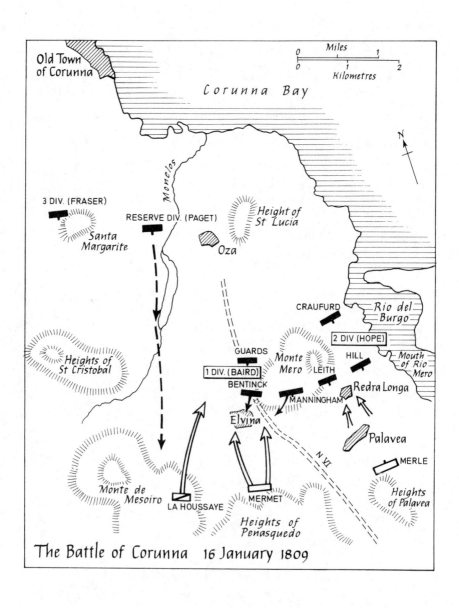

The Battle of Corunna 16 January 1809

CHAPTER TWELVE

The Battle of Corunna

Moore's Plan

Moore had reached Corunna, but he now faced much the same grim decisions as did Gort at Dunkirk in 1940. Like Gort, he saw his overriding responsibility to be to save his army, rather than fighting a battle; the question was whether he could hold off his pursuers until the fleet arrived. To his relief Soult was slow to close in, and so gave the exhausted British troops time to recover.

As soon as the main body was assembled in Corunna, they were re-equipped from the depots there. The remaining stores were then destroyed, including a magazine containing 4,000 barrels of gunpowder, which exploded with such force that it broke every window in the town and caused a tidal wave.

At last, on **14 January**, after three days of anxious waiting, came the welcome sight of 110 transports sailing into the harbour; loading began at once, with priority being given to the sick and wounded, artillery and cavalry. It was a race against time to get away before the French were upon them, but, thanks to a fine last stand by the rearguard at El Burgo on the Rio Mero, it was the **15th** before Soult finally closed in.

Moore was now faced with that most difficult and unwelcome military operation – an embarkation under fire, particularly as his force of 15,000 infantry and 12 guns was inadequate for the task. He would have liked to hold the outer ring of hills, the Heights of Penasquedo, but he had to settle for an inner line, centred on Monte Mero. He therefore kept as many men as possible in reserve, ready for the crises that he felt must come.

On his left flank, which was protected by the impassable Rio Mero, he placed Hope's 2nd Division. The key feature of Monte Mero in the centre was held by Baird's 1st Division, with Bentinck's Brigade in the village of Elvina. The right flank was open and vulnerable, and he therefore placed almost two-thirds of his force (3rd and Reserve

Divisions) on that side, but well back, so as to cover the approaches to Corunna.

The French Plan

Soult had around 24,000 men, with more closing up behind, and his 36 guns were able to rake the whole British line from the Heights of Penasquedo.

He appreciated that the weakest part of Moore's position was his right, which was also the most direct route to Corunna. He planned therefore to use Delaborde and Merle to make holding attacks against the British centre and left, while Mermet, with 7,500 infantry and 1,300 cavalry, would make the main breakthrough against Moore's right, and so cut off his escape route to Corunna.

The Battle

The morning of **16 January** passed with no French attack, and Moore used the respite to hurry on with the embarkation.

At about 1300 he rashly remarked, "Now, if there is no bungling, I hope we shall get away in a few hours."

It was a fair comment, for at that moment the Reserve Division were actually marching to the quayside, heading, as they thought, for safety and home. Then, at about 1345, Soult finally launched his attack. As they heard the firing behind them, every man of the Division halted, turned about, and within minutes they were striding back inland to their positions round Oza.

The main fighting was round Monte Mero. The feature itself was held, but Elvina was lost in heavy fighting, in which Sir David Baird was severely wounded. Lord William Bentinck took over command of 1st Division and led his own brigade forward and re-captured the village. A further French attack drove them out again, but, with support from the two battalions of Foot Guards, they managed to hold on to Monte Mero itself.

Soult now launched his strong thrust to the west of Elvina, confident that the way to Corunna was clear. But he soon met the two divisions barring his way. Despite having no cavalry, Paget's Reserve Division not only halted the French advance, but then drove them steadily backwards, through Elvina and up into the hills.

On the left, too, the French were falling back, and Moore, directing the battle from a hilltop behind Elvina, could see victory within his reach. But at that moment a round shot struck his left shoulder, tearing the arm from his body. As he lay in a house by the harbour, mortally wounded, he was heard to murmur, "I always wanted to die this way."

Command now devolved on Sir John Hope, but he was out on the left flank and it took some time for him to take control. The pursuit lost momentum and, as dusk fell, the fighting petered out.

Embarkation continued that night and all **next day** with little interference from the French, except long-range artillery fire which damaged some ships. The troops stumbled exhausted onto the transports, with the satisfaction that they had at least given the enemy the licking that they had been thirsting to do throughout the long, nightmare days of the Retreat.

On **18 January**, around 19,000 men of Moore's army sailed for home, where their desperate appearance caused an unprecedented outcry and public concern.

They left behind the body of Sir John Moore, "alone with his glory"[1] together with some 800 other dead. The Spanish garrison in Corunna gallantly fought on until the fleet was safely out to sea, and then they had to surrender.

THE BATTLEFIELD OF CORUNNA

Where To Go

The town has expanded enormously since 1810, though the old part to the north and the harbour are little changed. The whole battlefield is now built over, and the motorway N.VI runs between Monte Mero and Elvina; but this at least makes it possible to work out the site of the battlefield by finding the village of Elvina. (The Spanish call it the Battle of Elvina.)

Take the N.VI south out of the town of Corunna, and before reaching the Autopista, you can see a high ridge ahead, which is the Heights of Penasquedo.

Where the Autopista signs stand on the N.VI the village of Elvina is alongside the road on the right (west) and Monte Mero is to the left (east).

It is possible to drive into Elvina, on to Monto Mero and also on to the Heights of Penasquedo.

Looking at the ground one feels that this was a battle that the French really should have won, instead of being driven back by the Reserve Division almost to the Heights themselves.

What To See

ELVINA

The church, which was the centre of much fighting, still stands, and the village is a good point from which to orientate oneself. To the west is the plain across which Soult launched his main thrust towards Corunna. Beyond the plain can be seen the Heights of St Cristobal.

MONTE MERO

This feature blocks the main approach into Corunna today, as it did in 1809, but it is in turn completely dominated by the Heights of Penasquedo.

To the east is the estuary of the Rio Mero, and in front is the village of Palavea.

The fierce fighting by Bentinck's Brigade must have been in the middle of the N.VI. and covered a surprisingly small area. On the reverse slope is a marble plaque said to mark the spot where Moore fell.

HEIGHTS OF PENASQUEDO

The University of Corunna is on the forward slopes, and the golf course is on the reverse slope. Driving along the ridge, it is striking how much the French positions overlooked Moore's. One can see why Moore would have liked to hold these Heights, but he did not have the men.

HOUSE WHERE SIR JOHN MOORE DIED

Moore was taken to "a house numbered 12th in the Canton Grande". It is now the Banco Hispano Americano, and there is a plaque on the wall in memory of Moore.

SIR JOHN MOORE'S TOMB

This is in the "Jardin de San Carlos" in the Old Town, and verses of Charles Wolfe's famous poem (first published in 1817, dedicated to Moore) are inscribed on plaques (one in English) on the gate overlooking the harbour. Another plaque by the gate is a tribute by the Duke of Wellington to the Galician soldiers who fought in the war.

Notes

1 From *The Burial of Sir John Moore at Corunna* by Charles Wolfe.

Order of Battle: Corunna – 16 January, 1809

ALLIES					FRENCH	
Division	*Commander*	*Strength*	*Brigades*		*Division*	*Strength*
1st	Baird	5,100	Warde		Merle	6,200
			Manningham		Delaborde	5,500
			Bentinck		Mermet	7,500
2nd	Hope	5,600	Craufurd C.			
			Leith			
			Hill			
3rd	Fraser	2,600				
Reserve	Paget	1,500				
	(Edward)				*Cavalry:*	
					Lahoussaye	1,600
					Lorge	1,600
					Franceschi	1,300
Commander		Moore			Soult	
Strength		15,000			24,200	
Cavalry		—			4,500	
Guns		12			36	
Casualties		800			1,400	

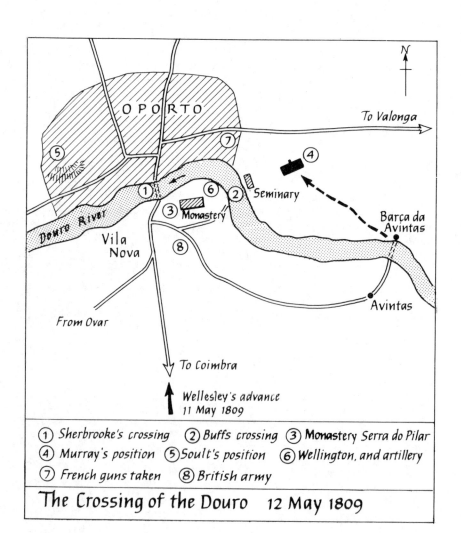

To Valonga

O P O R T O

⑤ Soult's position

⑦

④ Murray's position

Seminary

① Sherbrooke's crossing

⑥

②

Barça da
Avintas

③ Monastery

Douro River

Vila
Nova

⑧

Avintas

From Ovar

To Coimbra

Wellesley's advance
11 May 1809

① Sherbrooke's crossing   ② Buffs crossing   ③ **Monastery** Serra do Pilar
④ Murray's position   ⑤ Soult's position   ⑥ Wellington, and artillery
⑦ French guns taken   ⑧ British army

The Crossing of the Douro   12 May 1809

CHAPTER THIRTEEN

The Crossing of the Douro

Wellesley's Plan

When Wellesley returned to Portugal as C-in-C on **22 April, 1809,** he immediately prepared a plan to march north and attack Marshal Soult who was holding Oporto. Leaving 12,000 men to protect Lisbon, he sent 6,000 under Beresford to Lamego to cut off Soult's line of retreat to Spain, and led the main army himself.

On **1 May**, his 40th birthday, he entered Coimbra, and one week later set off for Oporto with 16,000 British and 2,400 Portuguese. They were almost all young soldiers and as yet untried in battle, but by a series of clever outflanking moves from the west, using the Navy in support, he forced Soult back 50 miles to Oporto.

On **11 May** Soult withdrew behind the River Douro, crossing by a bridge of boats, which he blew up at 0200 on the **12th**. He then had every boat brought over to the north bank, confident that the river, which was as wide as the Thames at Westminster and in flood, would now be impassable. But he under-estimated Wellesley's boldness, and also wrongly assumed that any attack would come from the west again.

Wellesley arrived in Vila Nova on the south bank of the Douro opposite Oporto **early on 12 May**, and immediately set up his observation post in the Monastery de Serra do Pilar. From here he noticed across the river to his right the Bishop's Seminary, which seemed to be unoccupied and was also apparently out of sight of most of the 11,000 French troops in the town itself, who were all facing west.

Hearing that a sunken ferry at Avintas, two miles upstream, could be salvaged, he sent two K.G.L. battalions and some cavalry under Murray to try to cross there, which they did.

At about the same time Colonel John Waters, a scout on his staff, appeared with a Portuguese barber who had rowed across from the north bank in his own skiff with news of four empty wine barges hidden on the river bank east of the city that were undamaged and unguarded.

Waters also confirmed that the Seminary had been unoccupied 30 minutes before.

Wellesley was delighted.

"By God! Waters has done it!" he exclaimed, and ordered the barges to be seized.

Waters promptly assembled "a splendidly mixed party of the barber, a Prior from Amarante and four peasants", who between them successfully brought the barges to the south bank.

"Well. Let the men cross," Wellesley ordered, and with those few words, he initiated one of his most daring offensive strokes ever, crossing a river 300 yards wide in broad daylight against a force of almost equal size. It was an immense risk, but it might succeed because of the sheer boldness and unorthodoxy of it.

Each barge carried only 30 men in addition to the crew, and all four could transport only 600 men per hour. A Lieutenant and his platoon of the 3rd Foot (The Buffs) crossed first, and incredibly reached the opposite bank unopposed. They immediately occupied the Seminary and began fortifying it.

The crossing continued steadily, with the 48th (Northamptonshires) and the 66th (Berkshires) reinforcing the 3rd. Amazingly it was an hour before the French realized what was happening, by which time 600 infantry were firmly established in the Seminary. It was now about 1130, but Soult was in bed, having been up all night, and there is a story that when he was woken with news of the crossing, he retorted, "Bah! It is just a party of red-coated Swiss going down to bathe."

General Foy, the local French commander, launched a hurried attack against the Seminary by three battalions, but it failed. The 18 British guns on the Serra heights gave most effective support, and one shrapnel shell burst directly over the first French gun into action, knocking out all the crew. Lt-General Edward Paget, who had crossed to the Seminary, was, however, seriously wounded and was replaced by Major-General Rowland Hill, aged 36.

A second French assault under Delaborde also failed, whereupon at about noon Soult mounted a brigade attack. But to do so he had to take the guards off the quaysides on the north bank, whereupon hundreds of Portuguese rushed out, seized the boats, and rowed them across to the British.

Wellesley was now able to launch a third crossing and he sent over Sherbrooke's 1st Division in the area of Soult's former bridge of boats. The Guards should have crossed first, but the 29th (Worcesters), who were already at the riverside, sent back word that they could not make way for the Guards in the narrow streets. It was not true, but it enabled them to have the honour of crossing first.

Advancing into the town itself, 1st Division broke up the third enemy attack against the Seminary.

Soult now realized that he was beaten and ordered a general withdrawal eastwards. Murray might have cut him off, but failed to do so, though the 14th Light Dragoons under General Charles Stewart did sterling work and took 300 prisoners.

The French retreated in complete disorder, but Wellesley only pursued them for a few miles, largely because of lack of transport. But Soult had lost 300 men killed and wounded as well as 1,500 taken prisoner and 70 guns, against a mere 123 British casualties.

Oporto had been liberated and Wellesley sat down that evening to enjoy the supper that had been prepared for Soult at the Palacio das Carrancas. It had been a dramatic and most satisfactory day.

THE CROSSING OF THE DOURO

Where To Go

The Crossing of the Douro is an easy and satisfactory battlefield to visit, once one knows just where to go. It can be combined with a tour of Oporto, or better still, with a trip to Vila Nova and some of the port "lodges" there.

There are two spots from which one can obtain an excellent idea of the operation. **Viewpoint A** is the Monastery de Serra do Pilar on the south bank of the Douro next to the Bridge de Luis.

Viewpoint B is the Seminary on the north bank, now an orphanage, but little changed from 1809.

What To See
Viewpoint A

Go south across the Bridge de Luis on the upper level on the Coimbra road. A quarter of a mile beyond the end of the bridge take the first turning left, across the dual carriageway, and immediately turn left again, uphill by a narrow road signed 'To the Monument'. After 300 yards one is at the carpark outside the church, with a viewpoint over the river to the city.

You are now standing where Wellesley stood early on the morning of 12 May, 1809, looking across at Oporto.

Soult had his headquarters just west of the Cathedral. The modern Bridge de Luis is the site of the bridge of boats that Soult destroyed at 0200 on 12 May, and is also where Sherbrooke made his crossing.

To the left on the south bank can be seen some wine barges belonging to the port firms in Vila Nova, and they are similar to those four boats in which the initial crossing was made by the Buffs.

The site of the initial crossing is just out of sight from this viewpoint, as is the Seminary, both being round the corner to the right where the river bends. Wellesley was able to ride through the Monastery grounds to the crossing site, but that is not possible now, as it is a military barracks and closed to the public.

Viewpoint B

Go south along the Rua de Saldanha till it ends in a small square called Largo do Padre Balthazar Guedes, where you can park. As you face the river, the Seminary is a large white building with a red roof to your left, with a path running between it and the high cliff along the river. There is one viewpoint opposite the west end of the Seminary (it is the municipal rubbish dump!), and another opposite the east end.

On the wall at the west end of the Seminary is a plaque recording the events of 1809.

To the right downstream it is possible to see the Bridge de Luis, but not Viewpoint A.

Directly opposite, at the far end of the railway bridge, is a wooded promontory, which is the Monastery (now a barracks) where Wellesley had another observation point, and where he posted his 18 guns covering the Seminary.

Below the railway bridge on the south bank, slightly upstream, is a sheltered bay and some level ground, and this is the embarkation point of the Buffs; one can see how it was out of sight of most of the French in Oporto, particularly if they were looking westwards.

Below the Seminary on the north bank are some stone steps, where the troops landed and then scrambled up to the Seminary.

Looking upstream to the left it is possible to see Avintas, where Murray crossed near John of Gaunt's house.

Order of Battle: Crossing of the Douro – 12 May, 1809

ALLIES				FRENCH	
Division	*Commander*	*Strength*	*Brigades*	*Division*	*Strength*
1st	Sherbrooke	6,706	Campbell	*At Oporto:*	
			Sontag	Delaborde	5,000
			Campbell A.	Merle	6,000
	Paget (Edward)	5,145	Stewart Murray		11,000
				South of the Douro	
	Hill	4,370	Hill Cameron	Mermet	6,300
				At Amarante	
				Loison	6,500
	Cavalry	1,504			
Commander		Wellesley		Soult	
Strength		17,378		11,000	
Cavalry		1,504		—	
Guns		24		Over 70	
Casualties		123		800 (plus 70 guns)	

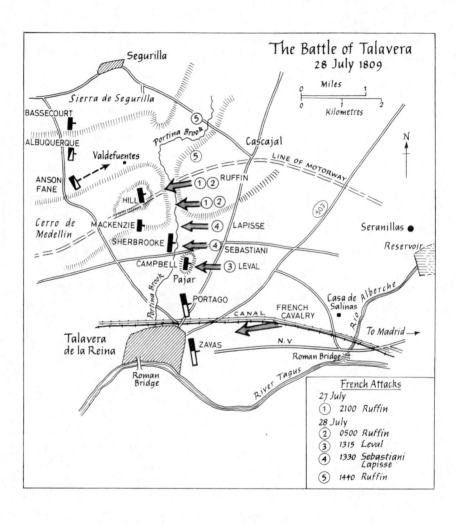

The Battle of Talavera
28 July 1809

Segurilla

Sierra de Segurilla

BASSECOURT

ALBUQUERQUE

Valdefuentes

ANSON
FANE

HILL

Cerro de
Medellin

MACKENZIE

SHERBROOKE

CAMPBELL

Pajar

PORTAGO

Talavera
de la Reina

ZAYAS

Roman
Bridge

Portina Brook

Portina Brook

Cascajal

LINE OF MOTORWAY

⑤

⑤

① ② RUFFIN

① ②

④ LAPISSE

④ SEBASTIANI

③ LEVAL

FRENCH
CAVALRY

Casa de
Salinas

CANAL

N.V

Roman Bridge

River Tagus

Seranillas

Reservoir

Rio Alberche

To Madrid →

N

Miles
0   1
0   1   2
Kilometres

French Attacks
27 July
① 2100 Ruffin
28 July
② 0500 Ruffin
③ 1315 Leval
④ 1330 Sebastiani
       Lapisse
⑤ 1440 Ruffin

CHAPTER FOURTEEN

The Battle of Talavera

Wellesley's Plan

In **May, 1809**, Wellesley with 20,000 British troops advanced into Spain and joined up with General Cuesta's Spanish army of 35,000 at Oropesa for operations against the French under Marshal Victor round Talavera de la Reina. Victor withdrew towards Madrid on **23 July**, whereupon Cuesta, against Wellesley's advice, pursued him, only to be counter-attacked and driven back to the line of the River Alberche on **25 July**.

The Allies were now in trouble, for King Joseph had joined forces with Victor, and was advancing with an army of 46,000 veteran troops and 86 guns. Wellesley knew that he could not rely on his 35,000 Spaniards, and he had therefore to face the French with only 20,000 British and German troops and 36 guns.

He quickly put out a screen along the Alberche, while he took up a stronger main position a few miles to the west. This was some three miles long with the right flank on the Tagus and the town of Talavera. The left was based on a prominent, rounded ridge called the Cerro de Medellin, which dominated the area. Just to the north of the Cerro was a flat valley about a mile wide, and beyond it were the steep slopes of the Sierra de Segurilla. His left flank was therefore reasonably secure, so long as he held the Cerro.

Opposite the Cerro to the east was a slightly lower feature called the Cascajal, which became the centre of the French positions, and the area from which they launched their main attacks against the Medellin.

Between the two sides flowed the Portina Brook; it was no obstacle in 1809, but it formed a dividing line.

Wellesley placed his 35,000 Spanish in the most easily defended sector of the front, running from the Tagus to the north edge of Talavera. A large, fortified farmhouse called Pajar de Vergara was held by the Spanish and also by Campbell's Brigade, with Kemmis behind him. On their left was Sherbrooke's 1st Division and then Mackenzie's 4th Division. The left flank and the defence of the vital Medellin was given to Hill and his 2nd Division.

27 July, 1809

Wellesley planned to occupy the new position on **27 July**, and it was a day of near disasters, starting with a surprise attack by the French against his outpost line on the Alberche. Donkin's Brigade, occupying a fortified building called the Casa de Salinas, were caught unawares and lost 440 men.

Then Wellesley himself was almost captured when he was forward at the Casa. A party of French cavalry attacked the building and he only just escaped, galloping off under fire.

The Allied army and its commander managed nevertheless to withdraw to the new positions, but there was more trouble when some French cavalry appeared that evening opposite the town of Talavera, which was held by the Spanish. At the sight, four battalions of Spanish infantry loosed off one massive volley at a range of 1,000 yards. Then, with cries of "Treason", they fled. Some were rounded up, but many others disappeared westwards, plundering Wellesley's baggage train on the way – a crime that he never forgave or forgot, and which led him never to trust Spanish troops again.[1]

He personally described the incident to Lord Castlereagh:

'Nearly 2,000 ran off (not 100 yards from where I was standing) who were neither attacked or threatened with an attack, and who were frightened only by the noise of their own fire; they left their arms and accoutrements on the ground, their officers went with them."[2]

As a result of this incident, Wellesley did not have time before dark on the 27th to position his troops personally as he normally did, and this again nearly led to disaster. That night at about 2100 the aggressive Marshal Victor, without telling King Joseph, launched a surprise night attack against the Medellin, hoping thereby to capture it before the main battle, due to start next day. It was one of the few night attacks of the war and it came very close to succeeding.

Due to a staff error, the two British brigades that were to hold the Medellin (Tilson and Stewart) were still half a mile behind the crest, intending to take up their positions the following morning. The forward slopes were only thinly held by two battalions of the King's German Legion.[3]

Ruffin's entire division (5,000 strong) crossed the Portina and soon drove back the forward troops. General Hill heard the firing as he was returning from a meeting with Wellesley, and he remarked somewhat unkindly that it was "probably the Buffs as usual, making some blunder".

Riding forward to investigate, he suddenly found himself surrounded not by the Buffs, but by men of the French 9th Light Regiment, one of whom seized his horse's bridle. The officer with him was killed and the General only just managed to escape.

He then personally led forward the 29th who managed to restore the situation, and the French withdrew, having lost just over 300 men.

Wellesley too appeared on the scene, saw to it that Hill's division was posted where it should have been in the first place, and then slept on the Medellin, wrapped in his cloak.

The Battle

As dawn broke at about 0500 on **28 July** a single French gun signalled the start of their main attack. It was again directed against the Medellin and was preceded by a heavy and accurate bombardment from 53 guns.

Hill ordered his men to lie down behind the crest, while he himself stood watching the skirmishers withdrawing. They fought well and moved back so steadily, as if on an exercise, that Hill is said to have shouted "Damn their filing. Let them come in anyhow," one of only two occasions throughout the war when he is supposed to have sworn![4]

The French attack was again led by Ruffin's Division, 4,300 strong, who advanced in three columns, each 60 men wide and 24 deep.[5] Hill had only 2,000 men available (29th and 48th),[6] but they were deployed in line, two deep, and could therefore muster some 1,500 effective muskets against a mere 400 in the massed enemy ranks.

The fire-fight lasted only three minutes and within half an hour the French had broken and fled, leaving 1,300 casualties.

It was not yet 0700, and for the next four hours there was an informal truce, while both sides collected their wounded. French and British soldiers met and talked and slaked their thirst from the Portina Brook. It must have been a strange scene, but it was to happen on several occasions, and showed the remarkable lack of any personal animosity between the fighting men on both sides.

Oman wrote on this subject: "This was the first example of that amicable spirit which reigned between the hostile armies throughout the war, and which in its later years developed into that curious code of signals (often described by contemporaries) by which French and English gave each other notice whenever serious work was intended, refraining on all other occasions from unnecessary outpost bickering or sentry-shooting."[7]

Meanwhile, the French generals held a council of war. Both Joseph and his Chief of Staff, Jourdan, were inclined to call off the battle until Soult's advance from the north. But Victor, belligerent as ever, argued fiercely that they must attack again – and he had his way. It was agreed to launch a feint attack against the Allied right, while the main assault went in yet again against the Medellin.

So, at about 1315, Leval's Division launched the diversionary attack against Campbell's 4th Division on the Pajar, and were duly repulsed, losing 17 guns.

Then at 1400, after a bombardment by 80 guns, the main French assault was launched by two divisions (Lapisse and Sebastiani), mainly against Sherbrooke's Division, just south of the Medellin. Again, the French columns were halted by the overwhelming fire-power of the British line, and were driven back.

But the Guards Brigade[8] and two K.G.L. brigades pursued the enemy too far, lost control, and were then themselves fiercely counter-attacked on the far side of the Portina Brook.

The Guards alone lost 611 men out of 2,000, and a dangerous gap appeared in the centre of the Allied line. There were 15,000 enemy, including 7,000 cavalry, poised to exploit it, and the situation was critical.

Wellesley was watching the battle closely from the top of the Medellin and, as always, he reacted swiftly. He dared not weaken his position on the Medellin, and so had only one battalion, 1/48th,[9] immediately available as his reserve. He pushed them forward, together with a battery of 6-pounders, to support the Guards while they re-formed. At the same time he ordered Mackenzie's Brigade[10] to move to their left and fill the gap.

The outcome of the battle depended on whether this thin line of 3,000 could hold against the 10,000 now advancing against them. In grim silence the four battalions waited until the French were within 50 yards and then their deadly volleys thudded into the enemy ranks, "one every 15 seconds from each of 80 half-companies". It was desperate bloody fighting, with both sides being mown down at point-blank range. Mackenzie was killed, and so was the French divisional commander, Lapisse. A timely charge by the 14th Light Dragoons drove back one French column. The Guards re-formed and joined in the fighting.

Finally, it was the French who broke first, and streamed back across the brook, leaving 1,700 dead and wounded.

Now a new threat appeared, as the French launched yet another attack, this time across the plain to the north of the Medellin. But Wellesley had anticipated this and had already positioned Bassecourt's Spanish Division, two British cavalry brigades (Anson and Fane) and 8 guns to protect that flank. Now he added Albuquerque's Spanish cavalry.

The French attack was led by Ruffin's battered division, who had already been through two hard battles, and their enthusiasm was not unnaturally weakening. They advanced hesitantly and, seeing this, Wellesley launched his cavalry at them as they approached the farm at Valdefuentes. Anson's Brigade cantered across the plain, with the 23rd Light Dragoons on the right and the 1st Light Dragoons of the King's German Legion on the left.

At first all went well, but then the 23rd broke into a gallop and disaster followed, for across their path, hidden by the long grass, lay a dried-up river bed, 9 foot across and 6 foot deep. They plunged headlong into it and half the regiment was lost. The survivors galloped on, but found themselves faced by a brigade of French chasseurs. Exhausted and out-numbered 5 to 1, they were routed and less than half the regiment returned.

Their charge had, however, made the French infantry form squares, which were now raked by the Allied artillery, and the attack petered out.

Only three hours remained before dusk and both sides were exhausted. Joseph now received news that the Spanish army under Venegas was advancing on Madrid, and he decided, despite angry protests from Victor, to call off the attacks.

Wellesley might at this point have been bold and pursued the retreating French, but he could not rely on his Spanish troops, and without them he was heavily at risk; moreover, he was still short of transport and his men were now on one-third rations, so he regretfully refrained.

It had been a grim, slogging match and, to add to the horror, grass fires now broke out, burning the wounded as they lay helpless on the ground. "I never saw a field of battle," wrote George Napier, "which struck me with such horror as Talavera."[11]

As dawn broke on **29 July**, there was no sign of the French, for they had withdrawn during the night, almost back to Toledo, and the Allies were left in undisputed possession of the battlefield.

Then, a few hours later, there appeared from the west the Light Brigade, just out from England, who had marched an incredible 43 miles in 22 hours in their determination to arrive in time for the fighting. They were just too late, but were a welcome reinforcement, for casualties had been heavy.

The British lost 5,365 which was 25% of their strength and the casualty list nearly included Wellesley himself, for he had been struck in the chest by a bullet, luckily spent, the first of three wounds that he would suffer during the campaign.

THE BATTLEFIELD OF TALAVERA

Where To Go

The battlefield is at Talavera de la Reina on the River Tagus 75 miles west of Madrid on the N.V. and it runs for about 3 miles north from the town to the motorway one mile south of Segurilla.

A motorway was built through the battlefield in 1990, running from east to west, but it does not prevent access to the battlefield and the features are still identifiable.

There are three possible viewpoints, and a fourth one for the bold.

Viewpoint A Just east of Talavera the N.V from Madrid crosses the River Alberche, and one can obtain a general view of the area of operations from here.

Viewpoint B This is the Cascajal, which gives the French view of the Allied positions. Take the road to Marrupe from the centre of Talavera, and soon after crossing the Alberche Canal take a turning to the left leading to Segurilla.

Viewpoint C is the road running over the Medellin, i.e. behind the British lines. It can be approached from Talavera by forking left from the Marrupe road immediately after it crosses the railway in the northern suburbs of Talavera. A memorial was erected beside the motorway by the Spanish Government in 1990 and makes a good viewpoint of the battlefield.

The spur of the Cerro de Medellin, which provides the best viewpoint, is private property, but a good view can be obtained from the road just south or north of the Cerro, looking east.

Viewpoint D is only for the very interested, for it entails driving on indifferent roads round the circuit from the Cerro to Segurilla and then across to the Cascajal. It does, however, give a good view of the battlefield as a whole, and the positions of both sides.

What To See

Viewpoint A The line of the River Alberche was held by the French under Victor on the 23rd, and then by Wellesley on the 25th, when the Spanish retreated back from Toledo. The original bridge can still be seen just downstream of the modern highway bridge, and the Alberche joins the Tagus just below it.

The Casa de Salinas, where Wellesley was nearly captured, now called Salinas, with its twin towers, stands out some 250 yards from the river. It can be seen from the main road bridge.

Looking north-west from the viewpoint, one can see Talavera and to the north of it the Cerro de Medellin, with the Sierra de Segurilla beyond. Just to the east of the Cerro is the Cascajal, but it is more difficult to distinguish.

Viewpoint B There are several points on the Cascajal where one can, subject to the motorway, look west across the Portina Brook and identify the features of the Allied positions; the Cerro dominates the scene and it is clear why the French made such efforts to capture it.

The Pajar de Pergara is not easy to pick out, but it lies to the left of the road from Talavera to Navamorcuande, 100 yards beyond the railway bridge. It was rebuilt in 1981.

Viewpoint C Approaching the Cerro from Talavera, the road crosses the Portina Brook soon after the railway, and it is clear that it was not an obstacle to infantry.

The Cerro de Medellin dominates the position and there is a

monument on it to commemorate the centenary of the battle in 1909. The house of the owner of the land stands on the spur where Wellesley and Hill must have stood. It is, however, possible to view the battlefield from the road on the south and north slopes of the Cerro.

Viewpoint D From the forward slopes of the hills round Segurilla one has a good view of the battlefield as a whole, with the positions of both sides identifiable, the Portina Brook running between them, and Talavera in the background.

Talavera

There is a plaque in the Town Hall in Talavera, dedicated to the battle, together with a map and some musket balls.

Notes

1 Cuesta ordered the units concerned to be "decimated" i.e. 1 man in 10 to be shot, a total of 200. But Wellesley interceded for them and the number was reduced to 40.
2 Despatches, V, 85.
3 5th and 7th Battalions of Lowe's Brigade.
4 The other was at the Battle of St Pierre in 1814 (see page 224).
5 This compares with 30 men across and 48 deep at Vimiero.
6 The Worcestershire and the Northamptonshire Regiments.
7 Oman, II, 526.
8 1st Bn Coldstream Guards and 1st Bn Third Guards.
9 Northamptonshire Regiment.
10 2/24th (Warwickshire); 2/31st (Huntingdonshire); 1/45th (Nottinghamshire).
11 *Passages in the Early Life of General Sir George Napier*, p. 110.

Order of Battle: Talavera – 28 July, 1809

ALLIES

Division	Commander	Strength	Brigades
1st	Sherbrooke	5,964	Campbell H. (Guards)
			Cameron
			Langwerth (KGL)
			Lowe (KGL)
2nd	Hill	3,905	Tilson
			Stewart
3rd	Mackenzie	3,747	Mackenzie
			Donkin
4th	Campbell A.	2,960	Campbell A.
			Kemmis
Cavalry	Payne	2,969	Fane
			Stapleton Cotton
			Anson

FRENCH

Division	Strength
1st Corps (Victor)	
Ruffin	5,286
Lapisse	6,862
Villatte	6,135
Cavalry	1,027
	19,310
4th Corps (Sebastiani)	
Sebastiani	8,118
Valence (Part)	1,600
Leval	4,537
Cavalry	1,201
	15,456
Madrid Garrison	5,797
Reserve Cavalry	
Latour – Maubourg	3,179
Milhaud	2,256
	5,435

	British	Spanish	Total	
Commander	Wellesley	Cuesta	—	Joseph and Jourdan
Strength	20,641	34,993	55,634	46,138
Cavalry	2,969	6,127	9,096	7,500
Guns	30	30	60	80
Casualties			5,365	7,268

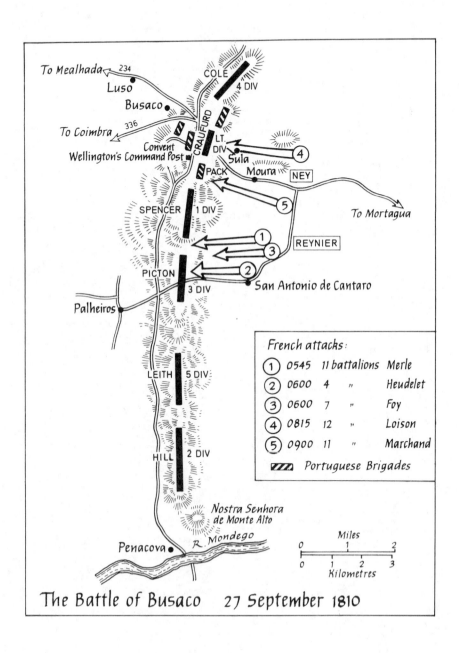

The Battle of Busaco   27 September 1810

To Mealhada   234
Luso
Busaco
COLE
4 DIV
To Coimbra   336
CRAUFURD
Convent
Wellington's Command Post
LT.
DIV
Sula
Moura
NEY
PACK
To Mortagua
SPENCER   1 DIV
5
REYNIER
1
3
PICTON
2
San Antonio de Cantaro
3 DIV
Palheiros
LEITH   5 DIV

French attacks:
1   0545   11 battalions   Merle
2   0600   4   "   Heudelet
3   0600   7   "   Foy
4   0815   12   "   Loison
5   0900   11   "   Marchand
▨▨   Portuguese Brigades

HILL   2 DIV

Nostra Senhora
de Monte Alto

Penacova   R. Mondego

Miles
0   1   2
0   1   2   3
Kilometres

CHAPTER FIFTEEN

The Battle of Busaco

Wellington's Plan

Wellington spent most of 1810 holding the 150-mile line of the Portuguese frontier in anticipation of another French invasion. He set out to block the three main approaches from Spain, reluctantly accepting the inevitable dispersion of his forces that this caused.

In the south he placed the trusty Hill with 20,000 men astride the road from Badajoz, which was the most direct route to Lisbon. In the centre he put Beresford and his Portuguese troops to cover the Tagus valley, while he himself took control of the northern sector, which he considered to be the likeliest approach, through Almeida or Ciudad Rodrigo.

He picked as his main defensive position the Busaco Ridge, which runs due north for some 10 miles from the Mondego River, rising steeply on both sides up to 1,800 feet, and dominates the entire countryside. Describing it, one of Wellington's staff remarked, "You only have to draw a damned long hill." It was considered "one of the finest defensive positions in Europe", but that was provided that it was attacked frontally, for it could be outflanked to the north.

The main road westwards to Coimbra and Lisbon ran across it through the village of Busaco, and was the only adequate road; there was a minor one from San Antonio, which was only just passable in 1810.[1]

Wellington considered that the ridge was more susceptible to attack in the north, and he therefore placed 34,000 men in the top four miles (8,500 men per mile as against only 3,000 per mile in the south).

He allotted the southern sector to Hill, with Leith's 5th Division on his left, which meant that three-fifths of his front was covered by only a third of his force.

The remaining four miles were more strongly held. Picton's 3rd Division guarded the San Antonio road, with most of 1st Division on the feature just to the north. The vital spur covering the main road was held by the Light Division and Pack's Portuguese Brigade, supported by Coleman's Portuguese Brigade. The northern flank was allotted to Cole's 2nd Division, Campbell's Portuguese Brigade and Lowe's K.G.L. Brigade.

Wellington's army of 52,000 was almost exactly half Portuguese, for whom it was their first real battle. He had only two squadrons of cavalry, but it was in any case not suitable country for them. He sited his artillery in "penny packets" along the whole position, rather than massing them.

An important factor was that he pushed forward an extra strong line of skirmishers, which not only prevented the French from finding out his positions, but also considerably hampered their assaults up the steep slopes.

The essence of Wellington's plan was flexibility. No positions were dug, and he planned to use his newly-built road to the west of the ridge to move troops swiftly from one sector to another. He positioned his men behind the crest, out of sight of the enemy, but he himself watched every French move from his observation post above Moura. He set up his headquarters in the Convent just south of Busaco and waited to see what Massena would do.

The French Viewpoint

Massena was so confident that he did not take as much trouble as he should have to reconnoitre Wellington's position. "I cannot persuade myself," he declared, "that Lord Wellington will risk the loss of a reputation by giving battle, but if he does, I have him. Tomorrow we shall effect the capture of Portugal, and in a few days I shall drown the leopard."

But he was under several misapprehensions. First, he did not know that Hill had joined Wellington, and that the British force was therefore 20,000 stronger that he thought. Second, he believed that the right flank of Wellington's position was on the San Antonio road, whereas that was in fact almost the centre. Finally, he thought that the Portuguese troops would not really fight and could be discounted.

Had Massena carried out a proper reconnaissance, he would have discovered not only the true strength of Wellington's position, but also the way round it to the north. As it was, he decided on a massive frontal attack such as had won so many victories already for the *Grande Armée*.

So, on the afternoon of **26 September** he advanced boldly to the foot of the Busaco ridge and formed up his three corps round Moura, watched closely by Wellington. That night the French lit their fires, but the Allied troops were ordered to eat cold food and show no lights, keeping completely out of sight over the crest; Massena thus remained in blissful ignorance of their strength and their dispositions. Wellington spent the night, wrapped in a cloak, sleeping among his troops on the Busaco Ridge, while Massena retired to his tent with Madame Lebrerton, and when an ADC from Ney arrived with urgent information, he was not even allowed in, but had to shout through the tent flap for half an hour.

The Battle

As dawn broke on **27 September, 1810**, a thick mist shrouded the Busaco Ridge. Wellington was confident that the French would attack initially along the San Antonio road and positioned himself there. Sure enough, at about 0545, Merle's Division emerged through the mist.

Despite the lessons of Vimiero and Talavera, they attacked 'in column', 40 men wide and 40–60 deep, and were promptly decimated by the disciplined 'rolling fire' of the British line and the grapeshot from two 6-pounders well sited to a flank.

Another French attack penetrated a ¾-mile gap in the Allied line, but was then charged by the 88th (Connaught Rangers) and driven off. "Upon my honour, Wallace," Wellington declared to their Colonel, "I never witnessed a more gallant charge than that just made by your regiment." Eleven French battalions had been driven off by four British, leaving 2,000 casualties.

At 0600 a further four French battalions under Foy attacked just north of the San Antonio road, but were repulsed by Picton's Division, led by him still wearing his night-cap.

By 0630 the fog had almost cleared and the third attack came in – seven battalions under Foy. They reached the crest of the ridge before they were driven off by Leith's 5th Division, which arrived just in time from further south. This was a good example of Wellington's remarkable sense of anticipation, for he had ordered Leith, if not attacked himself, to march north.

By 0830 all the enemy had been driven from the ridge; 23 out of 27 French battalions had been mauled and repulsed by five British and seven Portuguese battalions.

Firing could now be heard to the north, and Wellington galloped off there, saying to Hill, "If they attempt this point again, Hill, you will give them a volley and charge with bayonets." Then, recalling Talavera, he added: "But don't let your people follow them too far down the hill."

Wellington arrived in the area of Pack's Brigade[2] at about 0830, just as the French attack came in. It was launched by Ney's VI Corps, led by Loison's Division (6,000 strong). They advanced boldly and confidently, for they had seen their comrades gain the ridge further south, and thought victory was in sight. They little knew, however, first, that the attacks in the south had failed, and second, that awaiting them just over the crest, still out of sight, were the famous Light Division, with the 52nd just north of the road and the 43rd on their right.[3]

The French captured Sula and then struggled on up the steep slope, despite heavy casualties from Ross's Battery. Triumphantly, they reached the crest, only to find themselves faced, at a mere 25 paces, by the stolid lines of 1,800 men of the Light Division. At their head on his charger was 'Black Bob' Craufurd, calmly watching them approach.

"Now, 52nd," he shouted, as the astonished French paused, "Avenge John Moore!"[4]

At ten paces a deadly volley thudded into the packed French column, and 1,000 men fell. Then, with a cheer they charged, driving the enemy back down the hillside. Altogther, Ney lost 1,200 men, against a mere 177 in the Light Division.

Nothing had gone right for the French, but at 0900 they gallantly attacked yet again, this time with 11 battalions under Marchand; they came up against the four battalions of Pack's Portuguese Brigade, just south of the Light Division and, to their surprise, they were driven off as confidently as if they had come up against veteran British infantry. The Portuguese had 'come of age'.

By 1100 the French had given up attacking. Junot's corps had not been involved at all, but Massena had had enough. In three hours he had lost some 4,600 men out of 40,000, including 5 generals and almost 300 other officers, the highest French casualties of the war so far. No less than 45 French battalions had been trounced by 24 Allied battalions, and the Allied casualties were only 1,252 (exactly half of whom were Portuguese).

Wellington had won a great victory and was tempted to follow it up, but he had achieved what he wanted, and there was little to gain by advancing and risking heavy casualties that he could ill afford.

The Allied troops rested that night in their positions, and Wellington slept in a cell in the Convent just behind the ridge.

The very **next day** Massena's cavalry discovered the route to the north that outflanked Wellington's position, and he set out along it, hoping to redeem the disaster at Busaco.

But Wellington was already away on the next stage of his carefully thought-out plan. On **28 September** he disengaged his troops and withdrew to the Lines of Torres Vedras, 70 miles to the south. He had written earlier, "When we do go, I feel a little anxiety to go like gentlemen out of the hall door and not out of the back door or by the area."[5]

He certainly fulfilled his wish.

Summary

The Battle of Busaco was a great triumph for Wellington and his Peninsular Army, and a fine instance of his foresight and flexibility, e.g. the construction of the lateral road that proved so valuable.

It was also yet another example of the superiority of the British line over the French column, of Wellington's use of the reverse slopes, and of his employment of a strong skirmishing line to thwart the French *tirailleurs*. He deployed his artillery very effectively, making best use of the 1 gun per 1,000 men that he had against the 8 per 1,000 of the enemy.

A feature of the battle was that it was the occasion when the Portuguese Army really proved their worth; they fought bravely and well, and the French were both surprised and impressed by their effectiveness. As Wellington remarked succinctly, "It has given them a taste for an amusement to which they were little accustomed."

It was a demoralizing defeat for the French, particularly as they were led by so distinguished a Marshal as Massena. Wellington himself commented later that, "When Massena was opposed to me in the field, I never slept comfortably."

But on this occasion Massena had been over-confident, and had paid highly for his mistake. This decisive defeat of the French raised the morale of the Allied army to new heights and correspondingly lowered that of the French, who would never again have the same confidence in their ability to overwhelm Wellington and his "amateur army".

THE BATTLEFIELD OF BUSACO

Where To Go

The Battlefield of Busaco is one of the best and easiest to visit, particularly as there are several good hotels nearby as well as an interesting Military Museum.

Busaco is some 13 miles north of Coimbra, just east of Mealhada. Turn east off the N.1 (Oporto-Lisbon) at Mealhada, and take the 234 to Luso. Busaco is just beyond Luso, and where the road crosses the Busaco Ridge is the battlefield. **(Viewpoint A)**

A further mile along the 234 is Moura, which was the starting point of the final French attacks. **(Viewpoint B)**

Having looked at the Busaco Ridge from the French viewpoint, drive back to Busaco and stand at the Monument, which is where Wellington stood. **(Viewpoint C)**

A road from the Monument leads to the Military Museum in Busaco, which is well worth a visit, and contains many exhibits about the battle.

Near the Museum is the Palace Hotel, a former Royal Palace with fine formal gardens. It is worth a visit for its excellent wines, still produced by the traditional method of treading the grapes.

Adjoining the hotel is the Convent, which was Wellington's headquarters, and contains the monk's cell where he spent the night after the battle. There is an olive tree under which he is said to have sat.

There are several walks from the hotel up to the battlefield along the Busaco Ridge.

A road runs south from the Monument marked Cruz Alta, and about a mile along it a track runs off to the left and leads to Wellington's other Command Post above Moura, from where he controlled the earlier fighting.

Do not, however, continue on the road to Cruz Alta in order to see the battlefield, as this viewpoint faces south-east away from the battlefield, and this can confuse one's map-reading.

What To See

Viewpoint A The windmill and a slab mark where Craufurd stood, with the Light Division behind him, just over the crest. It is a dominating position, and the French had a very steep climb to get to it. Sula and Moura are visible to the front.

Viewpoint B If one stops just west of the village of Moura by the roadside there is a good view back to the Busaco Ridge, and it is clear what a strong position it was, particularly if attacked frontally. The Monument, the Windmill and road to Busaco are all clearly visible.

Viewpoint C The Monument, a stone pillar crowned with a star, marks Wellington's second Command Post, and is in the area of Pack's Portuguese Brigade. From it one can see the whole battlefield in the later stages. The ridge to the right is the position of 1st Division, and the Light Division were to the left. The Convent is behind one, and Sula and Moura are visible to the front.

The road from San Antonio no longer exists, nor does the road built by Wellington.

Today the Busaco Ridge is heavily afforested, but in 1810 it was covered only by scrub.

Anniversary Celebrations

The anniversary of the Battle of Busaco is celebrated every year on 27 September at Busaco, with parades in uniforms of 1810, and festivities to commemorate the distinguished part played by the Portuguese troops in this victory.

Notes

1   It is now impassable.
2   The area of the present monument.
3   43rd (Monmouthshire); 52nd (Oxfordshire).
4   Sir John Moore's Regiment had been the 52nd.
5   Despatch, 2 April, 1810.

Order of Battle: Busaco – 27 September, 1810

ALLIES					FRENCH	
Division	*Commander*	*Strength*	*Brigades*		*Division*	*Strength*
	Right Flank				II Corps (Reynier)	
2nd	Hill	4,743	Stewart		Merle	6,589
			Inglis		Heudelet	8,087
			Craufurd C.		Soult (Cavalry)	1,397
Portuguese	Hamilton	4,940	Campbell			16,073
			Fonseca			
					VI Corps (Ney)	
5th	Leith	7,305	Barnes		Marchand	6,671
			Spry		Mermet	7,616
			Baron Eben		Loison	6,826
					Lamotte (Cavalry)	1,680
	Centre					21,793
3rd	Picton	4,143	MacKinnon			
			Lightburne			
			Chaplemont (Port)		VIII Corps (Junot)	
					Clausel	6,794
1st	Spencer	7,053	Stopford		Solignac	7,226
			Blantyre		St Croix (Cavalry)	1,863
			Lowe			
			Pakenham			15,883
Light	Craufurd R.	3,787	Beckwith		Cavalry Reserve	
			Barclay		Montbrun	3,479
	Left Flank					
4th	Cole	7,400	Campbell			
			Kemmis			
			Collins (Port)			
Portuguese	Independent Brigades	8,363	Pack			
			Campbell			
			Coleman			
Cavalry		210				

Commander	Wellington	Massena	
Strength	51,345	65,974	
Cavalry	210	3,479	
Guns	60	114	
Casualties	1,252	4,600	

8. **Talavera.** The charge of the 23rd Light Dragoons into the ravine north of the Medellin. "They plunged headlong into it and half the regiment was lost". (p.97) (*Mansell Collection*)

9. **Talavera.** The plain north of the Medellin across which the 23rd Light Dragoons made their charge.

10. **Busaco.** The Busaco Ridge as seen from the French positions at Moura. Sula is on the shoulder in the centre, and the Light Division position is just over the crest immediately behind it. The Convent lies over the ridge to the left. "Busaco was a great triumph for Wellington and his Peninsular Army, and a fine instance of his foresight and flexibility". (p.107) (*Henry Radice*)

11. **Busaco.** The olive tree at the Convent under which Wellington is said to have sat.

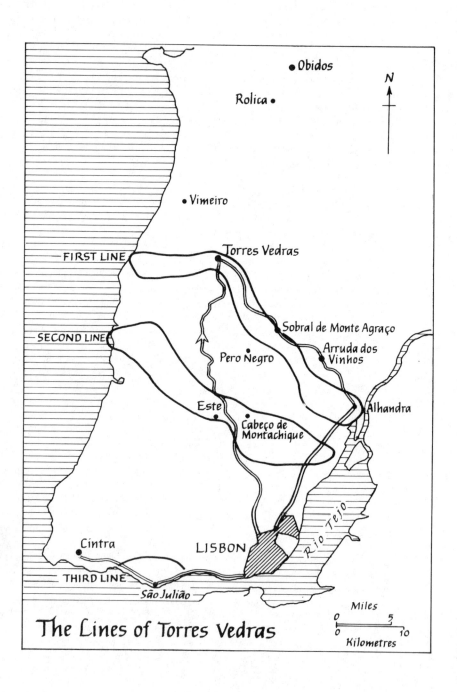

The Lines of Torres Vedras

CHAPTER SIXTEEN

The Lines of Torres Vedras

Wellington's Plan

When Wellington decided, in **October, 1809**, that he must construct the strongest possible lines of defence in Portugal, he had two aims in mind. First, he had to prevent the French from capturing Lisbon, and second, he must be sure that he could re-embark his army, should the worst happen.

To achieve this, he planned to build three lines of fortifications across Portugal between the Atlantic and the Tagus in the area of Torres Vedras, where it is only 30 miles wide, narrowing down to 18 miles nearer Lisbon. He had seen this piece of the country from the other side after the Battle of Vimiero in 1808, and he knew that it was a naturally strong defensive position. He had also studied reports by Marshal Junot's engineer, Vincent, and by the Portuguese surveyor, Neves Costa; but the concept of the Lines was his, and it was entirely on his initiative that they were constructed.

He rode over the whole area personally, some 500 square miles, and outlined his requirements in a 21-page memo to his Chief Engineer, Colonel Richard Fletcher,[1] sent to him on **20 October, 1809**.

He designed three main lines, blocking the four main routes to Lisbon.

    I. From the Atlantic along the south bank of the River Zizandre to Torres Vedras ("green towers"), then south-east to Alhandra on the Tagus. It was centred on Monte Agraco, and was 29 miles long.

   II. A Middle Line, roughly parallel to Line I, but five miles further south, and about 20 miles north of Lisbon. It was based on Cabeço de Montachique and was 22 miles long.

  III. A Third Line, 11 miles west of Lisbon, covering the harbour of Sao Juliao[2] as a port of embarkation, which could also be used to bring in supplies.

Line II was originally planned as the main line, but as there was more time than expected, Line I was built up into the main line.

The Lines cost about £100,000, and were "one of the cheapest investments in history". For this, Britain got 50 miles of fortifications, including 152 redoubts and 50 forts armed with 600 guns.

Construction of the Lines

The Lines were built entirely by Portuguese labour, under the guidance of only 18 British engineering staff. Lisbon Militia Regiments provided men at an extra 4d. a day, and 5–7,000 peasants worked at a shilling a day in gangs of 1,000 to 1,500 with some 150 British NCOs as overseers. The Lines were a great tribute to the Portuguese people who worked so loyally, and to the British who organized the project.

Every possible obstacle was constructed, using natural features where possible. Rivers were dammed, ravines blocked (one by a stone wall 16 foot thick and 40 foot high), and one hill was crowned by a wall 6 foot high, 4 foot thick and 3 miles long.

They were not a continuous linear rampart like Hadrian's Wall or the Maginot Line, but were a series of mutually supporting redoubts, 152 in all,[3] "crowning every dominant tactical feature along the defensive line, and enfilading all approach roads and defiles". They were so perfectly linked together that a message could be sent along the whole 29-mile front by semaphore in seven minutes, via nine main signal stations.[4] A written message from Wellington's headquarters at Pero Negro could reach any unit within an hour.

Each redoubt was designed to hold 3–6 guns and 200–300 men. The normal ditch was 16 foot wide, 12 foot deep, with a parapet 8–14 foot thick. The largest redoubt was just south of Sobral, with room for 25 guns and 1,600 men.

There were seven redoubts altogether in the Sobral area, mounting 55 guns with a garrison of 3,000, and the sector was "even stronger than Busaco". They were centred on Monte Agraco, and there was a paved road to the top.

The Tagus was patrolled by flotillas of 14 gunboats manned by the Navy, and they coordinated their firepower with the troops ashore. Wellington believed that "the one serious peril to the Lines came from the sea. If, by a sudden burst, he [Massena] could have got possession of the Tagus and kept it for a week, we must have starved. However, I had pretty well provided against that also."[5]

"If I am obliged to go," he wrote, "I shall be able to carry away the British Army."[6]

Occupation of the Lines

Wellington had been clear from the start that he would not tie up any first-line troops on static guard duties and he manned the fortifications, therefore, with his 25,000 Portuguese and 8,000 Spanish troops, supported by 2,500 British gunners and marines. His 34,000 British regulars were kept concentrated behind the Lines, ready to deal with any enemy break-through.[7] As part of the plan, he had several lateral roads built so that units could move rapidly to any of the dozen or so positions that were prepared for them.

The Peninsular Army withdrew to the Lines after the Battle of Busaco and were in position by **10 October, 1810**. Wellington set up his headquarters at Pero Negro, from where he rode out every morning to Monte Socorro to observe the enemy.

Massena was close on his heels, and saw the Lines for the first time on 10 October; it was in the area of Sobral and he was appalled.

When his staff tried to explain away their failure to warn him about their existence by saying that Wellington had built them very secretly, Massena retorted, *"Que diable. Il n'a pas construit ces montagnes."* ("To the devil with it. He never built those mountains.")[8]

On the **14th** the French launched a probing attack against Sobral, which failed completely, and this finally convinced Massena that he had no hope of penetrating such defences.

He now wrote off to Napoleon, saying, "The Marshal Prince of Essling [Massena's title] has come to the conclusion that he would compromise the Army of His Majesty if he were to attack in force lines so formidable, defended by 30,000 English and 30,000 Portuguese, aided by 50,000 armed peasants." Even Ney supported him in this view, which was a sure tribute to the strength of the Lines.

On the **16th** Massena rode to the village of Cotovios, near Arruda, to take another look from there. He was spotted by an alert artilleryman, and a gun in Redoubt 120 fired a shot to warn him not to press his reconnaissance too close. The shot hit the wall close to the Marshal, who lifted his hat in acknowledgement and retired out of range.

Wellington had expected that lack of food would force the French to withdraw within a week, but somehow they hung on for a month, in the hope that the Allies would tire first. But there was little chance of that, for they were sitting snugly and well-fed in their camps, with supplies coming in regularly through Lisbon. Indeed, they felt so sorry for the starving French that they tossed them biscuits and traded their rations and tobacco for brandy.

But there was a limit, and on 15 **November, 1810**, a cold, foggy night, the French slipped away, leaving straw dummies in the sentry posts in their front line.

They withdrew to Santarem and, except for a foray by Marmont as far as Guarda in April, 1812, would not set foot on Portuguese soil again. The Lines of Torres Vedras had served their purpose well.

THE LINES OF TORRES VEDRAS

Where To Go

A very good impression of the First and Second Lines can be obtained by driving north from Lisbon along the N.8 to Torres Vedras. This takes you through the Second Line at Este, while at Torres Vedras you can see a redoubt that has been reconstructed.

You then drive south-east along the 248 to Sobral-Arruda-Alhandra, following the First Line.

To see the Third Line, take the N.6 west out of Lisbon for about 10 miles and you come to Sao Juliao, a distinctive fortification on the left of the main road.

A detailed study of all three Lines requires 2–3 days, a marked map and a good deal of stamina.

What To See

Most of the 152 redoubts in the Lines are still visible, though in ruins, and as you drive through the hills north of Lisbon, they can be seen on every feature, giving a vivid impression of the astonishing scope and effectiveness of these fortifications.

MALVEIRA

Driving north on the N.8 from Lisbon, you pass through Malveira which is in the centre of the Second Line; it illustrates well the strength of the mountains as a defensive position, with redoubts still visible on the hilltops and in the valleys.

TORRES VEDRAS

The town itself is of interest, with its dominant castle, and a monument in the square, dedicated to the Peninsular War, and an Information Office nearby. There is a small but impressive Museum, which has a table on which it is said that the Convention of Cintra was signed.

SAO VICENTE

The strongpoint of Sao Vicente lies just to the north of Torres Vedras, on the west side of the main road to Lisbon. Forts 20–23 were combined to make one of the strongest positions in the First Line, and the fortifications have now been skilfully reconstructed, so that they give a very real idea of what they must have looked like in 1810.

It is intriguing to imagine how the defences might be manned today with modern weapons, and the conclusion reached in a Staff Study by Portuguese officers is that remarkably little change would be required.

SOBRAL DE MONTE AGRACO

This was the centre of the Front Line, and probably the strongest redoubt of all. It was the scene of the only French attack on the Lines.

PERO NEGRO

This was Wellington's headquarters, just south of Sobral, with Monte Socorro, which he used as his observation post.

ARRUDA

It was from here that Massena carried out a reconnaissance of the Lines on 16 October, and was shot at from Redoubt 120, which is identifiable from Arruda, but accessible only with difficulty and on foot.

ALHANDRA

This was the eastern end of the First Line, overlooking the Tagus.

The Monument to Colonel Fletcher is reached by turning off the A.1 just south of the overhead cableway of a large cement factory. It is erected on the site of Redoubt 2, and is a stone pillar crowned by a statue of Hercules and inscribed on one side with the words "Non Ultra. Lines of Torres Vedras."

There is a fine view from the Monument of the Tagus and the country to the east, the First Line to the west and the French positions to the north.

CABEÇO DE MONTACHIQUE

This dominant feature of the Second Line can be viewed from the bottom, but if you are energetic enough to climb to the top, you may, if visibility is good, get a view of both the Tagus and the Atlantic. It is 408 metres high, and was one of the signalling stations of the Lines.

SAO JULIAO

It is not possible to identify the Third Line in detail, as the area is so built up, but the fort is still intact and is impressive to see. It is now a Government Hospitality Centre.

Notes

1 The monument to him at Alhandra wrongly calls him "Henry". His assistant was Major John Jones, later General Sir John Jones, and the historian of the Lines.
2 The fort there was originally built between 1580 and 1640 as a defence against marauding British sailors such as Drake during the Spanish occupation of Portugal.
3 The redoubts were numbered according to their date of construction.
4 Manned by the Navy who were more used to signalling than the Army.
5 *The Lines of Torres Vedras*, A. H. Norris, p. 16.
6 Despatches, 14 January, 1810.
7 It is intriguing to compare this policy with that of the Allies for holding the Maginot Line in 1940, and with the German tactics for dealing with the Allied landings in Normandy in 1944.
8 This remark is recorded in the diary of General Pamplona, a renegade Portuguese officer on Massena's staff.

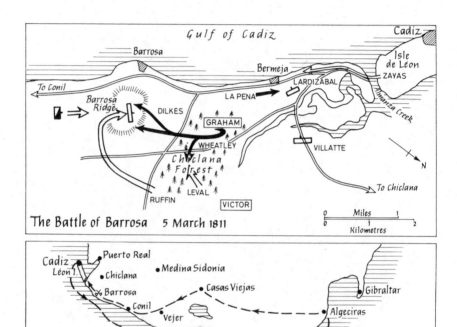

The Battle of Barrosa   5 March 1811

Gulf of Cadiz

Cadiz

Barrosa

Isle de León

Bermeja

ZAYAS

To Conil

LARDIZÁBAL

Barrosa Ridge

LA PENA

DILKES

GRAHAM

VILLATTE

WHEATLEY

Chiclana Forest

N

To Chiclana

RUFFIN

LEVAL

VICTOR

Manza Creek

Miles
0   1
0   1   2
Kilometres

The Barrosa Campaign

Cadiz

Puerto Real

León I.

Chiclana

Medina Sidonia

Barrosa

Gibraltar

Conil

Casas Viejas

Vejer

Algeciras

Tarifa

Miles
0   10
0   20
Kilometres

CHAPTER SEVENTEEN

The Battle of Barrosa

The Allied Plan

The important Allied harbour of Cadiz on the south coast of Spain was from **January 1810** besieged by some 25,000 French troops under Marshal Victor. But the garrison of 26,000 held out, thanks to the extremely strong defences and also the support of the Navy, who were able to keep the fortress well supplied.

Then in **January 1811** Victor was ordered to send almost a third of his strength to support Soult's assault on Badajoz, and was reduced to some 15,000 fighting troops. With such a force he could only await an Allied initiative, which was in fact imminent, for they were about to send a force of 13,000 men by sea from Cadiz to Tarifa, 50 miles to the south, and then march north and attack the investing French from the rear at Chiclana. At the same time 4,000 Spaniards, under General Zayas, would make a sortie from Cadiz.

A problem arose over who was to command the expeditionary force. The senior Spanish commander in Cadiz was the totally incompetent General Manuela La Pena, scornfully referred to by his own troops as "La Dona Manuela" (Madam Manuela).

The British commander was Major-General Thomas Graham, aged 62, but a fine, fighting soldier, described by Napier as "a daring old man, and of ready temper for battle".[1]

The Spanish Junta insisted that La Pena must be put in overall command, because there were 8,000 Spanish troops involved and only 5,000 British. This was directly contrary to the instructions that Graham had received from Wellington, but, for the sake of Anglo-Spanish accord, he reluctantly agreed to serve under La Pena. This was to prove a serious mistake, redeemed only by Graham's initiative and courage that saved the day.

The British element under Graham, consisting of 4,900 British, and 400 Portuguese infantry, 180 German cavalry, and 10 guns, sailed from

Cadiz on **21 February, 1811**, but, being unable to land at Tarifa due to bad weather, they went on to Algeciras. On the **27th** they joined up at Tarifa with La Pena and his 8,000 Spanish troops.

The combined force began its 60-mile advance to Chiclana the **next day**, but made slow progress, partly due to bad weather, but more because La Pena insisted on marching by night, which meant that they usually got lost.

As a result they were soon two days behind schedule. La Pena sent a message to General Zayas telling him to delay his sortie from Cadiz; but it never arrived, and Zayas duly launched his attack on **3 March**, as originally planned. He threw a bridge across the Almanza Creek and advanced southwards, but was defeated with 300 casualties by a French force under Villatte. He managed nevertheless to maintain a bridgehead just north of Bermeja.

La Pena finally reached Vejer on **4 March** and, when he learned of the situation, decided to abandon his original plan to attack Chiclana and instead, to join up with Zayas and return to Cadiz. He therefore advanced along the coast road and occupied the dominating ridge at Barrosa.

The French Plan

Victor was by now well aware of the Allied movements and saw a good opportunity to counter-attack. He ordered Villatte to hold the Bermeja Ridge and so block La Pena's line of advance to Cadiz. He then positioned two divisions (Leval and Ruffin) out of sight in the thick Chiclana Forest, where they were ideally placed to attack the Allies in the flank as they advanced towards Cadiz.

The Battle

On the morning of **5 March, 1811**, the Allied force was occupying the Barrosa Ridge, unaware of the two French divisions concealed in the thick forest just to the north.

Leaving Graham's division holding the ridge, La Pena now launched an attack north along the coast against Bermeja. After one failure, he succeeded, with the help of Zayas, in driving Villatte off his position and prepared to continue on into Cadiz.

At about noon he ordered Graham to move forward to Bermeja, leaving Barrosa Ridge undefended. Graham protested strongly that this exposed them to a French attack on the flank or rear of the whole Allied force, and La Pena reluctantly agreed to keep five Spanish and two British battalions on the ridge.

Graham now moved north as ordered, but when he was about halfway through the forest, he received news from Spanish guerrilleros that two massive columns of French troops were, as he had feared, advancing against him from the east. It was Leval's Division attacking the Allied flank, while Ruffin's Division was advancing against Barrosa Ridge, supported by 500 cavalry to the south. Victor himself was leading the assault.

Graham realized that the entire Allied force was in grave danger of being surrounded and destroyed and, disregarding his orders to join La Pena, he turned about and prepared to support the few Allied troops still on Barrosa Ridge.

He galloped back towards Barrosa, only to find that the Spanish troops had fled. Colonel Browne's battalion[3] alone remained on the feature, and they were being rapidly driven back by overwhelming numbers.

It was a desperate situation, and Graham decided that the only possible hope lay in a bold counter-attack. Within three minutes he had issued his orders.

Wheatley's Brigade[2] was to move to the east and confront Leval's Division. Dilkes's Brigade[3] was to counter-attack Ruffin's Division, who had by now seized the ridge.

Knowing that it would take time for the two brigades to deploy, Graham ordered the two flank battalions, commanded by Colonel Browne[3] and Colonel Barnard[2] to engage the enemy immediately. It was a "forlorn hope", but it was all he could do to buy time and so save the whole Allied force.

The 536 men of Browne's famous "Flankers" advanced up the steep Barrosa slope against Ruffin's 5,000. The first salvo from the French artillery and muskets knocked out 200 men, but the remainder pressed on till they could go no further. They then held their ground, and so bought precious time for the counter-attack by Dilkes's Brigade.

Graham himself led Dilkes's Brigade into the attack. His horse was shot under him, but he continued on foot. They now advanced, 1,400 strong, on Browne's right. Just as they neared the crest, they were charged by 2,500 French infantry in six columns. A furious fire-fight developed, the British line against the French columns. Once again the

Line won and it was the French who withdrew, having lost 859 against Dilkes's 413.

Meanwhile, to the east, Barnard's Light Battalion led the advance against Leval's Division. It consisted of 2,600 British in line, supported by 10 guns, against 4,000 French in column. The fire-fight here was even fiercer than on the ridge, some of it at 25 paces. Colonel Barnard[4] was wounded, and 1 man in 6 fell, but they checked the enemy long enough for Wheatley's Brigade to form up behind them.[5]

The Brigade advanced steadily, and for an hour it was merciless close-quarter fighting. Somehow the British held on and the 87th even managed to capture an Eagle from the French 8th Regiment. It was the first one taken in the campaign[6] and the Regiment became known thereafter as the "Eagle Takers" (unkindly corrupted later to the "Bird Snatchers".)

Finally, it was the French who withdrew, having suffered 2,400 casualties[7] against the Allies 1,740.[8] They had also lost four guns, in addition to the Eagle.

Thankfully, Graham withdrew his battered troops, who had lost a third of their strength. They were now too exhausted to pursue the enemy, having marched all night and fought all day.

La Pena had done nothing to support them during the battle, and now he refused to order a pursuit.[9] It was a great opportunity lost, and Graham, furious at La Pena's behaviour, marched his troops straight back to Cadiz. He was then accused by La Pena of having withdrawn without orders, and so having lost the battle for the Allies!

Summary

Barrosa was not a major battle, but it was a great victory and a fine feat of arms. A mere 5,000 British infantry took on 9,000 French and, against all the odds, defeated them.

The French divisional commander, Ruffin, spoke of "the incredibility of so rash an attack", and he was right. It was a supreme example of boldness earning its just reward, thanks to the courage and leadership of Graham.

It also proved yet again the superiority of the disciplined British line and its deadly firepower over the French column.

THE BATTLEFIELD OF BARROSA

Where To Go

Take the N.340 south from Cadiz following the signs to Chiclana. Five miles south of Chiclana, take a road to the right (west) marked Campano, and this leads to *Barrosa Hill.*

What To See

It is possible to climb *Barrosa Hill,* and from the top you look down on the British positions to the north prior to their attack.

The scene of Dilkes's attack lies due north, while Wheatley's attack against Leval was about a mile to the north-east.

The woods have long since disappeared, and the area is now mostly cultivated.

Cadiz is very industrialized, but some massive walls and fortifications survive in the old quarter. In the Plaza de Espana there is an impressive monument to the Peninsular War, and the Museo Historico Municipal on Calle Sagasta is interesting.

Notes

1 Napier, III, 100.

2 *Wheatley's Brigade*	3 *Dilkes's Brigade*
1/28th (less flank companies)	2/First Guards
2/67th	2/Coldstream Guards
2/87th	2/Third Guards
Two companies, 20th Port.	Detachment, 2/95th

Barnard's Battalion	*Browne's Battalion*
Two companies, 2/47th	Two companies, 1/9th
Four companies, 3/95th	Two companies, 1/28th
Two companies, 20th Port.	Two companies, 2/82nd

4 He and Colonel Bushe of the Portuguese 20th Regiment rode backwards and forwards through the intense fire, shouting *"Que bella musica"*, to encourage the men.

5 "Fire at their legs, and spoil their dancing," ordered Colonel Belson of the 28th.

6 It was presented to the Prince Regent and hung in the Chapel Royal until 1835. It then went to the Chapel at the Royal Hospital, Chelsea, but on 16 April, 1852, was stolen (by a patriotic Frenchman, it was thought).

7 The French 8th Regiment lost 726 out of 1,468.

8 Dilkes's Brigade lost 613 out of 1949.

9 He was later court-martialled, but was acquitted.

125

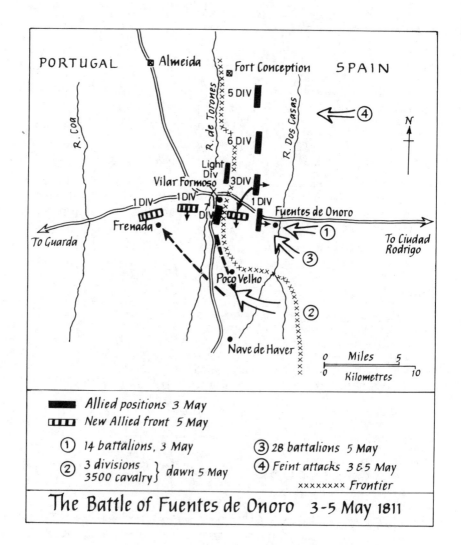

The Battle of Fuentes de Onoro   3–5 May 1811

PORTUGAL   ⊠ Almeida   ⊠ Fort Conception   SPAIN

R. Coa
R. de Torones
R. Dos Casas

5 DIV

6 DIV

Light Div
3 DIV

Vilar Formoso

1 DIV   1 DIV   1 DIV

Frenada

To Guarda

Poco Velho

Nave de Haver

Fuentes de Onoro

To Ciudad Rodrigo

N

① ② ③ ④

0   Miles   5
0   Kilometres   10

▬▬▬ Allied positions 3 May
▭▭▭ New Allied front 5 May

① 14 battalions, 3 May
② 3 divisions } dawn 5 May
   3500 cavalry
③ 28 battalions 5 May
④ Feint attacks 3 & 5 May
××××××× Frontier

CHAPTER EIGHTEEN

The Battle of Fuentes de Onoro

The Allied Plan

The Spring of 1811 was a difficult time for Wellington, who was very much on the defensive, holding the 150-mile line of the Portuguese frontier. The French had captured both Ciudad Rodrigo and Badajoz, and, if they concentrated their forces, they could muster at least 70,000 men against his 58,000.

Wellington set up his headquarters at Frenada in the north, and waited to see what the French would do. When he heard early in May that Massena was advancing from Ciudad Rodrigo with 48,000 men, he decided that he could afford to fight a battle against him, even though the Allied army was only 38,000 strong.[1] He picked as his position a long, low ridge that ran north and south through the village of Fuentes de Onoro on the Portuguese frontier. It stood astride the road from Ciudad Rodrigo to Coimbra, and provided the reverse slope position that suited Wellington's tactics.

The village itself was, and still is, a labyrinth of small, one-storey stone houses with stone walls enclosing patches of garden, and narrow alleys in between. It was on the forward slope of a low, rocky ridge over which the road climbed to Guarda, and behind which Wellington could place his troops out of sight.

In front of the village and at right angles to the road ran a small stream called the Dos Casas, which was no obstacle at this point, but, as it flowed north, it entered a steep ravine and was very much a barrier in the area of Fort Concepcion.

Wellington planned to make Fuentes de Onoro the strongpoint of his defence, and he placed the bulk of his forces in or behind it. He held the village itself with one battalion[2] and 28 light companies (2,260 men), under the command of Colonel Williams of the 60th, who had distinguished himself at Busaco. To the west of the village over the crest of the hill, he put four divisions (1st, 3rd, 7th and Light), effectively blocking the road into Portugal.

The Allied position was about five miles in length, and the whole sector north of Fuentes de Onoro was held by only two divisions (5th and 6th). The danger was his right flank, south of the village, which was open country, well suited to cavalry. The French out-numbered the Allies by more than 2 to 1 in this arm[3] and Wellington did not have enough troops to protect that flank properly. He could only hope that Massena would attack him frontally again, as he had done so obligingly at Busaco.

The Battle

On the afternoon of **3 May, 1811**, the French advanced straight down the road from Ciudad Rodrigo, just as Wellington had hoped, and at about 1400 Massena launched a massive frontal attack with five out of his eight divisions against Fuentes de Onoro. It was led by Ferey's Division in three columns, and the Allies were slowly driven out of the village, Colonel Williams being seriously wounded.

Wellington was, as usual, on the spot, and he sent in two Highland Regiments, (the 71st and 79th),[4] who re-captured it in fierce fighting. At the end of a day of bloody, hand-to-hand fighting the village was still in Allied hands and the French had lost 652 men to their 259.

The next day there was an unofficial truce, as had happened at Talavera. Both sides collected their wounded and there was some fraternization, as they met to drink and wash in the stream. The French then held parades, designed to intimidate their enemy, while the British played football.

The commanders meanwhile considered their next moves. Wellington was well satisfied with events so far, but he foresaw that the French might now attack his right, and he would then have two options. He could shift the bulk of his army south, which would expose Almeida, or he could remain where he was to cover Almeida and risk his communications to the rear being cut by a French out-flanking movement.

In the event, he compromised and strengthened his right flank slightly by sending the newly-arrived 7th Division to Poco Velho, and by sending some cavalry to Julian Sanchez, the Spanish guerrilla leader, who was holding Nave de Haver. He then waited to see what Massena would do.

Massena was well aware that he must do something to win the battle; he could not simply remain on the defensive. Mindful of his blunders at Busaco, he reconnoitred thoroughly on the **4th**, and soon appreciated that his best hope lay in turning Wellington's right flank, which would also cut off the Allied line of retreat to Portugal.

He therefore ordered Reynier to make a feint attack in the north, and Drouet to attack Fuentes de Onoro again, as it was the key to the enemy position. His main thrust would come from the south against the Allied flank west of the village.

It was a good plan and it came very near to succeeding.

At dawn on **5 May**, 17,000 French infantry and 4,000 cavalry swept up from the south and fell on the weakest part of the Allied line, held by the 7th Division, who were soon driven out of Poco Velho and retreated north-west in some disorder. Julian Sanchez and his Spanish guerrillas were forced out of Nave de Haver and Wellington's rear was threatened.

It was a serious crisis and defeat was close. Wellington had expected an attack but not on this scale, and his plans were not adequate to meet it. But he was at his best at moments like this and he now showed his power of reaction that could turn possible defeat into success. There is a story that he was told that some French prisoners had stated that "the whole French army was opposed to Wellington". His only comment was, "Oh. They are all there, are they? Well, we must mind a little what we are about."[5]

Rapidly and calmly, he re-aligned his whole position to face south, instead of east. Leaving the 5th and 6th Divisions where they were, he entrusted the defence of Fuentes de Onoro to the two Scottish regiments, (71st and 79th) with 1/24th in support. He moved the 1st and 3rd Divisions westwards to form a new line running towards Frenada, so that Fuentes now became the centre of his position rather than the right.

He also sent the Light Division to support the 7th Division, now fighting their way back from Poco Velho. So began one of the finest actions in their distinguished history, and it was also perhaps the "finest hour" of their commander, Craufurd, who had re-joined them only the night before.

The Light Division (2,900 British and 900 Portuguese) was supported by Cotton's cavalry[6] and by Bull's Battery of the Horse Artillery. Together they held off the confident advance of the French cavalry, infantry and artillery by forming squares and then moving back steadily, still in their squares, without ever allowing the enemy to break them.

The cavalry fought brilliantly, charging repeatedly against superior numbers until, in Wellington's words, the horses "had not a gallop in them".[7] Despite being out-numbered 3 or 4 to 1 and under constant pressure, they withdrew in good order for three miles, until the 7th Division was safely back in the Allied line.

William Napier declared that "there was not during the war a more dangerous hour for England", and Wellington admitted that it was "a near run thing". The danger from the French cavalry was demonstrated by the fate of three companies of Third Guards who failed to form square in time, and lost half their number, including their commander.

This phase of the battle also saw one of the most famous incidents in the history of the Royal Artillery, when Captain Norman Ramsay, commanding a pair of guns, stayed behind too long, firing at the French cavalry. He found himself cut off, but fought his way out with his guns at full gallop, and thus established a proud tradition for the Horse Artillery.

The casualties incurred during the withdrawal were surprisingly small. The Light Division lost only 67 men, but the cavalry lost 157 out of 1,400.

Meanwhile, bitter fighting had been continuing in Fuentes itself. Two hours after dawn, 5,000 French infantry, including three battalions of Grenadiers, attacked the 79th, who were driven back, having lost a third of their number, including their Colonel. Wellington fed in reinforcements, and the village was recaptured, but Massena in turn threw in no less than 18 battalions, including the Imperial Guard. They drove the defenders back as far as the church, but were then themselves thrown out by Mackinnon's Brigade, led by the 88th, the Connaught Rangers.

A final French attack at about 1400 failed, not surprisingly perhaps, for the troops involved had already attacked six times and were losing heart. Fuentes remained finally in Allied hands, bodies piled high between the narrow walls.[8]

Massena now gave up. He could not attack again from the south until he had captured Fuentes, and there was little chance of that. Wellington was still undefeated, Almeida was still invested, and there was little more that he could do about it.

Wellington was not, however, taking any chances, and he remained fully prepared that night for further attacks. Indeed, he ordered his troops to dig in, the only time that he did so in the whole campaign.

But on **8 May** Massena withdrew back to Salamanca, and Wellington let him go unhindered.

He had good reason to be pleased with the outcome. His army had performed magnificently, including the cavalry, who had excelled themselves. The Gunners too had played a decisive role, but he unfortunately failed to mention them in his Despatches, much to their indignation.

He had himself shown his usual outstanding close control of the battle, and his rapid decisions, such as the move of the Light Division, certainly saved the day.

It was another fine, defensive battle, and also a decisive victory,[9] which was welcome at home, and helped to sustain the Government.

THE BATTLEFIELD OF FUENTES DE ONORO

Where To Go

The village of Fuentes de Onoro is about one mile inside Spain, east of the frontier post of Vilar Formosa on the highway from Guarda to Salamanca (N.82 in Portugal and E.3 in Spain).

The battlefield, however, lies astride the frontier and is therefore tricky to visit. Almeida, Frenada, Poco Velho and Nave de Haver are in Portugal, while Fuentes and Fort Concepcion are in Spain.

Viewpoint A The easiest viewpoint, and one of the best is on the main road, 100 yards east of the bridge over the Dos Casas, looking back at Fuentes de Onoro.

Viewpoint B Drive south from Vilar Formosa on the Portuguese side of the frontier, and you can see the scene of the cavalry battle on 5 May.

What To See
FUENTES DE ONORO

The village can be clearly seen from Viewpoint A, and must be little changed from 1811. The present main road runs some 400 yards east of the old road of 1811, which is still there. The church still stands at the top of the village, and the Dos Casas flows through the village.

The forward slope on which the village stands is clearly unsuited for cavalry, and you can see how Wellington's main force would have been out of sight over the crest.

Walk into the village, and it is easy to imagine the bloody hand-to-hand fighting that occurred in the narrow alleys.

Viewpoint B It is interesting to drive through the area of the main fighting on 5 May, and to see the scene of the cavalry action. There are no easily identifiable landmarks, but the battlefield can be worked out from the locations of Poco Velho, Nave de Haver and Frenada.

Notes

1 35,000 infantry, 2,000 cavalry and 48 guns.
2 2/84th (York and Lancaster).
3 Massena had 4,500 to Wellington's 2,000.
4 Glasgow Highlanders and Cameron Highlanders.
5 Quoted by his Judge Advocate General, F.S. Larpent, as an example of Wellington's remarkable coolness. (Private Journal, I, 85)
6 1st Dragoons (The Royals); 14th Light Dragoons; 16th Light Dragoons; 1st Hussars, K.G.L.
7 Supplementary Despatches, VII, 177.
8 The village was in utter ruins, and Wellington asked the British Government for money to re-build it, saying that it had 'not been much improved' by the battle. (Despatches, VII, 571.)
9 The Battle is depicted on British £5 notes.

Order of Battle: Fuentes de Onoro – 3–5 May, 1811

ALLIES

Division	Commander	Strength	Brigades
1st	Spencer	7,565	Stopford
			Lowe
			Nightingall
			Howard
3rd	Picton	5,480	MacKinnon
			Colville
			Power (Port)
5th	Erskine	5,158	Hay
			Dunlop
			Spry (Port)
6th	Campbell	5,250	Hulse
			Burne
			Madden (Port)
7th	Houston	4,590	Sontag (Ger)
			Doyle (Port)
Light	Craufurd	3,915	Beckwith
			Drummond
Cavalry		1,854	Slade
			Arentschildt (KGL)
			Barbasena (Port)

Commander		Wellington
Strength		37,614[1]
Cavalry		1,854
Guns		48
Casualties		1,545

[1] British 23,026. Portuguese 11,471

FRENCH

Division	Strength
II Corps (Reynier)	11,064
Merle	
Heudelet	
VI Corps (Loison)	17,140
Marchand	
Mermet	
Ferey	
VIII Corps (Junot)	4,714
Solignac	
IX Corps (D'Erlon)	11,098
Claparede	
Conroux	
Reserve	2,514
Montbrun	
Cavalry	1,738
Bessières	

Massena	
48,268	
1,738	
38	
2,192	

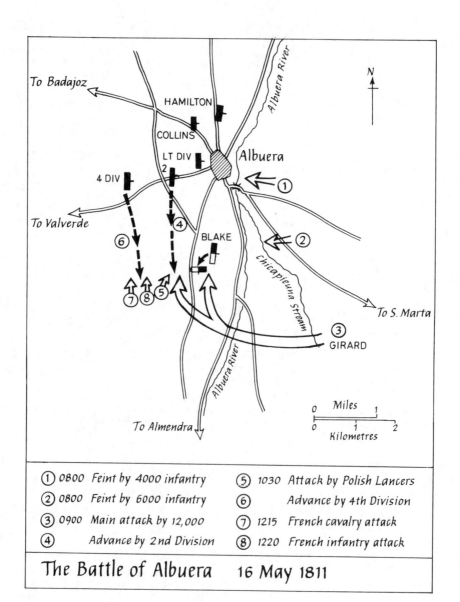

To Badajoz

HAMILTON

COLLINS

LT DIV

4 DIV

To Valverde

Albuera River

Albuera

N

① ⟵

② ⟵

BLAKE

Chicapierna Stream

To S. Marta

⑥

⑦ ⑧ ⑤

③ GIRARD

Albuera River

To Almendra

0	Miles	1
0	1	2
	Kilometres	

① 0800 Feint by 4000 infantry
② 0800 Feint by 6000 infantry
③ 0900 Main attack by 12,000
④   Advance by 2nd Division
⑤ 1030 Attack by Polish Lancers
⑥   Advance by 4th Division
⑦ 1215 French cavalry attack
⑧ 1220 French infantry attack

The Battle of Albuera   16 May 1811

CHAPTER NINETEEN

The Battle of Albuera

The Allied Plan

In **May, 1811**, General Beresford was besieging Badajoz when he heard on the 12th that Marshal Soult was advancing against him from the south with 25,000 men. He immediately abandoned the siege and moved south-east to the small town of Albuera, where he took up a defensive position, as discussed with Wellington the previous month. (See page 37)

On the afternoon of the **15th** he was joined by 14,000 Spanish under Blake and Castanos, who agreed to serve under him. He now had an army of about 37,000 with 50 guns.[1]

The country round Albuera is generally flat and open, with slight undulations; the Albuera River runs east of the town, dividing into two smaller streams, none of which were obstacles to infantry or even artillery. In 1811 there were quite a few trees along the Chicapieuna stream, which prevented the Allied Army from having a clear view of the French moves before the battle.

Beresford expected Soult to advance from the east, and he therefore made Albuera the centre of his position, which extended about one mile to the left of the town and two miles to the right. A low ridge, not more than 150 foot high, ran through Albuera, and he occupied this, with all his troops facing east.

He covered his left with Hamilton's Portuguese Division, Collin's Brigade and most of the Portuguese cavalry. He put Alten's K.G.L. Brigade in Albuera and behind them he put the 2nd and 4th British Divisions, and over 1,000 cavalry.

He left the right flank to Blake's 12,000 Spanish, with some cavalry; but they did not arrive at Albuera till late on the 15th and were not properly established by next morning.

The French Plan

Soult had 24,000 men, including 4,000 cavalry, together with 60 guns. He did not know that the Spanish had joined Beresford, and so thought he was opposed by only 23,000 Allied troops at Albuera.

He planned only to demonstrate against the Allied centre, and to send three-quarters of his forces in a wide sweep to the south to attack the Allied right flank; this would not only outflank Beresford's position, but might also cut him off from Badajoz. He gave the task of this sweep to Girard's V Corps and timed it for dawn on 16 May.

The Battle

Soult launched his attack early on **16 May, 1811**, and it began well, the demonstration in front of Albuera by Goudinot's Brigade leading Beresford to reinforce his centre, as Soult had hoped.

Then, suddenly, Zaya's Spanish Division in the south (4,800 strong) saw appearing from behind the trees to their right flank 8,400 infantry supported by artillery and 3,500 cavalry. It was Girard's V Corps, advancing in the "mixed order" so favoured by Napoleon.

It was "the most massive single attack of the Peninsular War"[2] – a solid mass of infantry, 400 yards across and 600 yards deep. It was a formidable sight, and it found the Spanish unprepared for such an onslaught. But they stood their ground most gallantly, despite losing a third of their strength.

Beresford too was taken by surprise, and he ordered Blake to move one whole division to face south instead of east. He did not, however, see for himself that it was actually done, as Wellington would have, and Blake, who still expected an attack from the east, moved only four battalions, instead of the whole division.

Beresford now ordered the 2nd Division to support the hard-pressed Spaniards. Its commander, the impetuous William Stewart,[3] was told to form a second line behind them, but, instead, he flung his troops straight into the battle. His leading brigade, Colborne's, attacked the left flank of the French column, using their 2,000 muskets to good effect, and checked them.

Then came disaster. A sudden rainstorm burst over the battlefield and none of the muskets would fire. Stewart had neglected to provide protection against enemy cavalry, and now, through the driving rain, thundered 3,500 French cavalry. Colborne's Brigade had had no time to form square and were virtually defenceless. Within five minutes they lost 1,300 out of 1,600[4] and five Colours. The 1st Polish Lancers did deadly execution, transfixing living and wounded alike. It was a grim reminder of the vulnerability of infantry caught unprepared by cavalry.

Some of the cavalry swept on and attacked Beresford and his staff. The general, a large, powerful man, parried one lance thrust and, seizing the trooper by the collar, pulled him off his horse and threw him to the ground.

Hoghton's Brigade of 2nd Division[5] now came up, followed by Abercrombie's, and formed line. "Seven British battalions, about 3,700, two deep, now faced two French divisions, about 7,800, in a fire-fight at close range perhaps never equalled in military history."[6]

At a range as close as 20 yards both sides fired volley on volley, closing in to the centre, as gaps relentlessly appeared in the ranks. The 29th lost 336 men out of 476, the 57th 428 out of 616, and the 48th 280 out of 646.

For almost an hour, on an area little larger than a cricket field, the grim killing continued. Neither side could advance, but neither seemed prepared to give way.

Strangely, no one knew how to end the impasse. Beresford seemed incapable of decisive action, while Soult had just discovered that the enemy were 15,000 stronger than he had thought, and from that moment he went on to the defensive.

The deadlock was resolved by 39-year-old Sir Lowry Cole. Urged on by a 26-year-old Major called Henry Hardinge,[7] he realized that something must be done to save the Regiments that were being steadily destroyed in front of him. On his own initiative, he moved his 4th Division forward to join the battle.

On a front of three-quarters of a mile, the 4,000 men advanced in line, with a square at each end as protection against cavalry. Sure enough, 1,600 French dragoons charged, but were beaten off.

Then three French columns, each of three battalions, advanced against them, supported by artillery. The British infantry were outnumbered by 3 to 1, but it was "line versus column" yet again – 2,000 effective muskets versus only 360. Very slowly, but very steadily, the British infantry, headed by three battalions of Fusiliers,[8] moved forward, and it was the French who broke first.

Belatedly, Soult threw in his reserve, 6,000 men of Werle's Brigade, but it was in vain. Attacked now from both flanks, his columns crumbled, and it became a general retreat.

At last Beresford brought forward units from his left and centre, and the French were driven back across the stream to the woods from where they had started. There was no pursuit and both sides remained in their positions exhausted and depressed by the appalling losses. The Allies had lost 5,956 out of 35,284, but the infantry had suffered grievously; their casualties were 4,407 out of 8,800 – nearly two-thirds of their strength. The French casualties are uncertain, but were probably around 7,000. They withdrew two days later, on the **18th**, and Soult complained bitterly of the British: "They could not be persuaded they were beaten. They were completely beaten, the day was mine, and they did not know it, and would not run."

Beresford, unnerved by the casualties, wrote a gloomy Despatch, but when Wellington read it, he declared, "This won't do. It will drive the people in England mad. Write me down a victory."[9] It was duly done, for it was the French, after all, who had retired from the battlefield.

There was much criticism of Beresford for his handling of the battle, but Wellington took pains to reassure him. "You could not be successful in such an action without a large loss", he wrote, "and we must make up our minds to affairs of this kind sometimes, or give up the game."[10]

On **21 May** Wellington visited the battlefield, and saw the dead "literally lying dead in their ranks as they stood". He also went to see some of the wounded and remarked, "Men of the 29th, I am sorry to see so many of you here." To which a veteran sergeant replied, "If you had commanded us, my Lord, there would not be so many of us here."[11]

Summary

Certainly Beresford made mistakes at Albuera that Wellington would probably have avoided. He had virtually no skirmishers out, and he did not protect his flanks adequately. Above all, he did not exercise close control over the battle and react to developments, as Wellington would have done, nor did he ensure that the orders he gave were properly carried out.

It is intriguing to consider how Wellington might have fought this battle, and it seems likely that, with his superior numbers, he would have retained the initiative and won a decisive victory at less cost.

Nevertheless, Albuera *was* a victory, though at a price, and it undoubtedly helped to sap French morale further when they discovered how hard it was to make the Peninsular Army accept defeat.

THE BATTLEFIELD OF ALBUERA

Where To Go

Albuera lies on the N.432, 14 miles south-east of Badajoz.

Stop about a mile north of the town on the road to Badajoz, and you are now on the rise from which Beresford controlled the battle. (**Viewpoint A**)

Drive on south through the town to the bridge over the Albuera River. Turn right just before the bridge and follow the road that runs between the stream and the ridge on the right. After about a mile the scene of the fiercest fighting is on your right. (**Viewpoint B**)

What To See

There are few obvious features to identify other than the town and the stream.

From Viewpoint A one can see why Beresford expected a frontal attack from the east, and the ridge along which he placed his troops is evident in the otherwise open country.

The trees that screened the French sweep round the Allied right are no longer there.

In the main square in Albuera is a monument to the battle, with a bust of General Castanos between two pillars, on which are the names of the Spanish and British generals who took part.

In the Town Hall are a collection of weapons, paintings and letters relating to the battle.

On the road running south towards the ridge where the main fighting took place there is a small monument erected by the Spanish Army in the 1970s in memory of two officers who were killed in the action.

Notes

1 British: 10,000; Portuguese: 12,000; Spanish: 15,000.
2 Jac Weller, *Wellington in the Peninsula*, p. 176.
3 He fought at Copenhagen with the light companies on board ship, and he recorded Nelson's historic reaction to Admiral Parker's signal.

4 The losses were: 1/3rd 85%; 2/48th 75.9%; 2/66th 61.6%.
5 They moved in such a hurry that Hoghton had to put on his tunic on horseback and under fire.
6 Weller, op. cit., p. 177.
7 He later became a Field-Marshal.
8 1/7th, 2/7th and 1/23rd.
9 Despatches, VII, 573.
10 Despatches, VII, 558.
11 Maxwell's *Peninsular Sketches*, II, 331.

Order of Battle: Albuera – 16 May, 1811

ALLIES

Division	Commander	Strength	Brigades
2nd	Stewart	5,460	Colborne
			Hoghton
			Abercrombie
4th	Cole	5,107	Myers
			Kemmis
			Harvey (Port)
Portuguese	Hamilton	4,819	Fonseca
			Campbell
Spanish	Blake (three divisions)	10,815	
	Independent Brigades	1,098	Alten (KGL)
		1,385	Collins (Port)
		1,778	Castanos (Spain)
	Cavalry		
	British	1,146	
	Portuguese	849	
	Spanish	1,887	

Commander			Beresford		
	Spanish	British	Portuguese	Total	
Strength	14,634	20,310		35,284	
Cavalry	1,887	1,146	849	1,995	
Guns	14	24	12	50	
Casualties	1,368	4,199	389	5,956	

FRENCH

Division	Strength
V Corps	
Girard	4,254
Gazan	4,183
	8,437
Brigades	
Godinot	3,924
Grenadiers	1,033
Werle	5,621
	10,578
Cavalry	4,012

Soult	
	24,260
	4,012
	60
	7–8,000

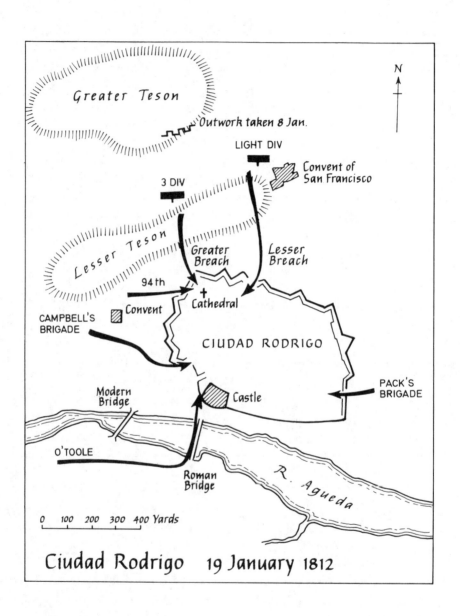

N

Greater Teson

Outwork taken 8 Jan.

LIGHT DIV

Convent of
San Francisco

3 DIV

Lesser Teson

Greater
Breach

Lesser
Breach

94 th

Convent

Cathedral

CAMPBELL'S
BRIGADE

CIUDAD RODRIGO

PACK'S
BRIGADE

Modern
Bridge

Castle

O'TOOLE

Roman
Bridge

R. Agueda

0   100   200   300   400 Yards

Ciudad Rodrigo   19 January 1812

12. **Lines of Torres Vedras.** Some of the reconstructed fortifications in the Redoubt Sao Vicente at Torres Vedras.

13. **Lines of Torres Vedras.** "One of the cheapest investments in history". (p114)

15. **Ciudad Rodrigo.** The Cathedral and the site of the Greater Breach viewed from the north, i.e. from the Lesser Teson.

16. **Ciudad Rodrigo.** The house in which Wellington stayed. (p.146)

17. **Ciudad Rodrigo.** The town viewed from the south. To the right is the Roman Bridge crossed by O'Toole to attack the Castle (centre). The Cathedral is just visible to the left.

18. **Badajoz.** The Castle seen from San Cristobal. Picton's assault went in from the left of the picture and Leith's from the right. The River Guadiana is in the foreground. "Wellington lost more British soldiers at the siege of Badajoz than in any battle of the Peninsular War except Albuera and Talavera". (p.151)

19. **Salamanca.** The Greater Arapile as seen by Wellington from his position on the ridge behind the village of Los Arapiles, just off the picture to the right. The heaviest fighting took place just to the right of the Greater Arapile. "The Battle of Salamanca was an outstanding 'opportunist' encounter, launched with remarkable boldness, and executed with perfect timing and control". (p.159)

CHAPTER TWENTY

The Capture of Ciudad Rodrigo

Wellington's Plan

Towards the end of 1811, Wellington decided that he could capture Ciudad Rodrigo early in 1812. He gave the task of investing it meanwhile to Julian Sanchez[1] and his Spanish guerrillas, who did so well that they actually captured the Governor, a Swiss called Reynaud.[2] He himself moved his army across the Portuguese frontier on 4 January and by the 7th was in position round Ciudad Rodrigo.

The town was oval in shape and only about 700 yards by 550 yards, standing on a plateau above the Agueda River. It was strongly fortified, but had two weaknesses; first, the garrison of around 2,000 was not enough for its defence, and second, there were to the north two low ridges, the Greater and Lesser Tesons, which were 700 and 200 yards respectively from the walls. The Greater Teson was actually 14 feet higher than the ramparts, and the French had built the Reynaud Redoubt there in order to hold it.

Wellington planned to use his superior numbers to attack from several directions, with the main assault coming from the north. His first move was to capture the Reynaud Redoubt and, as part of his plan, he "advertised" a "field sports day" as a diversion for the troops. The French cheered from the ramparts as the "mad English" galloped around, apparently having innocent fun, but in fact carrying out a reconnaissance.

Then on the night of 8 January 300 picked men of the Light Division, under 33-year-old Colonel John Colborne of the 52nd,[3] attacked the Redoubt without the usual preliminary bombardment. They captured it in 20 minutes, together with its garrison of 60, losing only 26 themselves.

The engineers started work immediately, but there were no miners or sappers (a weakness throughout 1812) and the digging had to be done by the infantry, working in bitter cold for 24 hours at a time under enemy fire. When news reached Wellington that Marmont was concentrating only 50 miles away, he decided not to wait, even though an attack was somewhat premature. Two passable breaches had been made in the northern ramparts, and on **19 January** he gave the laconic order "Ciudad Rodrigo must be stormed tonight".[4]

His plan[5] was that Picton's 3rd Division would attack the Greater Breach in the north-west corner of the ramparts at 1900, advancing from behind the Lesser Teson. The Light Division would at the same time attack the Lesser Breach, starting from the Convent of San Francisco.

There were to be two diversions starting ten minutes earlier. First, Colonel O'Toole, with the 2nd Cacadores and the light company of 2/83rd, was to advance from the south, cross the river by the Roman Bridge, storm the Castle and then silence two cannon below it that enfiladed the ramparts. Second, Campbell's Brigade was to advance from the Convent of Santa Cruz on the west, scale the walls and then attack the Greater Breach from the south.

A final diversion was that Pack's Portuguese Brigade would attack from the east at the same time as the main assault.

The Assault

At 1900 a signal rocket launched the assault. The diversions had been very successful, and both Colonel O'Toole and Campbell's Brigade were already on the ramparts.

The "forlorn hope"[6] of the 3rd Division consisted of 500 men of the 88th, and Picton addressed them in typical style. "Rangers of Connaught. It is not my intention to expend any powder this evening. We'll do this business with a cauld iron." The challenge was met with loud cheers.

But even they could not get beyond the breach. Then the French exploded a huge mine under the walls, which killed most of the assault troops of Mackinnon's Brigade, including its commander.[7] But it was more powerful than intended, and did so much damage to the defenders as well that the 3rd Division were able to force their way into the town.

The Light Division stormed their breach successfully. Their "forlorn hope" was led by Lt Gurwood of the 52nd,[6] who was knocked out and lay unconscious for a time in the ditch. When he came to, he set off on his own into the town, entered the Castle and found the

Governor seated at dinner with his staff. He immediately demanded their surrender and the Governor duly handed over his sword, which Gurwood sent to Wellington.[8]

Pack's Brigade had also penetrated into the town and the garrison now surrendered. The action had lasted only half an hour and had cost about 500 casualties, plus another 600 during the 10 days of the siege. The French lost around 530 and 2,000 survivors were taken prisoner. A more severe loss to them was their siege train, which included 150 heavy guns, which would come in very useful against Wellington's next objective – the even stronger fortress of Badajoz.

Among the British casualties was Major-General Robert Craufurd of the Light Division who died of wounds; it was a serious loss to the Army, for he was an outstanding commander and very much a "soldier's soldier". His troops paid a fine farewell tribute to him, when returning to camp after his burial by the Lesser Breach. The entire Light Division marched in silence, thigh deep in icy water through a marshy pool, 50 yards wide, in accordance with his edict that no man should ever divert round any obstacle to avoid physical discomfort.

There had been heavy officer casualties in the assault and this contributed perhaps to the loss of discipline that night, when the troops went on the rampage in the captured town. Plundering was not unusual after the storming of a defended fortress, but it was not excusable when the inhabitants were allies, as in this case, especially when combined with rape and murder.

Wellington spent that night in the Palace de los Castros near the Salamanca Gate, already planning the capture of Badajoz. The British Government now elevated him from Viscount to Earl, while the Spanish Junta made him Duke of Ciudad Rodrigo and a Grandee of Spain.

THE CAPTURE OF CIUDAD RODRIGO

Where To Go

Ciudad Rodrigo lies astride the main road from Salamanca to the Portuguese frontier at Fuentes de Onoro.

Viewpoint A Approaching from the Portuguese side, stop just short of the new bridge over the Agueda River for a general view of the town from the south-west.

Viewpoint B Drive on round the west side of the town, with the ramparts on your right and enter by the entrance nearest to the Cathedral, which is the site of the Lesser Breach.

Viewpoint C Park by the Cathedral and walk to the town centre, and then on to the ramparts just north of the Cathedral, where you are standing on the site of the Greater Breach.

Viewpoint D Walk round the ramparts anti-clockwise to the Castle, now a Parador.

Viewpoint E Walk to the Lesser Teson (now several blocks of flats) and look back at the town from the north-west.

What To See

Viewpoint A This gives a general view of the town, with the Castle on the south-west corner, and below it the Roman Bridge, crossed by Colonel O'Toole.

Viewpoint B The arched entrance into the town by the Cathedral is the site of the Lesser Breach, and the repairs to the ramparts are still visible. There is an official Information Office just inside the walls.

Viewpoint C The Palace de Los Castros where Wellington stayed is a private house, but the outside can be seen with its distinctive fluted columns either side of the entrance.

The Cathedral, standing within 50 yards of the ramparts, is still pockmarked by shot and shell. Between it and the ramparts is an impressive memorial to Julian Sanchez, the guerrilla leader. There is also a small garden made during the reign of Isabel II to honour the Spanish Governor, Herrasti, who resisted Marshal Ney so gallantly in 1810.

The ramparts here are the site of the Greater Breach, and look out to the Tesons.

Viewpoint D Walking along the ramparts, look westwards to the line of Campbell's advance (roughly from the bullring). Ahead is the Castle, at the foot of whose walls were the two guns enfilading the ramparts, which were silenced by Colonel O'Toole.

Beyond the Castle is the Roman Bridge by which he crossed.

Inside the Castle is a plaque commemorating the capture of the town by Wellington.

Viewpoint E From the Lesser Teson you see the town as viewed by the troops who assaulted the Greater Breach.

Notes

1 His tomb is outside the Cathedral in Ciudad Rodrigo.
2 It is said that he got himself captured deliberately, because his brother was Vice-Master of Trinity College, Cambridge, and he wanted to join him in England.
3 He later distinguished himself at the Battle of Waterloo.
4 It matched his "Well. Let the men cross" at Oporto, and "By God. That will do" at Salamanca.
5 It was written on the Greater Teson, while under constant enemy fire.
6 Commanding a "forlorn hope" was a recognized way of achieving promotion – provided one survived. Promotion was normally extremely slow, except for the 10% who could afford to purchase it. Lt. Gurwood, for example, was 33rd on the Lieutenant's Roll in the 52nd, but after Ciudad Rodrigo he was promoted Captain – but even then it was only in the Royal African Corps. He later edited Wellington's Despatches.
7 He was buried by his nephew, Dan Mackinnon, who was serving with the Coldstream Guards in the 1st Division.
8 It was formally returned to Lt Gurwood next day as a tribute to his bravery and initiative.

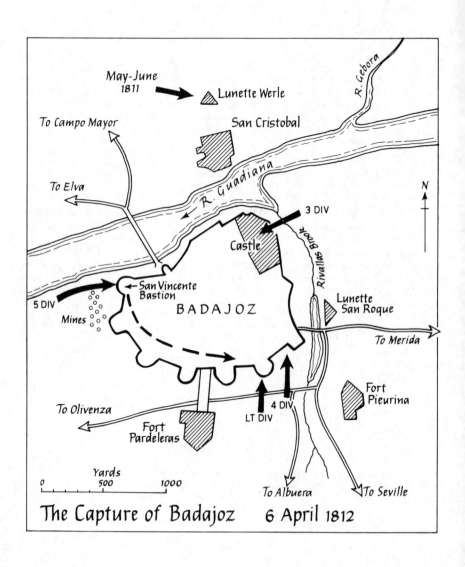

May-June
1811

Lunette Werle

San Cristobal

To Campo Mayor

To Elva

R. Gebora

R. Guadiana

3 DIV

Castle

Rivallas Brook

N

San Vincente
Bastion

5 DIV

Mines

BADAJOZ

Lunette
San Roque

To Merida

To Olivenza

Fort
Pardeleras

4 DIV

LT DIV

Fort
Pieurina

Yards

0   500   1000

To Albuera

To Seville

The Capture of Badajoz   6 April 1812

CHAPTER TWENTY-ONE

The Capture of Badajoz

Badajoz

Having seized Ciudad Rodrigo in January, 1812, Wellington now turned his attention to the fortress of Badajoz, which was, like Ciudad Rodrigo, a gateway into Spain, which must be captured before he could conduct any offensive operations across the frontier.

It had been taken by the French in March, 1811, and twice besieged unsuccessfully since then by the Allies.¹ By the time Wellington started the Third Siege in **March, 1812**, the French garrison of 5,000 under its resourceful commander, General Armand Phillipon, had considerably strengthened the defences. San Cristobal, north of the river, was well fortified, as was Fort Pardeleras in the south-west. The western side of Badajoz was heavily mined, while the east was made largely impassable by damming the Rivallas Brook for 600 yards. An outwork called Fort Picurina had also been constructed in the south-east corner.

It was now a formidable stronghold, but Wellington was for once well equipped for a siege. He had 52 guns and an adequate siege train, and he was not as short of time as at Ciudad Rodrigo; he had 60,000 troops altogether, but he had to be prepared for attacks from either Marmont or Soult. To guard against this, he detached Hill with 14,000 men to protect his north flank against Marmont, while Graham with 19,000 was sent south to keep Soult at bay. He was thus left with about 27,000 for the storming of Badajoz.

Wellington's Plan

By **16 March, 1812**, Badajoz was closely invested, and Wellington made his usual thorough reconnaissance. He was helped in his planning by a French sapper sergeant who deserted with a plan of part of their defences.

He built a pontoon bridge across the Guadiana River and invested San Cristobal, but floods on the **22nd** swept away the bridge, dividing his forces.

He finally decided to make his main effort against the south-east corner and began by capturing Fort Picurina on the **24th**. This enabled him to batter the walls there with 38 guns. But progress was slow and the flooded Rivallas made movement difficult; the French were constantly making spirited sorties, and Allied casualties mounted steadily.

News now came that Soult was on the move in the south, and a bigger threat was that Marmont seemed about to advance into Portugal in the north. Wellington had to react, but only three incomplete breaches had been made in the walls, and he would have preferred to wait longer. But, as at Ciudad Rodrigo, he felt that he could not afford to do so, and he reluctantly gave the order that Badajoz must be attacked on **6 April**. It happened to be Easter Sunday.

His plan was that the main effort would be an assault on the breaches in the south-east by the Light and 4th Divisions. As diversions, the 3rd Division was to attack the Castle from the east, while the 5th Division moved against the bastion of San Vincente in the north-west. A feint attack would also be made on the important Lunette San Roque by 1,000 men.

The Storming

From the start things went badly wrong. The assault was planned for 1930, but had to be delayed till 2200. The 3rd Division attacked a quarter of an hour early and the 5th Division an hour late; columns got lost and confusion followed.

The Light and 4th Divisions came up against fearsome defences held by determined troops. There were barriers of sword blades and planks studded with nails; barrels of gunpowder were exploded by fuses and fires started in the ditches; every French soldier had three muskets, and a storm of shot and shell swept the walls. The two "forlorn hopes" of 500 each were virtually annihilated and 40 assaults were thrown back, the ditches filling with dead and dying. The gallantry was incredible and the carnage was appalling. After more than an hour of slaughter 2,200 men had fallen and no progress had been made, either at the breaches or on the diversionary attacks.

Wellington was on the point of admitting defeat, but he sent an urgent message to Picton to make one last attempt to storm the Castle. Against all expectations, it succeeded and the 3rd Division gained a foothold, though Picton was wounded. About the same time the 5th Division managed to scale the walls to the north-west and, moving through the town, attacked the defenders at the breaches from the rear.

It was too much for the gallant French and resistance suddenly collapsed. General Phillipon withdrew to San Cristobal, but he had no supplies there and surrendered next morning.

Badajoz had been taken, but at the terrible cost of 4,924 casualties, with a disastrously high proportion of officers and NCOs. Wellington lost more British soldiers in the siege of Badajoz than in any battle of the Peninsular War except Albuera and Talavera.[2]

The survivors of the carnage now broke out in a bestial rampage that lasted 48 hours, drinking, plundering, raping and robbing, and officers who tried to stop them were themselves shot. It was shameful, but understandable, given the horrors of that nightmare Easter Sunday.

One of the few happy events of the capture of Badajoz was the rescue by Major Harry Smith of the Light Division of a 14-year-old Spanish girl, Juana Maria de los Dolores de Leon, who appealed to him to rescue her from plundering soldiers, who had already torn the earrings from her ears. A few days later he married her and she accompanied him throughout the rest of the campaign, earning the affection and respect of all who met her.[3]

Summary

Wellington has been criticized over his plan for the storming of Badajoz, and also for not doing more to stop the plundering sooner. Certainly, he attacked the town before he was ready to do so, but he did capture it. Success was probably achieved because he launched five separate attacks, and it was their combined effect that broke the French resistance. No one assault could have succeeded on its own.

The casualties were certainly high, but this should not be allowed to obscure the fact that he had captured two strong fortresses in two months, taking only 11 days over Ciudad Rodrigo and 20 days over Badajoz.

Now he was in a position to go on to the offensive at last.

THE CAPTURE OF BADAJOZ

Where To Go

Badajoz lies just in Spain on the main road from Lisbon to Madrid. It is very built up today, but the Castle stands out, and most of the features of the siege can be identified.

Drive first to San Cristobal, just north of the Guadiana River (**Viewpoint A**) and look across the river to Badajoz. The fort is in excellent condition, and provides an impressive view of the town.

Then drive round the east side of the town, under the Castle walls, to the south-east corner (**Viewpoint B**).

Finally, go into the Castle, and study the ground from the ramparts (**Viewpoint C**).

What To See

Viewpoint A Look across the Guadiana River to the town of Badajoz, with the Castle dominating the north-east corner. One can also identify the area of San Vincente in the north-west corner, where the 5th Division attacked.

It is evident that San Cristobal enfilades any troops attacking Badajoz from the east or north.

Viewpoint B Driving along the road to the east of the town, the Castle towers above one. The ground to the left is low-lying and marshy, and it is easy to envisage how impassable it was when flooded by the French.

Fort Picurina can be located, but it is difficult to identify the breaches in the south-east corner, though the area of the assault is obvious.

Viewpoint C The view from the ramparts of the Castle covers all the east and north sides of Badajoz, and it is an extremely dominating position. One wonders how the 3rd Division ever managed to scale the walls and capture the position.

Some historians who have visited Badajoz have spoken of a strong feeling of gloom still hanging over the place, as if the horrors of that Easter Sunday still pervade the town. —

Notes

1 First Siege, 5–15 May, 1811, by Beresford.
  Second Siege, 19 May – 17 June, 1811, by Wellington.

2 Talavera   5,365
  Albuera   4,159
  Siege of Badajoz   3,660
  Vitoria   3,475
  Salamanca   3,127
  Storming of Badajoz (two hours)   2,983
  (Jac Weller, *Wellington in the Peninsula*, p. 204.)

3 He later became General Sir Harry Smith, Governor of the Cape in South Africa, and gave his name to the town of Harrysmith, while his wife gave hers to Ladysmith in Natal. Her story is told in Georgette Heyer's historical novel *The Spanish Bride*.

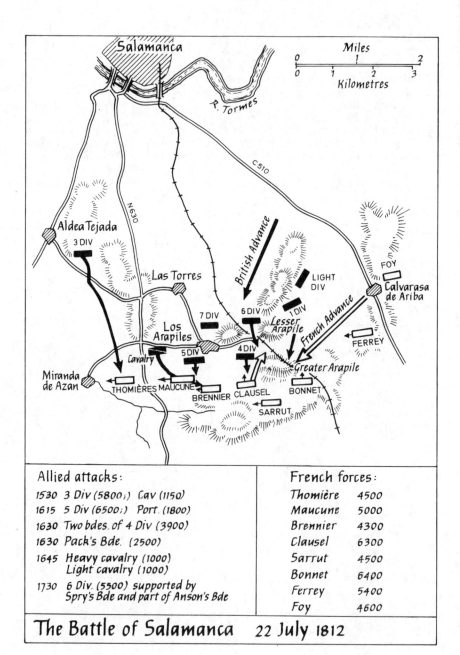

Allied attacks:

1530 3 Div (5800?) Cav (1150)
1615 5 Div (6500?) Port. (1800)
1630 Two bdes. of 4 Div (3900)
1630 Pack's Bde. (2500)
1645 Heavy cavalry (1000)
     Light cavalry (1000)
1730 6 Div. (5500) supported by
     Spry's Bde and part of Anson's Bde

French forces:

Thomière	4500
Maucune	5000
Brennier	4300
Clausel	6300
Sarrut	4500
Bonnet	6400
Ferrey	5400
Foy	4600

The Battle of Salamanca   22 July 1812

CHAPTER TWENTY-TWO

The Battle of Salamanca

Background

With both Badajoz and Ciudad Rodrigo now in his hands, Wellington was at last in a position to advance into Spain. He held the initiative, and he chose to make a bold thrust in the north against Salamanca, which he liberated on **17th June, 1812.**

He was opposed by Marshal Marmont, who had 48,500 men against Wellington's 50,000, and for some weeks during July the two commanders manoeuvred back and forth near Salamanca, each seeking an advantage, but it never came to a battle. By **20th July** the Allied Army was back in Salamanca, while the French were some 10 miles to the east round Heurta.

The **next morning**, both armies began crossing the River Tormes and moving south. That night, while the crossing was still going on, a tremendous thunderstorm lashed the 100,000 men on both sides with hail and torrential rain. The Inniskilling Dragoons had several men killed by lightning, hundreds of horses stampeded, and the river rose to such a flood that the rearguard, found by the Light Division, only just got across.

The British army spent a miserable night, but later, first at Sorauren in 1813 and then at Waterloo, they would recall Salamanca, and look on a storm the night before battle as an omen of victory.

Once across the river the ground was open farmland, though rather more wooded than today, and there were undulations that provided a surprising amount of concealment. It was bordered to the north and east by the Tormes River.

Three features dominated the area round the village of Los Arapiles, which lay in the centre of a plain roughly nine miles across. First, a long ridge ran north-east from the village; second, there was the Lesser Arapile, a rounded spur projecting from this ridge; third, there was, about half a mile to the south, a very distinctive 400-foot hill called the Greater Arapile.

The Battle

22 July, 1812, was a crucial day for Wellington, for he had to decide whether he could afford to stay at Salamanca, or must withdraw, in order to prevent the French from cutting him off from Portugal, which was clearly what Marmont was trying to do.

That morning the French advanced south-west from Calvarasa de Ariba and at about 0800 seized the Greater Arapile.

Wellington moved parallel to them, keeping out of sight just north of the ridge, and he duly occupied the Lesser Arapile. The two armies were now only about a mile apart, but, whereas Wellington could, as usual, watch every French move, they could see virtually nothing of his dispositions.

At about 1115 it looked as if Marmont might attack the village of Los Arapiles and Wellington therefore formed up two divisions (4th and 5th) south of it, with two more (6th and 7th) behind. The 1st Division and the Light Division were on the Lesser Arapile and the ridge to the north of it.

The attack against Los Arapiles never materialized and Wellington joined his staff on the ridge just north-east of the village for a bite of lunch, but keeping a close eye nevertheless on the enemy. He was described at this point as "stumping about and munching", chewing a chicken leg – a fact that lingered in the memory of his loyal Spanish aide, the Duke de Alava, because it was one of the rare occasions when the austere Iron Duke did *not* have plain cold meat for his meal.

Marmont meanwhile had just decided that his moment had come at last. Seeing Wellington halted round Los Arapiles, he saw an opportunity to get ahead of him and cut him off from Portugal. The leading French division (Thomière) was already a mile west of the Greater Arapile and was now ordered to push on and try to head off the Allied army.

Between 1400 and 1500 Wellington observed that a gap of about a mile had opened up between Thomière and the next French division (Maucune), and also that Marmont's army was now strung out altogether over at least four miles[1] with the tail stretching back as far as Calvarasa de Ariba. He himself, on the other hand, had almost his complete army concentrated round him, and was in a position, for a fleeting moment, to launch 34,000 against 18,000 French.

Suddenly he threw away his chicken leg, snapped shut his telescope, and exclaimed, "By God. That will do."

Cantering up to the crest of the Lesser Arapile, he took another look, and cheerfully declared, "Mon cher Alava, Marmont est perdu" (which might be freely translated "My dear Alava, Marmont has had it").

It was an amazing example of decisiveness and boldness, on a par with the Crossing of the Douro three years before. It was also the start of one of the most impressive opportunist battles in history.[2]

So at this particular moment both commanders believed that their great chance had come. But what Marmont did not know was that Wellington had his 3rd Division positioned wide on his right flank, at Aldea Tejada, to guard against just the threat that Marmont was making. It was now ideally placed to launch a surprise attack against the head of Thomière's unsuspecting column.

True to form, Wellington saw to it personally that things were done exactly the way he wanted. He out-distanced his staff in a 3-mile gallop to Aldea Tejada, where he himself gave the order to attack to his brother-in-law, Major General Edward Pakenham, who was commanding the 3rd Division.[3]

"Ned. Do you see those fellows over there? Throw your division into column, and drive them to the devil."[4]

Pakenham wasted no time and at about 1640 his division struck Thomière's column, in Napier's words, "like a meteor", just south of Miranda de Azan. The French were taken completely by surprise, Thomière was killed, his division was virtually destroyed,[5] and every one of his guns was captured.

Wellington meanwhile had galloped back to Los Arapiles and personally ordered Leith to attack the French centre with his 5th Division when he was given the word; Bradford's Portuguese Brigade and Cotton's cavalry would attack at the same time on his right. Wellington knew that he had only some three hours of daylight left and he meant to make full use of it.

As Marmont watched Thomière's division disintegrate, he must have realized the terrible mistake that he had made. Moments later he was badly wounded by a shell, possibly one of Major Shrapnell's new devices. General Bonnet took over, only to be killed shortly after, whereupon Clausel had to step in.

Wellington now launched the 5th Division against the flank of Maucune's division, the second in the long French column. The 5,800 infantry advanced in two lines, each two deep and extending for almost a mile, with some 1,500 muskets able to engage the enemy.

On their right a brigade of Dragoons trotted forward, led by Major-General Le Marchant,[6] one of the outstanding soldiers of the day, and he certainly commanded them superbly on this occasion. Seeing 1,000 sabres advancing towards them, the French infantry formed squares – a serious mistake, for they were first slaughtered by the muskets and guns of the 5th Division and then found themselves at the mercy of the cavalry, who thundered down at them, "with a terrible roar always remembered by the few who survived".

It was too much for any troops and the entire division broke.

Two French divisions had been shattered, and now a third (Brennier) was also cut down and scattered by Le Marchant's exultant dragoons. But in the last moments of the charge, Le Marchant was killed – a grievous loss not only to Wellington, but to the whole British Army.

Three French divisions had now been overwhelmed, and "40,000 Frenchmen had been defeated in 40 minutes."

But events did not go entirely Wellington's way. He had directed Cole's 4th Division, only 5,000 strong, against two intact French divisions, Clausel (6,300) and Sarrut (4,700). The odds were too great, and they were forced to withdraw.

At the same time Pack, with his 2,600 Portuguese, failed in his assault on the Greater Arapile.

Clausel now saw the chance of a counter-stroke. Using Sarrut's fresh division to hold off the British 3rd Division who were advancing from the west, he launched two strong divisions (his own and Bonnet's) northwards into the gap that had developed between the British 4th and 5th Divisions.

It was a brilliant move, involving 12,000 men, and it was well executed. Against almost any other commander, it would probably have succeeded, but Wellington, with his uncanny anticipation of his opponent's moves, had already moved to that spot himself and was prepared. He had deployed Clinton's 6th Division (5,500) just south-west of the Lesser Arapile, with Spry's Portuguese Brigade alongside them, ready for just such a manoeuvre by the French. The threat was thus countered before it was ever launched.

This encounter lasted about half an hour and followed the now familiar pattern of a British line stopping and then driving back a French column. (600 muskets against 210.)

The French fought bravely, but eventually broke. It was the final blow. Five out of their eight divisions had been shattered and they could do no more. They abandoned the Greater Arapile and retreated eastwards.

Ferrey's division was ordered to act as a rearguard across the Alba road, and they did so most gallantly, forming a three-deep line, almost a mile long, with a square at each end. They held off Clinton's men until dark and inflicted on them their heaviest casualties of the day. To add to the horror, the long, dry grass caught fire, as it had at Talavera, and many wounded from both sides were burned to death.

Wellington has been criticized for not pursuing the defeated French that night, but his troops were extremely exhausted. More than that, he believed that the bridge at Alba was firmly held by a Spanish force under Carlos de Espana, which would prevent the French from escaping across the Tormes. Unfortunately, de Espana had withdrawn against all orders several days before, and without informing Wellington; as a result, the French army lived to fight another day.

It had been a resounding victory nevertheless, and it raised the morale of the Allied army to new heights. Well satisfied at having inflicted 15,000 casualties on the French,[7] (half of them prisoners), as well as capturing 2 Eagles, 6 Colours and 20 guns, the troops were glad to rest in the cool of the evening.[8]

Summary

The Battle of Salamanca (referred to by the Spanish as the Battle of the Arapiles) was an outstanding "opportunist" encounter, launched with remarkable boldness, and executed with perfect timing and control.

Indeed, it was to some extent the conviction in Marmont's mind that Wellington would not be so bold as to attack him at Salamanca that led him to risk his army by over-extending them – a grievous error for which he paid dearly. The French would know better in future.

The French general, Foy, wrote only six days after the battle:

"It raises Lord Wellington's reputation almost to the level of Marlborough. Hitherto we had been aware of his prudence, his eye for choosing a position, and his skill in utilizing it. At Salamanca he has shown himself a great and able master of manoeuvres. He kept his dispositions concealed for almost the whole day; he waited till we were committed to our movements before he developed his own; he played a safe game; he fought in the oblique order – it was a battle in the style of Frederick the Great."[9]

Most significant of all, the French after Salamanca lost their legend of invincibility, a development that would give heart to all Occupied Europe – much as the Germans found after the Battle of Alamein in 1942.

The confidence and morale of the Imperial armies throughout the Peninsula suffered severely, and they would never again take risks against Wellington, whose reputation was now supreme.

Tactically, the battle proved yet again the superiority of the British line against the French column, and this time it had succeeded in attack as well as in defence. Wellington showed once again his outstanding control of the battle, particularly in forestalling Clausel's counter-attack. "Our Chief was everywhere," wrote Pakenham, "and sadly exposed himself." Indeed, a spent bullet pierced his holster and cloak, but happily without injuring him.

Strategically, Salamanca was the beginning of the end of French domination in Spain.

THE BATTLEFIELD OF SALAMANCA

Where To Go

Take the N. 630 south out of the city of Salamanca, and after 3 miles you see the village of Las Torres on your left, with a small road to it. You can now just see the Greater Arapile half-left.

After a further mile, turn left at a cross-roads to the village of Los Arapiles, and from now on you are on the battlefield. The Lesser Arapile is straight ahead, and the Greater Arapile half-right.

Drive into the village, which is probably little changed from 1812, and visit the Town Hall, where they have a large map of the battlefield, and a collection of cannon and musket balls from the battlefield. A plaque to commemorate the battle was also placed there by the Wellington Society.

Drive on through the village and stop on the road just beyond the eastern edge. On your left, about 300 yards from the road, is a ridge, from the slopes of which Wellington watched the French manoeuvring round the Greater Arapile. It is well worth climbing to the top (crops permitting). (**Viewpoint A**)

Drive on down the road for half a mile to the deserted railway station, from where it is possible to climb to the top of either the Greater or Lesser Arapiles, from which there is another grandstand view of the battlefield. (**Viewpoints B and C**)

Return to the N. 630, go straight across and this brings you to the village of Miranda de Azan, where Pakenham's 3rd Division struck Thomière's division. If, coming from Los Arapiles, you turn left (south) at the crossroads, there is a bend after about a mile, and this gives another view of the battlefield.

What To See

The country is today less wooded than it was in 1812, but it is interesting to see how much concealment is provided by undulations, and how the 3rd Division could have advanced unseen from Aldea Tejada.

Viewpoint A. The line of advance of Marmont's column was straight across the open fields to right and left of the Greater Arapile, and the plain just west of the hill is where the 5th Division launched their attack.

It is clear also how Wellington's line of advance to the north of the ridge was not visible to the French.

The fighting during Clausel's counter-attack would have been in the area of the deserted railway station.

Aldea Tejada can be seen to the west, and Salamanca to the north.

The above aspects of the battlefield can be seen from Viewpoints A, B or C, but the most dramatic is perhaps Viewpoint A, because one is standing where Wellington stood, and can see the battlefield as he did.

Viewpoint B – The Greater Arapile. It is quite a long walk and steep climb to the top of the Greater Arapile, but it does give a fine view of the whole battlefield, including the area round Aldea Tejada, and it is interesting to note how broken the ground there is, and how the 3rd Division could have advanced unseen, particularly if there were more trees, as in 1812.

The main fighting took place in the plain just west of the Greater Arapile, which was the scene of the 5th Division attack.

Viewpoint C. It is a shorter, if steeper, climb up the Lesser Arapile, but worthwhile because it shows clearly how the two armies advanced parallel and a mile apart, but the French could see virtually nothing of Wellington's dispositions.

Viewpoint D. There are no landmarks in the area of Miranda, but it is interesting to work out the line of advance of Pakenham's and Thomière's Divisions, and also to relate their encounter to the main battle.

Notes

1 Opinions vary as to the distance, but my calculations on the ground make it about four miles.
2 It is intriguing to think which World War Two commanders on either side would, or would not, have done as Wellington did at that moment.
3 Picton was away sick.
4 *Personal Reminiscences of the Duke of Wellington*, F. Ellesmere, p. 159.
5 The leading regiment lost 1,000 out of 1,450, and total casualties were 2,130 out of 4,500.
6 He was commanding the leading brigade because their former commander, Lord Henry Paget, had eloped in 1809 with Wellington's younger brother's wife, and so was *persona non grata* with Wellington. He was the founder of the Royal Military College at High Wycombe that was later to become the Staff College.
7 This included 3 generals killed and 4 wounded, 136 officers as casualties and 7,000 prisoners. The Allies had 2 generals killed and 6 wounded.
8 Private Wheeler found it a bit too chilly as night came, so he built himself a comforting wall of dead Frenchmen to keep out the cold wind, and slept well.
9 Oman, V, p. 472–3, translating Foy's *Vie Militaire*, 178.

Order of Battle: Salamanca – 22 July, 1812

ALLIES

Division	Commander	Strength	Brigades
1st	Campbell	6,023	Fermer Wheatley Lowe (KGL)
3rd	Pakenham	5,875	Campbell Wallace Power (Port)
4th	Cole	5,236	Ellis Anson Stubb (Port)
5th	Leith	7,091	Greville Pringle Spry (Port)
6th	Clinton	5,541	Hulse Hinde Rezende (Port)
7th	Hope	5,185	Bernewitz Halkett (KGL) Collins (Port)
Light	Alten	3,548	Vandeleur Barnard
	Independent Portuguese Brigades	4,499	Pack Bradford
Spanish	Espana	3,360	
	Cavalry	4,025	

FRENCH

Division	Strength
Foy	5,147
Clausel	6,562
Ferey	5,689
Sarrut	5,002
Maucune	5,244
Brennier	4,558
Thomières	4,543
Bonnet	6,521
Cavalry	
Light (Curto)	1,879
Dragoon (Boyer)	1,500

Commander	Wellington	Marmont
Strength	51,949	49,647
Cavalry	4,025	3,379
Guns	60	78
Casualties	5,214	14,000 (approx)

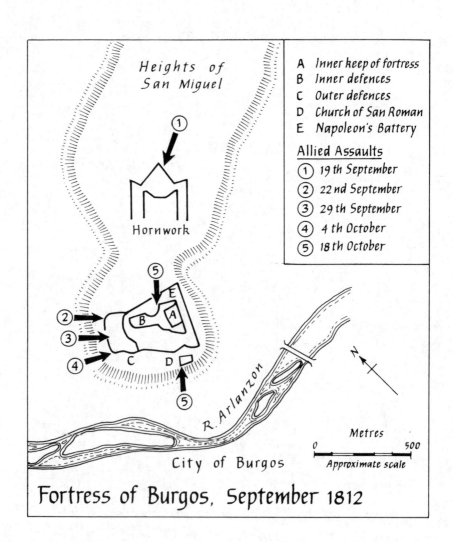

Heights of
San Miguel

① Hornwork

A Inner keep of fortress
B Inner defences
C Outer defences
D Church of San Roman
E Napoleon's Battery

Allied Assaults
① 19th September
② 22nd September
③ 29th September
④ 4th October
⑤ 18th October

⑤
E
B A
② ③ C D
④
⑤

R. Arlanzon

N

City of Burgos

Metres
0   500
Approximate scale

Fortress of Burgos, September 1812

CHAPTER TWENTY-THREE

The Siege of Burgos

Burgos

Burgos, the capital of Old Castile, was always a key communications centre, and as such it was a tempting target for the Allies.

In July, 1812, Wellington considered advancing against it after his victory at Salamanca, but chose instead to liberate Madrid. But then on 31 August he marched north with 35,000 troops[1] to besiege Burgos. The French withdrew, leaving only a garrison of 2,000 in the Castle under the command of General Dubreton.

Burgos was apparently not a particularly attractive town then, and was described by William Bragge as "one of the worst large towns I have seen in Spain . . . the people horribly ugly and . . . excessively dirty".[2]

The Castle guarded all the approaches, standing, as it does today, on a steep ridge just north of the Cathedral. It was surrounded by two lines of defences. It was roughly 450 yards long by 300 yards wide, and difficult to attack; but it had one major weakness, in that it was overlooked by an equally high ridge called San Miguel, some 500 yards to the north-east. The French were aware of this and had built a strong outwork there, known as the Hornwork.

The Siege (19 September–21 October, 1812)

Wellington invested Burgos on 19 September, five days before Napoleon entered Moscow. He was perhaps somewhat over-confident, for he was short of engineers and had only three heavy guns (18 pounders);[3] but he declined to send for more. He was also so short of ammunition that his gunners were reduced to collecting and re-using French cannon-balls.

He further restricted his chances of success by two decisions that show the human side of the Iron Duke. The 1st Division had complained bitterly that they had "missed out" at Salamanca, and had "not had Justice done them".

Wellington agreed that "they had been very ill-used, but he would see them righted at the first opportunity".[4] He therefore gave the honour of leading the assault on Burgos to them rather than to 3rd or Light Divisions, who were more experienced. It was not a success, and it was reported that "only the Guards did their duty in the trenches".

Second, Wellington regularly committed too few troops to the assaults. With grim memories of the terrible losses at Ciudad Rodrigo and Badajoz, he was reluctant to send in more men than he felt was absolutely essential, arguing that "if we fail, we can't lose too many men".[5]

His first move was in fact successful, when on the **night of 19/20 September** part of the 1st Division attacked and captured the Hornwork. It was a "silent attack" with no artillery support, but it failed to achieve surprise, because of the bright moonlight, and there were 421 casualties against 198 French. Indeed, success was largely due to units of the Light Division under Major Somers-Cocks who got behind the enemy lines.

Wellington commented in his Despatches, "I doubt, however, that I have the means to take the castle, which is very strong".[6]

The first assault on the walls of the Castle itself was made on **23 September** and was repulsed with 158 casualties; so was another on the **29th**, despite the firing of a 1,000 lb mine.

The failures continued. On **1 October** two of the Allies' three heavy guns were knocked out, and on the **4th** an attack against the north-west wall failed with 244 casualties. To make matters worse, the French captured a copy of Wellington's plans for the assault from an officer who was killed.

Apart from the strength of the defences, Wellington was up against an extremely competent commander in General Dubreton, who on **5 and 8 October** carried out two highly successful sorties, which inflicted three times as many casualties on the Allies as were suffered by the French.

Among those who died on the 8th was Major Charles Cocks. He had been on Wellington's staff, where he proved himself an outstanding officer. The Duke felt his death deeply, remarking at his funeral that if he had lived he would have been one of the greatest generals ever.[7]

On **18 October** another assault was launched, this time by two parties, each of 300 men from the Guards and the K.G.L. A mine was exploded under the Chapel of St Roman, but the attack failed with 200 casualties.

Three days later Wellington heard that the armies of Soult, Joseph and Suchet were all uniting to attack Hill in Madrid and he decided that the time had come to leave.[8] The operation had been an undeniable failure and the morale of his army had sunk to unprecedented depths. A Private of the 42nd commented bitterly: 'It was as foolish a piece of work as ever I saw Wellington encounter."

The British suffered 2,064 casualties against 623 French. Wellington was far from being at his best (perhaps he was mentally exhausted), and he was opposed by a commander whom he himself described as "a very clever fellow".

On the night of **21/22 October**, Trafalgar Day, the siege was abandoned, and the Allied army slipped away southwards, the wagon wheels wrapped in straw.

Retreat from Burgos (22 October–18 November, 1812)

Wellington's troubles did not end with his lifting of the siege of Burgos. He had managed to slip away unnoticed on **22 October**, but the French, with a 3 to 1 superiority in cavalry, were soon in hot pursuit. The Allied army covered 26 miles on **23 October**, but the enemy were hard on their heels, and there was a sharp engagement at Venta del Pozo.

At Torquemada, Wellington paused briefly behind the River Carrion, but, as on the Retreat to Corunna four years before, the angry, dispirited troops broke into the cellars and were soon on a drunken rampage for most of the night of the **24th**.

The withdrawal continued the **next day** back to Valladolid, where the Duke planned to make a stand behind the Douro. But on the **29th** a party of 56 French troops swam naked across the flooded river at Tordesillas, drove back a German unit and built a pontoon bridge. It was a very bold and brave effort, and was only foiled because Wellington managed to bring up reinforcements and contain the bridgehead.

On **6 November** the French called off the pursuit, but the Allies were still in a difficult position. Wellington had 80,000 men, but 25,000 of them were Spaniards in whom he had limited confidence, and he was faced by 50,000 veteran French along the Douro, while Hill, with only 28,000, was trying to hold Madrid against 60,000.

Faced with the threat of over 100,000 French troops converging on his scattered forces, Wellington now decided that both he and Hill must withdraw yet again to the security of Portugal. On 31 October Hill reluctantly abandoned Madrid and joined Wellington at Salamanca on 9 November.

But, as in July, Wellington still felt vulnerable there and ordered a further withdrawal back to Ciudad Rodrigo. Unfortunately the weather turned bad and, to add to the army's resentment at retreating, a blunder by the new Quartermaster General, Colonel James Gordon, meant that they were without supplies for four days and were reduced to eating acorns.

As they struggled back through the mud, 2,000 men collapsed and died, and 1,000 stragglers were taken prisoner. Among those captured was General Sir Edward Paget, commanding the 1st Division, who had only arrived during the siege of Burgos. He was attacked by three French dragoons and was unable to defend himself properly, having lost an arm in the fighting in Oporto in 1809.

Another mishap that might have been serious was that three of Wellington's divisional commanders (Clinton, Stewart and Dalhousie) ignored his orders and were lost for two hours. When he found them, the Duke is said to have remarked, after an icy pause, "You see, gentlemen, I know my own business best".

However, the whole Allied army was finally concentrated in Ciudad Rodrigo by 18 November, 1812, and there it settled down for the winter. The retreat from Burgos was for Wellington "the most agonising retreat of his career", but it was in no way the disaster that Moscow was for Napoleon, as events in 1813 would show.

THE SIEGE OF BURGOS

Where To Go

Burgos lies on the River Arlanzon about halfway between Valladolid and San Sebastian.

The Castle is clearly visible to the north of the town, standing on a prominent ridge, on which is a wireless aerial. It is best approached by a winding road which climbs the hill and approaches the Castle from the

north-east, passing the high ground on which stands the Hornwork
(Viewpoint A). The road continues for about a quarter of a mile
through the outer defences to the Castle itself, where it is possible to
climb on the ramparts, which have been partially reconstructed
(Viewpoint B).

Park by the Monument and walk through the arch into the centre of
the Castle (but with care, as it is a network of steep ditches). It is
possible to climb on to the ramparts (again with care), and there is a
magnificent view of the city of Burgos and the surrounding countryside.

What To See

Viewpoint A is the flat plateau at the north-east end of the ridge,
which was the Allied position and gun line. There is a wide view of the
surrounding countryside, but it is hard to see the Castle, as the area is
now covered in trees. The ruins of the Hornwork are clearly visible.

Viewpoint B is the Castle itself, and it is easy to see why it was so
important, since it dominates the four main roads that meet in Burgos.
It is clear too how strong the defences must have been in 1812. The
scenes of the various assaults can be worked out, but it should be
remembered that it was much less afforested in 1812.

Notes

1 24,000 British and 11,000 Spanish.
2 *Letters of Captain William Bragge*, edited by A. C. Cassels.
3 They were referred to by the troops as "Thunder", "Lightning" and "Nelson"
  (because it had only one trunnion).
4 *Letters of Captain William Bragge*, edited by A. C. Cassels.
5 *Burgoyne's Correspondence*, edited by G. Wrottesley, p. 235.
6 Despatches, 21 September, 1812.
7 *History of the British Army*, Fortescue, VIII, p. 580.
8 Despatches, IX, 466, 5 October.

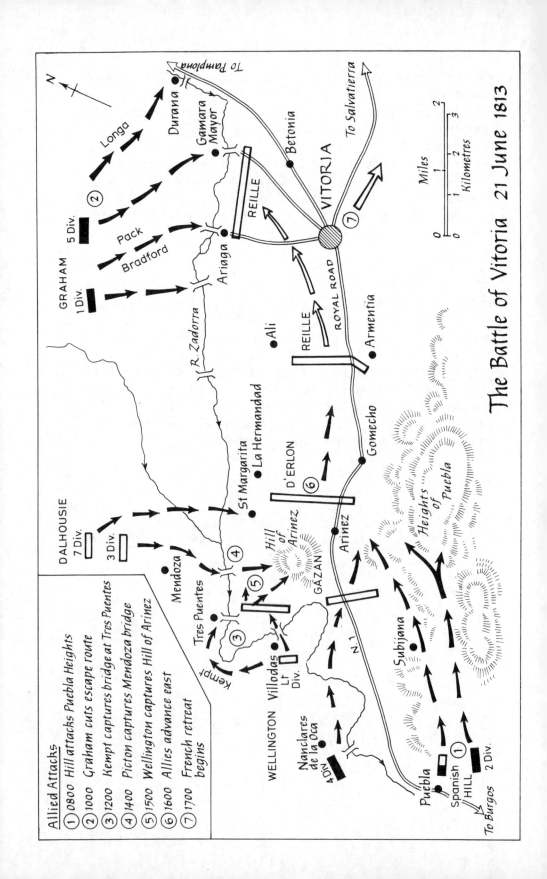

The Battle of Vitoria 21 June 1813

Allied Attacks
(1) 0800 Hill attacks Puebla Heights
(2) 1000 Graham cuts escape route
(3) 1200 Kempt captures bridge at Tres Puentes
(4) 1400 Picton captures Mendoza bridge
(5) 1500 Wellington captures Hill of Arinez
(6) 1600 Allies advance east
(7) 1700 French retreat begins

N

To Pamplona

Longa

Durana

Gamara Mayor

GRAHAM
5 Div.

Pack

Bradford

1 Div.

Ariaga

R. Zadorra

REILLE

Betonia

VITORIA

To Salvatierra

Ali

REILLE

ROYAL ROAD

Armentia

Miles
Kilometres

DALHOUSIE
7 Div.

3 Div.

St Margarita
La Hermandad

Mendoza

Tres Puentes

Kempt

D'ERLON

Hill of Arinez

GAZAN

Arinez

Gomecho

Heights of Puebla

WELLINGTON

Villodas
Lt Div.

Nanclares de la Oca

4 Div.

N.1

Subijana

Puebla
HILL

Spanish

2 Div.

To Burgos

CHAPTER TWENTY-FOUR

The Battle of Vitoria

On **22 May 1813** Wellington finally went onto the offensive and began his decisive thrust north-east from Portugal that would by the end of the year take him across the Pyrenees and into France itself.

His plan was to make a wide sweep north of Burgos and so outflank each French position in turn; he was able to do this because he had moved his supply base from Portugal to the north coast of Spain, and so was able to keep his army supplied, which the French had thought he could not possibly do.

As a result, Joseph was forced to abandon his positions first on the Douro, then at Burgos and finally on the Ebro. On **19 June** his army was gathered round Vitoria, and he prepared to make a stand there against the advancing Allies. He had 66,000 men against Wellington's 79,000, but he hoped to be joined shortly by Clausel from Pamplona.

The plain of Vitoria is some 8 miles broad and 10 miles long, with the town lying at the eastern end. Mountain ranges lie to the north and south, while to the west is a key feature, the rounded Hill of Arinez. The Zadorra River runs along the north and west sides, and was an obstacle to artillery.

The town is a major communications centre, with five major roads converging on it, including the main French supply line back to Bayonne.

Joseph assumed that Wellington, advancing from the west, would attack frontally from that direction, and he therefore placed his divisions in three defensive lines west of Vitoria.

The front line was held by Gazan with 35,000 men on the forward slopes of the Hill of Arinez, with strong artillery support. D'Erlon's division was just east of Arinez astride the main road, while Reille's division was behind him, half a mile west of Vitoria. It was a reasonably strong position against an attack from the west, but it had two serious weaknesses. First, Joseph should have realized by now that Wellington was unlikely to oblige by taking the obvious line. Second, his whole position was extremely vulnerable to a flank attack, particularly from the north, and, unfortunately for him, that was exactly what Wellington was planning to do.

Wellington's Plan

Wellington spent the whole of **20 June** carrying out his usual thorough reconnaissance, and soon decided against any head-on attack. Instead he planned to divide his army into four separate columns, and to attack Joseph not only from both flanks, but also in the rear. In this way he would make full use of his own superior strength, and would also have maximum freedom of manoeuvre; at the same time he would force the French to defend 12 miles of front rather than just 3, and he knew that they did not have enough troops to do this.

Hill, with 2nd Division and Morillo's Spanish Division, was to climb the Heights of Puebla and threaten Gazan's left. This was a secondary attack, designed to make Joseph reinforce that flank at the expense of his right, where the main Allied effort would be made.

This was to be carried out by the 3rd and 7th Divisions, both under Dalhousie, and they were to make a long and difficult approach march behind the mountains to the north, in order to emerge at Mendoza and attack Gazan's right flank from that direction, soon after Hill attacked in the south.

Following these flanking attacks, the centre column, consisting of 4th and Light Divisions, was to advance against Gazan frontally from the direction of Nanclares, where Wellington had his command post.

Gazan's force of 35,000 would thus be attacked from three directions by 50,000 Allied troops. But this was not all.

The final blow to complete Joseph's defeat was to be struck by Graham, who was to make an even wider sweep to the north and emerge beyond Vitoria at Durana, thus cutting the main road from there to Bayonne. His force of 20,000 consisted of the 1st and 5th Divisions, Pack's and Bradford's Portuguese Brigades, the Spanish Brigade of General Francisco Longa,[1] two brigades of cavalry and 18 guns.

The Battle

21 June, 1813, dawned, according to Napier, "rainy, with a thick vapour", but it soon cleared. It would be a day full of drama and memorable incidents, and was to see one of Wellington's greatest victories.

He took up his position on a hilltop west of the Zadorra, from where he could maintain his customary close control of the battle. Opposite him, a mere mile away, he could see Joseph and his staff on the top of Arinez.

The Allied columns all had long and difficult approach marches before they could get into position, and it was 0800 before the attack began, with Hill's corps crossing the Zadorra near Puebla. He sent Morillo's Spaniards and Cadogan's Brigade up into the hills, where they were soon involved in heavy fighting, in which Cadogan was killed.[1] The attack made slow progress, but it had the intended effect of making the French reinforce that flank.

Graham, meanwhile, had emerged from the hills opposite Durana, a full 12 miles away from Hill, and by 1000 Longa's Spaniards had the road from Vitoria to Bayonne under fire; by noon, it was cut. So far, Wellington's orders had been carried out exactly as planned.

It was now noon and time for the attack by Dalhousie against Gazan's right flank. But he had got delayed up in the hills and was not yet in position; as a result, the whole plan was in jeopardy.

Wellington now decided to launch the 4th and Light Divisions in their frontal assault, even though Dalhousie had not yet appeared. Then, just as the orders were being issued, a Spanish peasant was brought to him with information that the bridge at Tres Puentes was not only intact and unguarded, but was not even under proper observation by the French.[3]

Wellington reacted with his usual speed and decision, and immediately ordered Kempt's Brigade of the Light Division to seize the bridge. Thanks to the lie of the land, they were able to approach unseen round a bend in the river, rush the bridge and capture it, closely followed by the 15th Hussars, who galloped across one by one.

Sadly, the guide who had brought the vital news that led to this spectacular success was decapitated by one of the few round shot fired at Kempt's Brigade.

This dramatic incident is matched by the well-known tale of the next attack. Dalhousie and his 7th Division had still not appeared on the scene, but the fiery Picton, with his 3rd Division, had arrived and was champing for action. Having watched Kempt's capture of the bridge, he expected orders from Wellington to join the fighting.

"Damn it! Lord Wellington must have forgotten us," he declared angrily.

Just then, an aide-de-camp rode up, and asked whether the general had seen Lord Dalhousie.

"No, sir," retorted Picton. "I have not seen his lordship. But have you any orders for me, sir?"

"None," replied the aide-de-camp.

"Then pray, sir," Picton demanded, "what are the orders you do bring?"

"Why," came the reply, "that as soon as Lord Dalhousie with the 7th Division shall commence an attack upon that bridge, the 4th and 6th are to support him."

Whereupon Picton, in a fury, shouted at the astonished officer, "You may tell Lord Wellington from me, sir, that the 3rd Division under my command shall in less than 10 minutes attack the bridge and carry it, and the 4th and 6th Divisions may support if they choose."

He then put himself at the head of his troops, and sent them into battle with the unique orders. "Come on, ye rascals! Come on, ye fighting villains!"

As Elizabeth Longford puts it. "This grave and grand insubordination was the beginning of victory."[4]

Picton's Division was opposed by two French divisions, well supported by artillery, but they were not to be stopped now, and stormed across the bridge and ford at Mendoza. Kempt's Brigade supported them from the south, and the 4th and Light Divisions were by now crossing too at Villadas.

Gazan was under attack from three sides and was driven steadily back. By 1500 both the hill and the village of Arinez were in Allied hands.

At the same moment the 7th Division finally appeared and, attacking on the left of 3rd Division, threatened the village of St Margarita, which was the hinge of the French defences in the north. But again, Dalhousie was to be beaten to it, this time by the Light Division.

As he was somewhat hesitantly debating what to do next, he was approached by Major Harry Smith, the firebrand Brigade Major of Vandeleur's Brigade of the Light Division, who had been sent to support the 7th Division.

20. **Burgos.** The ruins of the Castle, with the town in the valley behind. "(The siege of Burgos) was as foolish a piece of work as ever I saw Wellington encounter". (p.167)

21. **Vitoria.** The battlefield as seen from Wellington's viewpoint at Nanclares. The Heights of Puebla are to the right, the village of Arinez is in the centre and the Hill of Arinez to the left. A motorway now runs through the centre of the battlefield. (*Henry Radice*)

22. **Vitoria.** The initial battlefield with the Hill of Arinez in the background, as seen from Nanclares. "A brilliant piece of generalship by Wellington". (p.176)

23. **Vitoria.** In the foreground is the bridge of Tres Puentes, seized by Kempt's Brigade, with the village to the left. Further up the river in the trees is the Mendoza Bridge, stormed without orders by Picton's Division. "Picton's Division was opposed by two French divisions, well supported by artillery, but they were not to be stopped now, and stormed across the bridge and ford at Mendoza". (p.174)

"What orders, my Lord?" Smith asked twice, without receiving any reply.

Dalhousie turned to his Quartermaster General and asked him, "Had we better take the village?"

It was an aside, but Smith heard the words and pretended they were his orders.

"Certainly, my Lord," he shouted and galloped off before Dalhousie could change his mind. His brigade promptly advanced and seized St Margarita under the noses of the 7th Division.

It was the breakthrough, and the French resistance began to crumble everywhere. They were being overwhelmed from three sides, and were in grave danger of being cut off by Graham's skilful pressure against their rear at Durana.

The battered remnants of Gazan's force tried to form another line, based on D'Erlon's position, but Wellington launched the 4th Division, as yet hardly involved, eastwards down the main road. Despite heavy fire from 80 French guns, they struck at the point where Gazan and D'Erlon's Divisions joined, and soon broke through.

Seeing this, Graham pushed forward against Reille's troops holding the river line north of Vitoria, and there was fierce fighting for the bridges at Gamara Mayor and Ariaga. With Wellington and Hill pressing from the south and west, it was too much for the French and they suddenly broke and scattered.

About 1700 Joseph issued orders for a general retreat eastwards, but his army had already disintegrated. Reille's Division fought a skilful rearguard action round Vitoria, but they too were driven back, and the retreat became a rout.

Vitoria was now one vast chaotic confusion, jammed solid by the mass of baggage and impedimenta that was inextricably piled up in the streets. The retreating French army had no option but to abandon all its transport, and they even lost 151 guns out of 153, together with 415 caissons, 100 military wagons and 2,000 prisoners.

In addition to the military maelstrom, there were legions of camp followers, *le bordel ambulant*, and vast quantities of loot. "The wealth of Spain and the Indies seemed to be here," wrote one cavalryman.

It was ironically this that probably saved the French army from complete destruction, for Wellington's troops could not possibly resist the temptation of such wealth, as well as wine and women. First, the cavalry and then the infantry surged into the town and an orgy of plundering began that brought all discipline and thoughts of further fighting to an end. Never in history had an army found such an abundance of booty, which they traditionally looked on as their well-earned right and reward. The soldiers filled their pockets with dollars, jewellery and other treasures, and then got drunk on the ample stocks of wine.

The 14th Light Dragoons all but captured King Jospeh himself. Captain Henry Wyndham, together with Lieutenant Lord Worcester of the 10th Hussars, galloped up to his carriage as it struggled to escape from the turmoil. As they fired their pistols through the nearside window, Joseph leapt out of the other side, jumped on a horse and escaped. They did, however, acquire immense Royal booty, including the magnificent silver Royal *pot de chambre*, now a prized regimental trophy, known as "The Emperor".

Another well-known trophy was Marshal Jourdan's baton, which was "acquired" by a corporal of the 18th Hussars. It was handed over to Wellington, who in turn sent it to the Prince Regent. He wrote back, "You have sent me among the trophies of your unrivalled fame the staff of a French Marshal, and I send you in return that of England."

The only snag was that there was no such thing, and one had to be very hurriedly made, to signify Wellington's new rank of Field-Marshal.

Summary

Wellington did not pursue the French hard that night, and has been criticized for it. But his army was in no mood for further fighting, and he could not get them on the move again.

Joseph's army had been completely defeated, losing 8,000 men against only 5,100 Allied casualties; in addition, they lost virtually all their transport and artillery.

It was a brilliant piece of generalship by Wellington. After a month of successful manoeuvring, he had put together an imaginative attack one day before Clausel could join Joseph. He beat the French by careful planning, speed of concentration, and, above all, by his own personal control of the battle. His orders to Graham enabled that Anglo-Spanish force to cut the only major line of retreat open to the enemy, but without undue risk to Graham's isolated force. He broke the French front line by his double flanking movement, which worked because Wellington exercised such close control of the four widely separated forces in his plan.

THE BATTLEFIELD OF VITORIA

Where To Go

The main road N.1 (Burgos to Vitoria) runs straight through the battlefield, and it is possible to get a reasonable idea of events by just driving along it, as the area is largely undeveloped, and the main features are easily identified. It is, however, well worth making a deviation to Tres Puentes to obtain a fuller picture of the fighting.

Viewpoint A Coming along the N.1 from Burgos, stop at the junction with the L.622 to Nanclares de la Oca. Walk up the knoll on the left of the road, and you can then view the battlefield, as seen by Wellington.

Viewpoint B Turn north off the N.1 towards Tres Puentes, and you are in Gazan's position on the forward slopes of the Hill of Arinez. It is possible to drive to the top of the feature by a track on the north-west, but it is rough going.

Viewpoint C Drive to the village of Tres Puentes and you first cross the Mendoza Bridge, the scene of Picton's charge. Turning left along the Zadorra, you come to the Tres Puentes Bridge that was seized by Kempt's Brigade.

Viewpoint D From the N.1 just east of the village of Arinez, you can see the battlefield from the point of view of Reille in the French second line of defence.

What To See

Viewpoint A (Wellington's position near Nanclares) The 4th Division were in this area, and so was Wellington, though probably nearer Villodas. He could see Joseph and his staff on the top of the Hill of Arinez immediately opposite.

He could also watch Hill's diversionary attack on the right along the Heights of Puebla, and note that the French were reacting just as he had hoped by reinforcing their right.

He would be less happy about the left flank, where Dalhousie should by now be approaching Tres Puentes, but is not in sight.

Far away to the left he can hear firing as Graham advances on Vitoria from the north.

Viewpoint B (Gazan's position forward of Arinez) Gazan can see the 4th and Light Divisions opposite near him Villodas, but is puzzled that they are not attacking as expected.

There is firing in the hills round Puebla to his left, and he keeps getting orders from the staff on the hill behind him to do something about it. "Is that the main attack or not?"

There is firing too way back north of Vitoria, but that cannot be anything serious, as it is too far away.

Then there are some troops to his right round Mendoza. "It looks like that old firebrand, Picton. There's bound to be some fighting wherever he is. It's a pity the bridges over the river in that corner were not blown. An attack against the right flank would be awkward, particularly if we are also attacked in front and from the left."

Viewpoint C (Position of Picton and Kempt) This area must be little changed from 1813, and it is easy to imagine the events that took place here.

The bridge that Kempt seized still stands, but Picton's one at Mendoza is new.

It is interesting to see how effectively Wellington's main attack from here outflanked the whole French position and led to the capture of the Hill of Arinez.

Viewpoint D (Reille's position) Standing on the French second line of defence, one can see how Reille was under pressure from three sides. Gazan was being driven back from Arinez, while Picton was thrusting up from the north, capturing Arinez and St Margarita.

Worse still, the Allied attack north-east of Vitoria was proving not to be a feint at all, but a serious threat, and before long Reille had to send most of his division in that direction to deal with it.

Notes

1 His portrait hangs in the Hall of Fame in the Military Museum in Madrid.
2 Mortally wounded, he asked to be carried to the edge of the cliffs from where he could watch his former regiment, the 71st, in action. His last words were, "I trust to God that this will be a glorious day for England."
3 How many battles in history have hinged on the discovery and capture of bridges, guarded or unguarded?
4 *Wellington. The Years of the Sword*, p. 384.

...der of Battle: Vitoria – 21 June, 1813

...sion	Commander	Strength	Brigades
	Hill (*Right*)		
	Stewart	10,834	Cadogan
			Byng
			O'Callaghan
			Ashworth (Port)
	Wellington (*Centre*)		
	Cole	7,826	Anson
			Skerrett
			Stubb (Port)
...ht	Alten	5,484	Kempt
			Vandeleur
		13,310	
	Dalhousie (*Left*)		
	Picton	7,459	Brisbane
			Colville
			Power (Port)
	Dalhousie	7,297	Barnes
			Grant
			Le Cor (Port)
		14,756	
	Graham (*Far Left*)		
	Howard	4,854	Stopford
			Halkett
	Oswald	6,725	Hay
			Robinson
			Spry (Port)
...rtuguese	Indep. Brigades	4,689	Pack & Bradford
...anish	Longa	3,130	
	Morillo	4,551	
		23,949	
...rtuguese	Silveria	5,287	Campbell
			Da Costa
...h	Pakenham	7,347	Stirling
			Hinde
			Madden (Port)

...ommander	Wellington
...rength	79,000
...avalry	8,317
...uns	90
...asualties	5,148

FRENCH

Division	Strength
Army of the South	
Leval	4,844
Villatte	5,874
Conroux	6,589
Maransin	2,927
Daricau	5,935
Soult P. (Lt.Cav)	1,671
Tilly (Dragoon)	1,929
Digcon (Dragoon)	1,869
	31,638
Army of Portugal	
Sarrut	4,802
Lamartinière	6,711
Mermet (Lt.Cav)	1,801
Boyer (Dragoons)	1,471
	14,785
Army of the Centre	
Darmagnac	4,472
Cassagne	5,209
Casalpalacios (Span)	2,167
Guards	2,380
Cavalry	2,607
	16,835

Joseph	
66,000	
11,300	
153	
7,999	

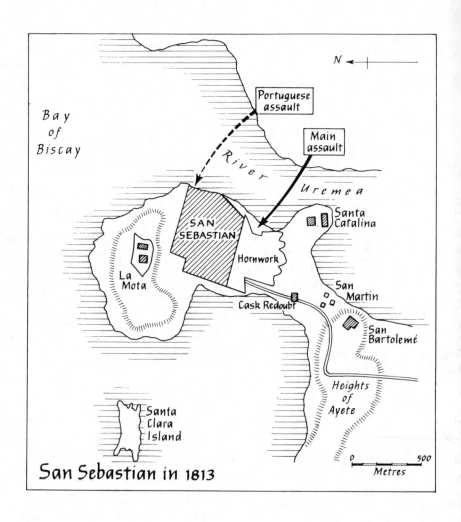

N

Portuguese
assault

Main
assault

Bay
of
Biscay

River

Uremea

SAN
SEBASTIAN

Santa
Catalina

La
Mota

Hornwork

San
Martin

Cask Redoubt

San
Bartolemé

Heights
of
Ayete

Santa
Clara
Island

0   500
Metres

San Sebastian in 1813

CHAPTER TWENTY-FIVE

The Sieges of San Sebastian

San Sebastian

In 1813 San Sebastian was a small, compact town, only some 400 yards square, and dominated by the castle on the height of La Mota. It had been under French control for five years and was held by 3,000 troops with 60 guns under General Rey, a determined and capable commander. It was regularly supplied by sea and the Navy could not prevent this. The defences were strongest to the south, and the best chance of success was an attack from the east.

First Assault (25 July, 1813)

San Sebastian was blockaded by Graham from **28 June, 1813** and, after a visit by Wellington on **12 July**, an assault was planned for 24 July, but had to be postponed until the **25th.**

It was carried out from the east by Oswald's 5th Division and Bradford's Portuguese Brigade, but failed. It provided an example of "troubles coming in threes", for Colonel Sir Richard Fletcher was killed. He had been Wellington's trusted and brilliant Chief Engineer throughout the war and had been the mastermind behind the construction of the Lines of Torres Vedras.

The third misfortune was that the failure made Wellington ride straight to San Sebastian on the morning of 25th to investigate, and so he was absent from his headquarters at Lesaca at the crucial moment when Soult launched his offensive across the Pyrenees.

Second Assault (31 August, 1813)

It was now decided to wait for the arrival of more siege guns, and it was not until August that a sufficient breach had been made in the walls.

After a reconnaissance in force on **29 August**, the major assault was set for the 31st.

It was to be carried out again by 5th Division and Bradford's Brigade, but with the addition of 750 volunteers from the 1st, 4th and Light Divisions. H Hour was set for 1055, because that was low tide, and it was preceded by a heavy bombardment.[1]

The assault went in against the 300-foot breach in the east wall, but almost every man in the "forlorn hope" was mown down by the defender's guns. After 35 minutes 800 Portuguese volunteers waded up to their waists across the 300-yard-wide estuary further north, and managed to get into a lesser breach, but not through it into the town.

After an hour of bitter fighting, the attack was on the verge of failure, when Graham ordered his artillery commander, Colonel Dickson, to open up again, firing this time over the heads of the assaulting troops. It was almost unprecedented, and there was only a 40-foot clearance at 1200 yards range. But the Gunners managed it, causing severe casualties to the defenders.

Then the magazine containing all the French ammunition exploded, and these two setbacks turned the scales; by 1240 the Allies had finally broken into the town. Street fighting continued for an hour, with 1,300 survivors of the garrison finally withdrawing to the Castle, where they held out for a further nine days.

Allied losses had been 856 killed and 1,520 wounded, and as in previous sieges, the troops went on the rampage, plundering and drinking, and could not be brought under control. To make matters worse, fires started, and, fanned by a strong wind, destroyed much of the town.

There was much indignation in both London and Madrid, because the inhabitants were allies, and the Spanish Government actually accused Wellington of burning down the town deliberately in order to hamper their trade with France.

San Sebastian Today

Today the town has expanded considerably and is heavily built up, but it is still possible to identify the original isthmus and the scenes of the assaults. The Castle still stands, dominating the old part of the town.

The Museum Historico Militar houses a remarkable collection of shot and shell from the siege that makes one wonder how the French survived under such a bombardment day after day.

Notes

1   There was a large crowd of spectators watching.

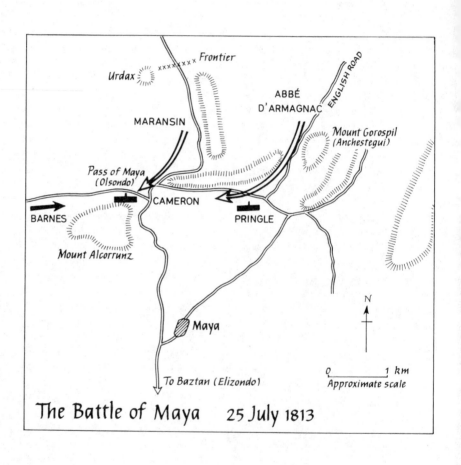

Urdax xxxxxxxx *Frontier*

ENGLISH ROAD

ABBÉ
D'ARMAGNAC

MARANSIN

*Mount Gorospil
(Anchestegui)*

*Pass of Maya
(Olsondo)*

CAMERON

BARNES

PRINGLE

Mount Alcorrunz

N

Maya

To Baztan (Elizondo)

0   1 km
Approximate scale

The Battle of Maya   25 July 1813

CHAPTER TWENTY-SIX

The Battle of Maya

Wellington's Plan

The Battles of Maya and Roncesvalles were the opening blows of Soult's brilliant counter-offensive across the Pyrenees in July, 1813.

Wellington had paused after his advance of 400 miles in 40 days, and his army was spread out along the south side of the Pyrenees from Fonterrabia on the coast to Pamplona, some 50 miles to the south. He had only 60,000 troops available for the task, and his plan was to hold the passes with the minimum numbers, while his main strength was positioned behind, ready to deal with any enemy breakthrough. He placed Hill in command of the northern sector and Cole in the south.

Allied Positions

The defence of the Pass of Maya[1] in July, 1813, was entrusted by Hill to Stewart, commanding the 2nd Division, who had under him for this task two of his brigades[2] totalling some 6,000 men.

Stewart placed Cameron's Brigade on the left, covering the main road from Bayonne to Pamplona, where it crosses the pass, 4 miles south of Urdax. They were on the slopes of Mount Alcorrunz, with good observation of their front.

Pringle's Brigade was on the right, covering the secondary road, which runs about a mile further east,[3] roughly parallel to the main road. They had a much wider front, as the pass is a plateau 2 miles wide; their task was made more difficult by the broken country, and their observation was very limited.

Pringle had only arrived from England 24 hours before, and so was unacquainted either with the ground or with his troops. He adopted a peculiar system of defence, in that he had only one company of about 80 men in the front line. They formed an outpost on Mount Gorospil,[4] and were supported by 400 men from four light companies 800 yards further back. Half a mile behind them was an "alert battalion", with the other two battalions encamped a further two miles to the rear behind Maya.

The Battle

At dawn on **25 July, 1813** 21,000 men under D'Erlon[5] advanced against the Pass of Maya. Stewart was not at his headquarters, having ridden off to the right to investigate some firing there, and so command fell upon the inexperienced Brigadier Pringle.[6]

By about 1000 D'Armagnac's Division had approached unseen to within half a mile of Pringle's outpost on Mount Gorospil. The light companies had joined the outpost, but it was 500 men against 7,000, and, after 40 minutes of fierce fighting, they were overrun with heavy casualties. The plan had been that the other battalions would be able to reach the ridge in time to prevent the enemy capturing it, but this had not worked, and the French columns now pushed westwards towards Mount Alcorrunz.

Pringle could only throw in his battalions as they became available. First, the "alert battalion", the 2/34th, hurried forward and attacked, but were repulsed, and the same happened to the 1/39th. Finally, the 1/28th came up from Maya, but they could not dislodge the French, who remained in firm possession of the Maya Plateau.

The 1/50th from Cameron's Brigade also attacked the advancing enemy columns, but could not check them.

Pringle now took command of both brigades and led forward the 1/92nd (Gordon Highlanders) eastwards from Mount Alcorrunz. For 20 minutes 400 men faced an entire French Division, but, despite magnificent courage, they too were driven back.

Maransin's Division was now also closing in on Cameron's Brigade from the Urdax road, while Abbé was following D'Armagnac along the secondary road. By 1630 the French were firmly in occupation of the pass, but did not for the moment press on.

Stewart had by now returned, and he took over. He re-grouped and took up a defensive position on the slopes of Mount Alcorrunz. Then at about 1800 Barnes's Brigade[7] arrived from Eschalar to the west and launched a highly effective counter-attack, which halted any further enemy advance.

It was now getting dark and the fighting had lasted 10 hours. The battle died down, with the French still in possession of the pass, but the

Allies were in strong positions, and it would not be easy for D'Erlon to advance further.

The French had lost 2,000 and the British 1,500, but for the latter this was 25% of their strength. They also lost four guns, the first and only time that Wellington lost a gun.[8]

Late that evening Hill appeared and ordered Stewart to withdraw to Irurita, which he did, and luckily the French did not follow up.

Summary

Stewart's dispositions were faulty in that the French were able to close in unobserved, and he was also at fault in leaving an inexperienced Pringle in command.

Pringle launched his counter-attacks piecemeal, but he did at least check the enemy and prevent them breaking through. This was crucial, as a breakthrough at Maya as well as Roncesvalles would have been serious for the Allies.

THE BATTLEFIELD OF MAYA

Where To Go
FROM FRANCE

Take the D.918 to Espelette, and then the D.20 to Ainhoe and Urdax (the frontier) where it becomes the N.121 in Spain.

The pass is about 5 miles from the frontier.

FROM SPAIN

Take the C.133 along the Bidassoa valley from Irun or the N.121 from Pamplona. Turn north-east at Mugaire along the N.121 to Baztan (Elizondo).

What To See

Identification is tricky, because many names have been changed, and so have the roads (and even the frontier!).

The Pass of Maya (Olsondo) is clear, despite being signposted (in 1988) as "Otxondo 602 m". Mount Alcorrunz is to the west of the pass, close to the road.

A gravel road runs east from the pass along the south side of the line of hills which form the crest of the Pyrenees. This road is joined after about a mile by a track coming in from the north, which is known as the "English Road".

The peak to the east (right) of the English Road is Mount Gorospil (Anchestegui). The crest of the pass is a strong position, and it should have been possible to hold it, had Pringle had more men forward, because the French could not deploy in full strength.

The line of the French advance after capturing Gorospil was westwards along the gravel track to Mount Alcorrunz, but the only signs of warfare today are the pigeon shooters' hides and piles of cartridge cases that litter the crest of the ridge.

The village of Maya is far below the crest, deep in the valley, and the battalions that climbed up to the ridge at the double must have been exhausted before they ever started fighting.

Notes

1 Now called the Pass of Elisondo.
2 *Pringle's Brigade* (Formerly O'Callaghan's)
    1/28th. 2/34th. 1/39th.
    Cameron's Brigade(Formerly Cadogan's)
    1/50th. 1/71st. 1/92nd.
3 It was known in 1813 as "the English Road".
4 Called Anchestegui on modern maps.
5 2nd Division   (D'Armagnac)   7,000
    3rd Division   (Abbé)   8,000
    6th Division   (Maransin)   6,000
6 He was senior to Cameron.
7 1/6th. 3rd Provisional Battalion. One company of Brunswick Oels.
8 Beresford lost one at Albuera.

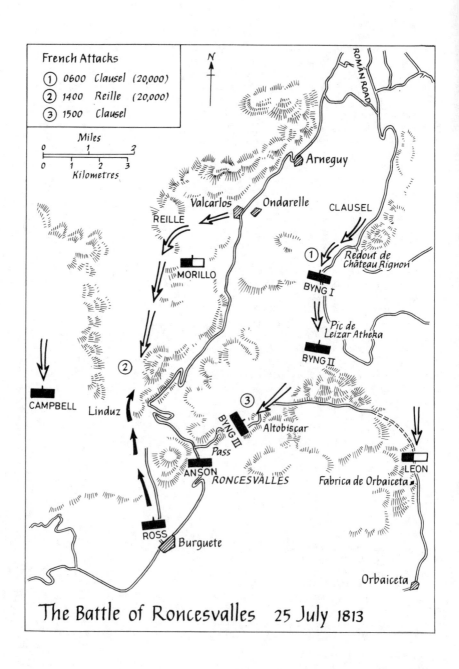

French Attacks

① 0600 Clausel (20,000)
② 1400 Reille (20,000)
③ 1500 Clausel

Miles
0   1   2
0   1   2   3
Kilometres

N

ROMAN ROAD

Arneguy

Valcarlos   Ondarelle   CLAUSEL
REILLE

① Redout de
   Château Rignon
MORILLO
              BYNG I

                    Pic de
                    Leizar Atheka
                BYNG II

②
CAMPBELL   ③
        Linduz   BYNG III
                  Altobiscar
              Pass   LEON
        ANSON RONCESVALLES
                              Fabrica de Orbaiceta

ROSS Burguete

                              Orbaiceta

The Battle of Roncesvalles 25 July 1813

CHAPTER TWENTY-SEVEN

The Battle of Roncesvalles

Allied Positions

Wellington planned to hold the Pass of Roncesvalles with a rather scratch force of 13,000 under Sir Lowry Cole of 4th Division, whom he had ordered "to maintain the passes to the front of Roncesvalles to the utmost, but to disregard any wider turning movement to the Allied right."

The pass consists of two parallel ridges running NNE towards St-Jean-Pied-de-Port and almost a mile apart. The highest point (3,648 feet), with its memorial to Roland who was killed there in 778, is a mile north of the village of Roncesvalles.

The only passable road in 1813 was the Roman Road,[1] which ran along the eastern ridge through Château Rignon, and this was held by Byng's Brigade, 2,000 strong, from 2nd Division.[2]

The present main road through Valcarlos was then only a track, and was covered by Morillo's Spanish Brigade, and one British battalion, the 1/57th.

Campbell's Portuguese Brigade, also 2,000 strong, was posted to the left rear on the Linduz Plateau, where another track running along the north ridge approached the Pass.

French Plan

Soult knew that Wellington's forces must be widely dispersed, and he hoped that a strong thrust through the Pass of Roncesvalles would enable him to cross the Pyrenees without too much difficulty and break through to Pamplona.

He allocated 40,000 men, almost two-thirds of his whole force, to the attack on Roncesvalles, and himself moved with them. He divided them into two corps under Reille and Clausel, and sent one against each ridge.

The Battle

Soult launched his offensive at 0600 on **25 July, 1813**. Clausel's leading division (Vandermaesen) advanced along the Roman Road, and soon came up against Byng's skirmishers at Château Rignon. They outnumbered the British 7 to 1 at this stage, but the ground strongly favoured the defenders, who fought so doggedly and skilfully that they held up the whole of Clausel's corps for four hours.

From about 1000 to 1200 there was a lull in the fighting, but at 1500 the French attacked again, this time using infantry in column, and Byng was driven back to the Altobiscar. This was a strong position, but it could be outflanked to the east through Orbaiceta; the French did this, but were then thwarted when a thick mist suddenly came down.

Morillo's Brigade and the British 1/57th at Valcarlos were not engaged because Reille's troops by-passed the village and advanced along the western spur that led to the Linduz Plateau.

Seeing this, Cole sent Ross's Brigade,[3] which he had brought up from Burguete, to the Linduz area to support Campbell's Portuguese.

The two forces met at about 1400 on the narrow ridge near Linduz, where neither side could deploy more than a battalion. The 1st/20th fought until they had exhausted their ammunition, and then the 1st/7th took over. Although heavily outnumbered, they held on, and then suddenly, around 1600, a thick mist enveloped both sides. Visibility was down to 20 yards and the fighting stopped.

The French were still not within a mile of the pass itself, but Cole was extremely worried nevertheless. He had only 13,000 men to hold his position against 40,000 and foresaw his force being engulfed by the enemy in the eerie mist. He was unquestionably brave, but he had never had command of so many before; he had had no sleep for two nights, and his nerve was not equal to the intense pressure. That evening, despite the specific orders he had received from Wellington, he ordered a withdrawal back down the road to Pamplona.

THE BATTLEFIELD OF RONCESVALLES

Where To Go

Approaching from Spain take the C.135 from Pamplona through Burguete and on to the village of Roncesvalles, a mile beyond.

From France take the D.933 from St Jean-Pied-de-Port.

What To See

The Pass is easily identified by the memorial to Roland[4] and the small chapel just beside the main road, which did not exist in 1813 except as a track.

The road over the Pass then was the Roman Road through Château Rignon. It still exists today and is passable.

It is also possible to drive up to the Linduz Plateau.

Much depends on the weather, and mists are still liable to come down suddenly and reduce visibility to 20 yards.

The Altobiscar, which was occupied by Byng's Brigade, is a feature that is not marked on all maps and is not the same as the village of that same name.

The village of Roncesvalles, a mile south of the Pass, is worth visiting to see the 13th century Augustinian abbey and the 12th century chapel. There are also two small restaurants there.

Notes

1 It still exists, but is a secondary road.
2 1/3rd. 1/57th. 1st Provisional Battalion.
3 1/7th. 1/20th.
4 In 778 the rearguard of Charlemagne's army, led by Roland, was cut off and overwhelmed by the Basques. In 1367 the Black Prince crossed the Pass on his way to the Battle of Najera or Navarrette.

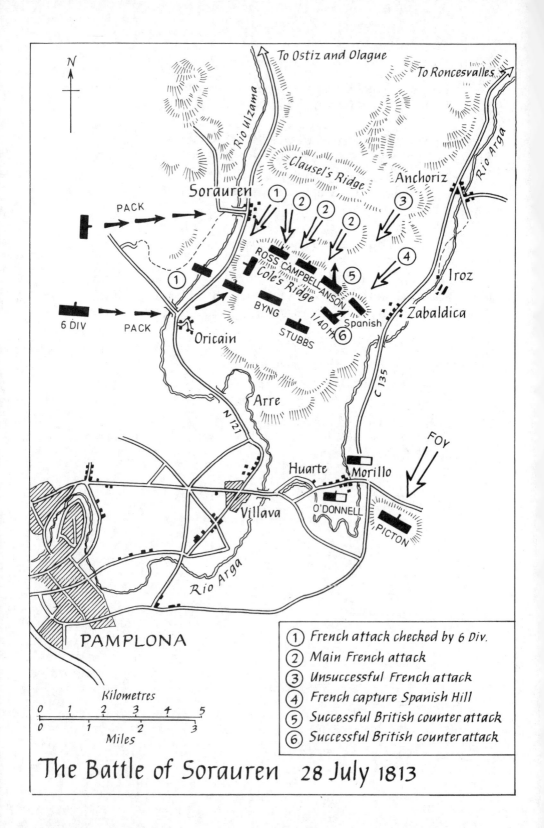

To Ostiz and Olague

To Roncesvalles

N

Rio Ulzama

Clausel's Ridge

Anchoriz

Rio Arga

PACK

SORAUREN

① ② ② ③

④

Iroz

ROSS CAMPBELL ANSON
Cole's Ridge
BYNG
STUBBS

⑤

Zabaldica

1/40 H²

Spanish ⑥

6 DIV   PACK

①

Oricain

C 135

Arre

N 121

FOY

Huarte   Morillo

Villava   O'DONNELL

PICTON

Rio Arga

PAMPLONA

Kilometres

0 1 2 3 4 5

0   1   2   3

Miles

① French attack checked by 6 Div.
② Main French attack
③ Unsuccessful French attack
④ French capture Spanish Hill
⑤ Successful British counter attack
⑥ Successful British counter attack

The Battle of Sorauren   28 July 1813

CHAPTER TWENTY-EIGHT

The Battle of Sorauren

Allied Plans

When Sir Lowry Cole abandoned his positions on the Roncesvalles Pass on the night of **25 July**, he withdrew along the road back towards Pamplona until he came to Sorauren, where he took up a strong defensive position on the morning of the **27th**. With his 18,000 men, he occupied a ridge to the south-east of the village, which blocked the road to Pamplona, and was later to be known as "Cole's Ridge".

Soult was close on his heels and reached Sorauren with around 30,000 men on the morning of the 27th. An immediate thrust southwards might well have taken him to Pamplona, but Soult was a cautious commander, and, despite being urged by Clausel to attack at once, he hesitated.

Wellington did not hear of Cole's withdrawal from Roncesvalles until 2000 on 26 July, and early on the 27th he galloped south to find Cole. Accompanied only by his Military Secretary, Major Fitzroy Somerset, he reached Sorauren, and saw Cole's troops on the ridge ahead; but he then noticed that the French were moving on to the opposite ridge to the north of the village.

Sitting on the stone bridge over the River Ulzama (then called the Lanz), he scribbled a 13-line message to his QMG, General Murray, at Olague, telling him to move Pack's 6th Division to Sorauren at top speed, but by a new route to avoid the advancing French.

Handing the message to Somerset, who galloped off with it, Wellington put his spurs into Copenhagen, and, with the French actually in pursuit, headed towards the British lines.

The first Allied troops that he met were Campbell's Portuguese Brigade, who set up a great shout of "Douro! Douro! Douro!", and the cheering was taken up by the British soldiers.

His appearance had a dramatic effect on both sides. His own army began to regain confidence and morale after their unwelcome retreat from Roncesvalles. "We would rather see his long nose in the fight," declared Captain Kincaid, "than a reinforcement of 10,000 men any day."[1] A Private commented more pungently " 'Ere's 'Atty, 'ere's that long-nosed bugger that licks the French," while an officer wrote home pompously that he would "never forget the joy beamed in every countenance when his lordship's presence became known."

French Plans

Soult, on the other hand, was distinctly worried by the bursts of cheering, and Wellington, with his remarkable insight into his opponent's thinking, set out to exploit it to the full. He deliberately stood on the most prominent point that he could find, opened his telescope and calmly focused it on the French Marshal, who had been pointed out to him by a double agent.

It is an intriguing example of psychological warfare. Wellington knew that Soult was by nature cautious, and he considered, quite rightly, that the Marshal would "delay his attack to ascertain the cause of these cheers; that will give time for the Sixth Division to arrive, and I shall beat him."[2]

It worked. Although Pamplona was a mere two hours march away and the French out-numbered the Allies nearly 2 to 1,[3] Soult refused to attack without a further reconnaissance. Clausel urged him not to delay, but instead, he actually took a siesta, leaving Clausel "leaning against an oak tree . . . beating his forehead with rage, muttering, 'Who could go to sleep at such a moment?'"

The Battle

So the afternoon of the **27th** slipped by, with Soult asleep, while Wellington welcomed the delay, knowing that 6th Division could not arrive before 1000 the next day.

That evening a fierce thunderstorm swept down from the Pyrenees. It prevented Hill and Dalhousie from bringing their divisions to join Wellington, but it was welcomed by the British troops, who remembered Salamanca and took it as a good omen.

Having carefully reviewed Cole's dispositions, Wellington made only one change, though it was to prove a significant one. Noting that a key feature south-west of Zabaldica was held only by Spanish troops, he placed the 1/40th behind the Spaniards as a reinforcement.

As dawn broke on **28 July**, (the fourth anniversary of the Battle of Talavera) Wellington expected the French to attack at any moment, but it was 1230 before Soult finally took the plunge. By then it was too late, for Pack and his 6th Division were now in position to the west of Cole's Ridge.

The first French attack was made by Conroux's Division, which advanced south from the village of Sorauren, but met 6th Division and came under fire from three sides; they were driven back, pursued by Pack, who even tried to capture Sorauren, but failed and was himself severely wounded.

The main French attack, by six divisions, now came in against the Allied centre, while one more division (Lamatinière) advanced against the Spanish Hill. The French had a superiority of 2 to 1 and succeeded in reaching the crest of Cole's Ridge in several places. For a while the situation was serious. But as Maucune's Division crossed the land bridge on the Allied right and climbed confidently up the slope beyond in column, they suddenly found themselves confronted by two of Anson's battalions[4] in the familiar two-deep line. The British advantage in firepower was around 1,200 against 300 and, one after another, the French battalions were driven back, losing 660 men out of 2,200.

On the left, however, the French had captured the chapel after some hard fighting. But Wellington was there and sent two victorious battalions of Anson's Brigade diagonally down the hill against the French flank.

The outcome is vividly described by Jac Weller: "Never in the Peninsular War did two battalions accomplish so much so quickly. The 3/27th and 1/48th smashed each successive enemy battalion, apparently by charging each after a short period of fire. With remarkable tactical skill, Wellington contrived to gain a two to one numerical advantage at each encounter, although he was out-numbered in the general area by more than two to one. Ross and Campbell returned to the fray with new vigour, while Wellington committed the physically fresh brigades of Byng and Stubbs. The entire French attack between Sorauren and the land bridge was defeated and cast down into the transverse valley, but the Allied infantry were ordered not to press their advantage too far."[5]

To the east, however, the Spanish, after bravely repelling one French attack, had been driven from their hill by Lamatinière's Division. But as the French troops reached the peak, they found themselves facing the 1/40th, placed there by Wellington for just such a contingency.

The usual deadly volley rang out and the enemy advance was checked. But they came on again, whereupon the Spaniards withdrew, leaving a mere 400 British infantry facing 2,000 French.

Despite heavy losses, they held on grimly, and suddenly it was the French who broke and were driven back into the valley. It was such a dramatic sight that some of Wellington's staff began cheering, but he silenced them.

The battle ended at about 1600 with some four hours of daylight remaining. Both sides remained in their original positions, but Soult had to admit that his assault had failed. The French had lost around 4,000 against 2,652 Allied casualties, and they had not reached Pamplona.

During the **29th** Wellington managed to get some artillery up on to Cole's Ridge and on the morning of **30 July** he launched his own powerful, well-coordinated attack. Picton advanced up the Arga valley, while Cole attacked the ridge opposite his positions and Pakenham led three columns against the village of Sorauren. The enemy was driven back everywhere with heavy losses, and a disorganized remnant of 10,000 withdrew back to France under General Foy. Soult fought a last battle in Spain against Hill at Lizaso on the same day, and then himself withdrew to Vera and back into France. His nine-day offensive had failed.

Summary

"The 28th was fair bludgeon work," Wellington wrote later, and he told his Judge Advocate, Larpent, "Why, at one time it was rather alarming, certainly, and it was a close-run thing."[6]

It was certainly yet another example of Wellington's remarkable personal control of the battle, and it showed how much this was a battle-winning factor. It was also proof of the confidence that his troops had in his leadership. Morale rose immediately he appeared, and with justification, for he was invariably at the crucial spot at the crucial moment, acting swiftly and decisively to cope with crises and to seize opportunities.

He was, as always, in the thick of the fighting, and he confided to his brother William, "I escaped as usual unhurt, and I begin to believe that the finger of God is upon me."[7]

THE BATTLEFIELD OF SORAUREN

Where To Go

Take the N.121 north from Pamplona (which is itself best avoided) and the village of Sorauren sits astride it after some three miles.

Then drive back towards Pamplona and take the C.135 running north-east towards Roncesvalles and France. Pass through Huarte, and after two miles you come to the village of Zabaldica, which was the eastern end of the Allied positions at Sorauren.

What To See

AT SORAUREN

The River Ulzama (now Lanz) runs beside the N.121, and in the village is a stone bridge (re-built in 1987), which is the actual bridge on which Wellington wrote his despatch before the battle.

From the bridge there is a good view of the battlefield, with the French ridge to one's left and Cole's Ridge across the valley on one's right. The valley runs away eastwards and ends in the land bridge and the hill that was occupied by the Spanish.

AT ZABALDICA

To the west of the road by the village is the hill held by the Spanish, and further north is the land bridge. It is not possible to look down into the Sorauren valley from this side except by climbing the steep ridge, but if one does so, there is an excellent view of the whole battlefield.

Notes

1 *Adventures in the Rifle Brigade*, p.53.
2 Napier, VI, 130. But he was not there himself, and there is no confirmatory evidence.
3 33,000 to 18,000.
4 3/27th and 1/48th.
5 *Wellington in the Peninsula*, p.295.
6 Larpent, I, 304, 24 August, 1813.
7 Raglan MSS, No.56, 3 August, 1813.

CHAPTER TWENTY-NINE

The Battle of the Bidassoa

(See Map p.48)

Wellington's Positions

Having repulsed Soult's great offensive of 25 July, Wellington renewed the siege of San Sebastian, and a further assault was ordered for 31 August. He had received information that Soult might at any moment try to relieve the besieged fortress, and he expected the attack to be made along the coast road through Irun.

For the first three miles from the sea the Bidassoa River is a slow, wide estuary, but it then runs for five miles through the steep Gorge of Bidassoa, before opening out again at Vera. The main bridge at Behobie had been destroyed, but there were several fords that could be used at low tide. The coast road was dominated at Irun by a long ridge crowned by the monastery of San Marcial; it ran parallel to the river about a mile south of it, and effectively blocked the route to San Sebastian.

Wellington fortified the ridge, and occupied it with three Spanish divisions under General Manuel Freire;[1] they held from opposite Irun to just beyond Behobie, with Longa's Spanish division on their right. The British 1st Division and Aylmer's Independent Brigade, who had just arrived from England, were in support behind them.

Wellington appreciated that Soult might also make a crossing at Vera, and so placed the Light Division in that area, ready for such a contingency. He also ordered Dalhousie to demonstrate at dawn on the 31st from the direction of Maya so as to distract the French troops round Vera.

French Plan

Soult did indeed hope to relieve San Sebastian by an advance along the coast, just as Wellington expected, but his plan was in fact more ambitious and imaginative. Three divisions under Reille were to attack

San Marcial frontally, supported by 36 field guns and some heavy artillery.

But at the same time, Clausel with four divisions was to cross the Bidassoa at Vera and then swing northwards towards San Sebastian. This would not only force the Allied army to face in two directions, but might cut off the strong concentration of Allied troops round Irun, and enable Soult to attack them from behind as well as in front.

D'Erlon with two divisions was given the task of protecting the French left flank east of Vera.

It was a bold, imaginative plan, typical of Soult, but it was not easy to implement and control and this was where it would fail.

The Battle at San Marcial

Dawn on 31 August, 1813, produced an early morning mist so dense that Soult's attack at Irun, planned for 0600, was held up for two hours. At 0800 Reille's three divisions began crossing the river in the area of Behobie, and climbed the slopes of San Marcial.

But the attack did not develop as intended. The final advance was launched before all Reille's divisions were across the river and before his artillery was ready.

The Spanish infantry were in strong positions and they adopted Wellington's tactics of advancing to meet the enemy as they struggled up the hill. Before they were half way up the French were met by disciplined volleys and by 1000 had been driven back to the river valley with heavy losses.

Soult rallied his troops and about noon launched them into a second assault. Again, the Spanish fought extremely well and repulsed it. For three hours Soult tried to organize a third attack, but without success.

Only at the western end of the San Marcial ridge did the French gain a foothold, which the Spanish could not dislodge. General Freire sent to Wellington asking for reinforcements, but the Duke, with considerable discernment, refused the request, saying, "If I send you the English troops you ask for, they will win the battle; but as the French are already in retreat, you may as well win it for yourselves."[2]

Sure enough, the French soon afterwards withdrew everywhere. San Marcial was thus an unqualified Spanish victory, with no other Allied troops being involved, and their morale rose accordingly. They lost 1,679 men, but inflicted 2,500 casualties on the French.

The Battle at Vera

At dawn on 31 **August** Clausel duly began crossing the Bidassoa at Vera with his four divisions. But he moved very slowly and cautiously, for he was aware of the Light Division watching him and threatening his flank. He could also hear firing in the direction of Maya, and this worried him. This was Dalhousie's demonstration, which had developed into more of a battle than had been intended, because a Portuguese brigade became over-enthusiastic and tried to capture the town of Urdax.

Clausel diverted one of his four divisions to deal with what he thought was the threat from the Light Division and never made any real progress.

Little was achieved during the morning and in the afternoon Soult, realizing that his whole plan had failed, ordered Clausel to withdraw back across the Bidassoa to Vera. Unfortunately it had been raining heavily and there was now over six foot of water at the fords by which the French infantry had crossed earlier that morning.

Some 10,000 of them[3] were stranded on the Allied side of the river, and for several hours they vainly searched the raging torrent for a possible crossing point. Finally they found a narrow stone bridge near Vera, which was still standing.

It was held by 80 men of the 95th (The Rifle Regiment) under Captain Cadoux, and they refused to give in. For two hours they fought off incessant attacks by the French division, who were desperately trying to seize what was their only possible escape route. Despite the odds, the dwindling "forlorn hope" held out, inflicting over 200 casualties on the enemy, including killing the divisional commander, General Vandermaesen. But, inevitably, they were eventually overwhelmed and Captain Cadoux was killed.

During the fighting Cadoux appealed repeatedly to the acting commander of the Light Division, General Skerrett, for help, but it was refused, and indeed the General declined to take any action to support him. This behaviour was so much resented by the whole Light Division that it proved impossible for the general to remain in command and he was shortly afterwards sent home and left the Army.

Had General Skerrett taken steps to support Cadoux, the French casualties might have been considerably higher, and the end of the war might have come sooner. As it was, they lost some 1,300 against 850 Allied casualties in the whole action.

The operation had been a complete failure for the French, and this had a very serious effect on their morale and confidence in the future. It was the last major offensive that they would launch in the Peninsular War.

Notes

1. He commanded the Spanish Army of Galicia. Wellington thought highly of the Galician troops, particularly after the Battle of Vitoria.
2. Stanhope, 22.
3. Vandermaesen's Division.

CHAPTER THIRTY

The Crossing of the Bidassoa

(See Map p.48)

French Positions

After his attack on **31 August** failed, Soult went on to the defensive; he had a 16 mile front to defend, stretching from Maya to the sea, and he could not tell where Wellington would attack. He did not have enough troops to cover all likely approaches, and he could only manage to retain an inadequate reserve of 8,000.

For weeks he had been building fortifications, similar to the Lines of Torres Vedras, but in no way as formidable, and he was grateful for every day that Wellington did not attack.

What he feared most was that Wellington would launch a major assault against his left flank which, if successful, would come in behind his line of fortifications, and pin him against the sea. Such a move would be very similar to what he had himself attempted five weeks before, and he anticipated that Wellington might well think the same way.

He therefore made the centre of his line the strongest sector, basing it on the 2,800 foot feature of the Great Rhune, just north-east of Vera. He divided his front line into three, allotting his troops between them:

Left	D'Erlon	14,000
Centre	Clausel	15,000
Right	Reille	10,000
Reserve	Villatte	8,000
		47,000

He believed that the Bidassoa estuary was impassable, and the weakest part of his front was thus near the sea. But, unfortunately for him, this was just where Wellington planned to launch his main attack.

Wellington's Plan

By the **end of September, 1813**, Wellington was ready to move forward again, and his plan was to cross the Bidassoa and enter France on 7 October.

Pamplona was near surrender, the Peninsular Army had had the time it needed to reorganize, and he had built up a great deal of information about the enemy. He knew that Soult was trying to hold the whole line of the Bidassoa from the sea to Vera, and was therefore vulnerable to a concentrated attack at one point.

His plan was to launch his main assault in the west near the coast. He had discovered from local shrimpers that the seemingly impassable flats of the estuary could in fact be crossed on foot at low tide, and, as the next convenient one was on 7 October, he decided to attack that day.

There were two major advantages to making his main thrust up the coast. First, there was a good chance of achieving surprise, but above all, it enabled him to keep in close touch with the Navy and obtain supplies from them through the ports of Hendaye and St Jean-de-Luz.

On **1 October** Wellington rode to Roncesvalles and took good care to be seen there, so that Soult might think that the Allied attack was coming from that direction.

On **5 October** he issued his orders. On his right flank 2nd Division at Maya and the 6th Division at Roncesvalles were to remain where they were, but keep the French opposite them fully occupied.

In the centre he gave the Light Division the challenging task of capturing the Great Rhune, supported by two Spanish divisions (Longa's on their left and Giron's on their right). The best hope lay in a sudden thrust, and the Light Division was undoubtedly the formation most suited to such a role. The attack across the estuary would be the task of the 1st and 5th Divisions, supported by Freire's Spaniards and nine Portuguese battalions.

The Battle at Irun

Long before dawn on **7 October, 1813**, the soldiers of the 5th Division were in position on the south bank of the Bidassoa estuary at Fuenterrabia, waiting for the shrimpers who were to guide them across three separate crossing places.

On their right the 1st Division were ready to cross by the same fords at Behobie that the French had used in their attack five weeks before. Behind them were Wilson's Portuguese Brigade and Aylmer's British Brigade. Further to the right were Freire's Spanish Division and Bradford's Portuguese Brigade.

At 0725, as the early morning mist cleared, three batteries of artillery opened up at Irun, and the infantry waded into the 500-yard-wide expanse of water. It came up to their armpits, but they got across; the assault achieved complete surprise, and they were ashore before the French realized what was happening.

The assault at Behobie was equally successful, and by 0900 Reille had been forced out of all his defences on the coast. By 1130 the Allies were firmly established in a bridgehead round Hendaye, and the French withdrew to Urrugne.

It had been a highly efficient and successful operation, and the risks taken had paid off. By the time Soult arrived from Ainhoe, his whole line had been turned where he had least expected, and there was little that he could now do about it. But Wellington ordered that there should be no pursuit.

Allied losses in this sector were 400 against 450 French, but the latter also lost all their guns, most of their baggage, and, perhaps most serious of all, more of their self-confidence.

The Battle at Vera

The fighting round Vera was fiercer than at the estuary, although there were fewer troops involved. The main French positions were centred on the massive feature of La Rhune, three miles north-east of Vera, and it was held by two divisions,[1] behind earthworks and redoubts in depth from the river back to the spine of the Pyrenees.

The plan was that the Light Division would advance north-east from the river at Vera along two almost parallel ridges about a mile and a half apart. Colborne, on the left, was to follow a long spur, almost two miles in length, called La Bayonnette. Kempt, on his right, moved along quite a good track, while, between the two columns, Longa's men filled the gaps and also protected the left flank. No attack was to be made on La Rhune itself initially, but the defenders there were to be kept engaged by Giron's Spaniards, and their position would be untenable once the ridge to the west of La Rhune was captured.

At dawn on **7 October** the men of the Light Division drove in the

24. **Maya.** The Pass from the east, with Mount Alcoruunz to the left. The French advanced from the right of the picture and the village of Maya is to the left.

25. **Roncesvalles.** The Pass looking east towards the Roman Road. "The only passable road in 1813 was the Roman Road". (p.191)

26. **Sorauren**. Wellington writes his despatch on the bridge at Sorauren, while Major Fitzroy Somerset waits to ride off with it. The French Ridge is to the left and Cole's Ridge to the right. (*The Duke of Wellington*)

27. **Sorauren**. The bridge in 1988.

French outposts on the north bank of the Bidassoa and began the long, steep climb towards the crest of the Pyrenees.

On the left Colborne's men and his Cacadores advanced steadily along La Bayonnette until, at about the halfway point, they came up against a strong-point called the Star Redoubt; the 52nd, attacking in line, soon cleared it and such was the impetus of their attack that they seized the peaks, driving the French down the other side into France.

On the right Kempt's Brigade also made good progress, seizing a large hill called the Hog's Back. They then advanced on a broader front with a formidable line consisting of two battalions of the 43rd, two of the 95th and two Portuguese battalions. They too carried all before them, and by midday joined up triumphantly with Colborne's Brigade on the crest of the Pyrenees.

It had been a remarkable achievement by the Light Division, and the soldiers now made themselves comfortable in the enemy's huts and bivouacs, which formed "squares and streets, and had names placarded up such as 'Rue de Paris', 'Rue de Versailles', etc."[2]

Summary

The crossing of the Bidassoa was a masterpiece of both planning and execution. The bold and imaginative fording of the estuary at Fuenterrabia achieved complete surprise; the diversion at Maya effectively prevented any reinforcements being sent to Vera, and, as a result, Wellington was able to achieve a local superiority of some 6,500 to 4,700 at Vera. The French there should have been able to hold their positions, fortified as they were, but they were overwhelmed by the impetus of the Light Division attack.

There were two other reasons why the French failed to hold their strong positions on La Rhune. First, their morale was low, and second, they had had little experience of defensive fighting in fortified earthworks and allowed the Light Division to take each line in turn, often by an outflanking movement. Allied casualties were surprisingly low, being only 800 in both attacks, compared with 1,250 French.

The highly successful crossing of the considerable obstacle of the Bidassoa and the Pyrenees, followed by an invasion of "the sacred soil of France" raised the morale of the Peninsular Army to new heights, and they had no doubts now that they had the enemy on the run and would continue to thrash them.

But Wellington was still not yet prepared for a full-scale invasion of

France, and he let Soult withdraw to the line of the Nivelle, where he started preparing another line of defences.

THE CROSSING OF THE BIDASSOA

Where To Go

Leave the A.63 at Irun and follow the C.133 along the south side of the Bidassoa River, past San Marcial to Vera, five miles upstream. Turn east in Vera along the D.406, drive past La Rhune, and cross the frontier to Sare.

What To See

SAN MARCIAL

The long ridge on which the battle was fought is a distinct feature on the south bank opposite the frontier post at Irun. The Ermitage de St Marcial stands on the crest and can be reached by a winding track.

THE BIDASSOA ESTUARY

Fuentuerrabia (now called Honirrabia) is heavily built up, but it is possible to identify the rough area of the crossing, and Behobie is just upstream.

VERA DE BIDASSOA

The road from Irun goes through the Gorge of Bidassoa, and one sees how steep the hills are. At Vera, on the south side of the village, is a narrow, old stone bridge (400 yards downstream of a modern bridge), and this is Cadoux's Bridge, with a plaque to that effect. It also offers a good view of La Rhune.

LA RHUNE

From Vera one looks up at the dominating mass of La Rhune crowned with white buildings, and one must be impressed that this was made the objective of just one division, and that they achieved it. The ridges up which the Light Division advanced can be worked out, and some of the earthworks remain.

Notes

1 Taupin and Conroux.
2 Gronow, 1, 4.

Order of Battle: The Crossing of the Bidassoa – 7 October, 1813

ALLIES				FRENCH	
Brigades	*Commander*	*Strength*	*Position*	*Brigades*	*Strength*
	Left			*Right* (Reille)	
1st	Howard	6,898	Maitland	Maucune	3,996
			Stopford	Boyer	6,515
			Hinuber (KGL)		
5th	Hay	4,553	Robinson		
			Greville		
			De Regoa (Port)		
Spanish	Freire				
British	Indep. Brigade		Aylmer		
Portuguese	Indep. Brigades		Wilson		
			Bradford		
		15,250*			10,511
	Centre			*Centre* (Clausel)	
Light	Alten	4,970	Kempt	Darmagnac	4,400
			Colborne	Abbé	6,051
Spanish	Longa	2,607		Conroux	4,962
	Giron	7,843		Taupin	4,778
				Villatte (reserve)	8,018
		15,420			28,209
	Right			*Left* (D'Erlon)	
2nd	Stewart	8,480	Byng	Foy	4,654
			Walker	Maransin	5,575
			Pringle	Daricau	4,092
			Ashworth (Port)		
6th	Clinton	6,718	Pack		
			Lambert		
			Douglas (Port)		
		15,198			14,321

	ALLIES		FRENCH	
Commander	Wellington		Soult	
Strength	44,000		55,000	
Cavalry	—		—	
Guns	—		—	
Casualties	Irun	400	Irun	450
	Vera	800	Vera	1250

*Figures are not available for all brigades.

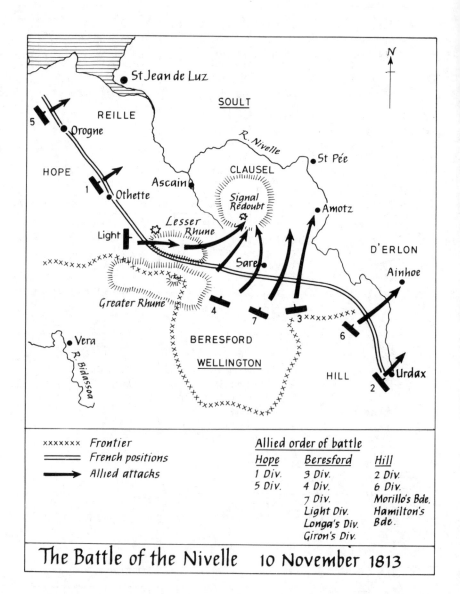

St Jean de Luz

SOULT

REILLE

5 Orogne

HOPE

R. Nivelle

St Pée

CLAUSEL

1 Othette

Ascain

Signal Redoubt

Lesser Rhune

Amotz

Light

D'ERLON

Ainhoe

Sare

Greater Rhune

4   7   3

6

Vera

BERESFORD

WELLINGTON

HILL

Urdax
2

R. Bidassoa

xxxxxxx   *Frontier*

    French positions

    Allied attacks

Allied order of battle

Hope	Beresford	Hill
1 Div.	3 Div.	2 Div.
5 Div.	4 Div.	6 Div.
	7 Div.	Morillo's Bde.
	Light Div.	Hamilton's
	Longa's Div.	Bde.
	Giron's Div.	

The Battle of the Nivelle   10 November 1813

CHAPTER THIRTY-ONE

The Battle of the Nivelle

French Positions

Soult, having been forced to abandon the Pyrenees, next tried to defend a line that ran just south of the Nivelle River from St Jean-de-Luz to the Mondarrain Mountains east of Urdax. It was a front of 16 miles as the crow flies, but over 20 miles on the ground, and, just as on the Bidassoa, he did not have enough troops to cover it properly. He constructed what fortifications he could in the time, and declared somewhat over-confidently that it would cost the Allies a third of their strength to dislodge him.

The sector from the sea to Ascain was the most heavily fortified and was strongly defended by three divisions, with a fourth in reserve; all were in positions west of the Nivelle.

The rest of the front was not so well fortified and was held by only five divisions. The key feature in this sector was the Lesser Rhune, a prominent ridge running parallel to the Greater Rhune and some 700 yards to the north; if that were taken, the whole French line would be threatened. Soult did not have enough troops to hold both that and the coastal sector in strength, and he chose to concentrate on the coast.

Wellington's Plan

The surrender of Pamplona on **25 October** freed Wellington to take the offensive again, and he wasted no time. His troops were across the Bidassoa, and he had a superiority in numbers of 82,000 against Soult's 63,000; 22,000 of his strength were, however, Spanish, and as yet unproven in battle.

He fully appreciated that the enemy were over-extended and he made the point to his commanders when they were studying the French positions with him from the top of the Greater Rhune.

211

Colborne commented on some of the difficulties, whereupon Wellington remarked, "Ah, Colborne, with your local knowledge only, you are perfectly right. It appears difficult, but the enemy have not men to man the works and lines they occupy. They dare not concentrate a sufficient body to resist the attacks I shall make upon them. I can pour a greater force on certain points than they can concentrate to resist me."

This incident, which is recounted first-hand by Harry Smith, is of interest on two scores. First, it shows the thinking on which Wellington would base his plan, and second, it shows that he was by now taking his experienced commanders more into his confidence than in the past, and training them to think more for themselves.

Wellington's plan was to engage the enemy along the whole front, but to attack overwhelmingly in the centre, where he rightly considered Soult's defences too weak. If he broke through there, he knew that he would be in a position to thrust north-west and cut off the whole French army along the coast.

On the left, Sir John Hope,[1] with 1st and 5th Divisions and Freire's two Spanish divisions (19,000 men), was to keep occupied the 23,000 French troops in the sector between the sea and Ascain.

The main thrust would be in the centre in the area of Sare and Amotz, aimed at the junction between the sectors of Clausel and D'Erlon. Here 55,000 Allied troops with 54 guns would be concentrated against 40,000 French.

Beresford commanded the main striking force, which consisted of 3rd, 4th, 7th and Light Divisions, and two Spanish divisions, a total of 36,000 men and 24 guns. On his right was Hill with 26,000 men[2] and 9 guns.

The attack was ordered for dawn on 10 November and Wellington positioned himself with Beresford on the crest on the Great Rhune to watch it start.

The Battle

The first and crucial task of taking the Lesser Rhune was allotted to the Light Division. Attacked frontally from the south, it was virtually impregnable, with a deep ravine running between it and the Greater Rhune. But it could be approached from the west, and an assault from that direction along the crest might roll up the French defences one after the other, since they were mostly facing south. That is just what the Light Division achieved with outstanding success.

As dawn broke on 10 **November** at about 0600, signal guns on Mount Atchubia boomed out and the men of the 43rd[3] and 52nd began scrambling up the steep, craggy slopes of the Lesser Rhune from the west. They took the enemy by surprise, but there was fierce hand-to-hand fighting as they came up against one stronghold after another. But they pressed on, and finally at 0800 captured the "Donjon", the last fortress at the eastern end of the ridge.

"Nor did we ever meet a check," wrote Harry Smith exultantly, "but carried the enemy's works by one fell swoop of irresistible victory."

Now the way was open for Wellington's main thrust – an advance by nine divisions on a front of five miles; it must have been an impressive sight as they advanced north-east from the Greater Rhune towards the Nivelle.

By 0900 4th Division had taken Sare, and by 1100 3rd Division had pushed on to seize the bridge at Amotz, so dividing the French army into two.

As the assault swept on, the Light Division joined in and drove forward again, until they came up against a formidable stronghold known as the Signal Redoubt. Twice the 52nd attacked, but were repulsed with heavy losses. Then the brigade commander, Colonel John Colborne, tried bluff. Under a flag of truce he called out to the enemy commander, "See. You are surrounded on every side. There are Spaniards to your left. You had better surrender at once."

The French had a particular horror of falling into the hands of the vengeful Spanish, and they promptly laid down their arms, their commander handing over his sword with the words, "There, Monsieur, is a sword that has ever done its duty."

Meanwhile to the west Reille's 23,000 had hardly moved from their positions, in the face of effective feint attacks by Hope's force.

To the east the French had a moment of success, when Foy advanced with his division from Bidarray towards Maya, and so came up behind Hill. He captured some baggage, but was halted by three Spanish battalions and forced to withdraw to Cambo.

A swift counter-attack by the French might yet have restored the situation, but Soult hesitated until the opportunity had gone. By 1400 the centre of his line was broken and his army was in retreat over the Nivelle.

The Allied breakthrough against the French centre offered Wellington a chance of cutting off the enemy forces near the coast, and he might well have done so but for three considerations.

First, there was not enough daylight left for him to reorganize before dark, and he never liked attacking by night. Second, some troops (notably the 6th Division) had been slower than planned in reaching their objectives. Third, an advance north-west by Beresford and Hill would expose them to a counter-attack by Soult; his troops under Reille were virtually intact and could attack eastwards against Ascain, which was the pivot of the Allied line. This area was held by Spanish troops, and he did not want to risk any reverse at this stage.

He had achieved a handsome victory, driving the French out of a strong, fortified position at little cost (2,450 Allied casualties against 4,351 French) and he was content to let Soult withdraw unharassed to the line of the Nive. But he did admit two days later to his brother, William: "I did not do as much as I had wished; if there had been more daylight and less mud, I should have given Soult a terrible squeeze. As it is, they are more frightened than hurt."[4]

Nevertheless, it had been a most satisfactory encounter as far as the Peninsular Army was concerned; they had shown themselves to be superior to the French in every respect, and, to quote Arthur Bryant, "the Allied army was irresistible that day."

THE BATTLEFIELD OF THE NIVELLE

Where To Go and What To See

It is not easy to pick any particular viewpoints, as the fighting covers such a large area. But it is well worth driving along the D.406 from Vera, past the Greater Rhune and on to Sare, a charming village in the foothills.

Then drive from Sare along the D.4 to Ascain, which takes you between the Greater and Lesser Rhunes, and you can see the line of advance of the Light Division.

Join the D.918 just beyond Ascain and turn east along the Nivelle to St Pee and on to Amotz, by which time you will have covered most of the battlefield.

It is very broken country, and it is interesting to try to envisage just how the battle developed.

Notes

1 He had replaced Graham who had eye trouble.
2 2nd and 6th Divisions. Morillo's Spanish Division and Hamilton's Portuguese Brigade.
3 They were commanded that day by the historian, William Napier, whose account of the battle is a superb, first-hand story. (Napier, V, 368–9).
4 Wellington to William, 13 November, 1813, Raglan MSS, No. 64.

Order of Battle: Nivelle – 10 November, 1813

Division	Commander	Strength	Brigades	Division	Strength
	Hope (*Left*)				
1st	Howard	6,898		Foy	5,136
5th	Hay	4,553		Darmagnac	4,705
Spanish	Freire			Abbé	6,326
	(two divisions)	10,284		Conroux	5,399
	Three Indep.			Maransin	5,579
	Brigades	5,729		Daricau	5,782
				Leval	4,539
		27,464		Taupin	4,889
				Boyer	6,560
	Beresford (*Centre*)			Villatte (Reserve)	8,310
3rd	Colville	2,684			
4th	Cole	6,585			
7th	Le Cor	6,068			
Light	Alten	4,970			
Portuguese	Hamilton	4,949			
Spanish	Longa	2,607			
Spanish	Giron	7,653			
		35,516			
	Hill (*Right*)				
2nd	Stewart	8,480			
6th	Clinton	6,729			
Spanish	Morillo	5,129			
		20,338			

Commander	Wellington	Soult
Strength	82,000	63,000
Cavalry	—	6,788
Guns	54	97
Casualties	3,400	4,351

CHAPTER THIRTY-TWO

The Battle of the Nive

(See Map p.48)

French Positions

Having been driven out of his position along the Nivelle, Soult withdrew to Bayonne, which was a strongly fortified military base. He had some 63,000 men, and could expect reinforcements now that he was in France.

He took up positions just south of Bayonne and along the east bank of the Nive from Bayonne south-east to Cambo. He established a bridgehead on the west bank of the river round Cambo, and held four divisions there, so that he was in a position to attack westwards against the flank of any Allied advance up the coast.

The city of Bayonne was easy to defend, as it was well protected by water; the Atlantic lay to the west, while the River Adour flowed in from the east. Any Allied advance along the coast, which was the obvious approach, meant entering an ever-narrowing triangle formed by the Atlantic and the River Nive to the east.

Wellington's Plans

Wellington's plan, however, was to close in on Bayonne from the east as well as from the south, because this would threaten Soult's line of withdrawal and so force him to evacuate the city. The problem was that this meant that the Allied army would be divided by the Nive, which was liable to flood. Indeed, this happened soon after the Allies had driven in the French bridgehead at Cambo on **16 November**, and they were then held up for three weeks.

By **early December** it was possible to resume offensive operations and the crossing of the Nive was set for 9 December.

Hill, with the 2nd Division and Le Cor's Portuguese Division, was to cross by three fords at Cambo and advance northwards along the east bank.

Beresford, with the 3rd and 6th Divisions, was to cross by a pontoon bridge at Ustaritz and would be followed by 4th and 7th Divisions.

Hope was to advance up the coast direct on Bayonne with the 1st and 5th Divisions and three independent brigades.[1] His task was to protect the left flank and also to demonstrate against Bayonne.

The Light Division had the role of linking up the three attacks, which covered a front of some five miles, while Morillo's Division was to engage the troops under General Paris which were just south of Cambo.

The Battle

Just before dawn on **9 December, 1813**, a beacon was lit to signal the start of the battle.

Hill and Beresford both got across the Nive on a front of five miles against little opposition; three French divisions were opposed by four Allied divisions and Soult was forced to withdraw north towards Bayonne.

Hope also met little resistance and by nightfall was established on a line from the village of Biarritz on the coast through Anglet to Arcangues. He then reconnoitred up to the Adour; that done, he posted a line of picquets and sent the whole of 1st Division, together with Aylmer's Brigade, back to St Jean-de-Luz, leaving 5th Division in reserve, some three miles behind the picquets. He and his troops relaxed that night, satisfied with a good day's work and confident that they would continue to drive the French back next day.

But they were opposed by Soult, a brilliant strategist, and he had the great advantage that he was working on interior lines, i.e. he was on the inside of the circle, and could therefore easily move his troops from one sector to another. He could thus achieve surprise and attack with superior numbers at any one point before his opponents could react.

Soult decided to concentrate nine divisions (50,000 troops) just south of Bayonne and to attack Hope's scattered 30,000, in the hope of defeating them before Wellington could get any reinforcements across the Nive to come to their support.

Leaving their camp fires burning, the French, under General D'Erlon, moved on the night of the 9th from the east side of Bayonne to the southern outskirts, in heavy rain, and formed up, ready to attack Hope's unsuspecting picquets.

At 0900 on the morning of **10 December** Soult struck southwards down the roads to St Jean de Luz and Ustaritz, and the whole Allied line was driven back almost three miles.

The Light Division were the first to be engaged and were attacked by four French divisions under Clausel, who drove them back some two miles into Arcangues. Here they took up a strong position between the château and the church,[2] on a ridge some 1,200 yards long and protected on each flank by marshy areas.

No major French attack was made on them, but an unusual duel developed between some riflemen of the 43rd and some French artillery at a range of 400 yards. The riflemen had good cover in the church and churchyard and the enemy gunners could only fire at them by moving into exposed positions on a crest, where they were immediately picked off by the Light Division marksmen. Eventually the infantry seem to have won, and the French abandoned their 12 guns.

An attempt by the French to outflank Arcangues by moving further east along the Nive was thwarted by 7th Division, who had been posted there the night before by Wellington to protect the bridge at Ustaritz.

By early afternoon the French had been marching and fighting for over six hours in heavy rain and were exhausted; their morale was, in any case, not high and their advance ground to a halt.

Meanwhile, Reille had been thrusting down the coast road towards St Jean de Luz with three divisions, and he soon forced Hope's picquets to withdraw three miles to the area of the Château Barrouillet, the home of the Mayor of Biarritz[3].

Campbell's and Bradford's Portuguese Brigades, occupying hastily-prepared positions astride the road, managed to halt the first French division, but Reille sent in another, and also threatened the Allied right flank.

The 5th Division came up just in time to counter this development, but Hope's force was still out-numbered 3 to 2, and when Reille threw in a third French division, it looked as if the Allies might have to abandon their position. Then Aylmer's Brigade and elements of the 1st Division arrived from St Jean-de-Luz, just in time, and managed to check the enemy assault. The fighting continued until the afternoon, when, as at Arcangues, the French attack petered out and they withdrew. Honours were about even. The French had surprised and defeated the Allies, but they had not achieved the decisive victory they badly wanted.

All was quiet that night, but on the morning of the 11th Soult launched another attack, this time near the coast at Barrouillet. Despite the events of the day before, the Allies were taken by surprise yet again, were driven back for a mile and lost some 400 men in the first few minutes of the encounter.

Fortunately Hope now had ample troops to hand, including the 4th and 7th Divisions who had been moved by Wellington across to the west bank of the Nive. Soult realized that there was little hope of a decisive victory and he called off the operation; he had, however, struck a shrewd blow and checked the Allied advance. He suffered a setback himself on the night of 10 December when three whole battalions of German troops fighting with the French Army deserted with their officers and all their equipment.[4]

Undeterred, the French attacked for the third time on **12 December** and actually occupied the Mayor's Château at Barrouillet for a while. But they were driven out and could do no more. The Battle of the Nive was over, with total casualties of around 1,500 on each side.

THE BATTLEFIELD OF THE NIVE

Where To Go and What To See

This was another mobile battle covering a large area, from Cambo-les-Bains to Bayonne. Driving along the D.932 from Cambo-les-Bains northwards you pass through Ustaritz and Villefranque, and can see the areas of the crossings. It is interesting to note what an obstacle the Nive was, particularly in a flood.

The N.10 from Bayonne to St Jean-de-Luz passes through Anglet and also goes past the Lac de Mouriscot.

It is worthwhile making a detour to Arcangues. The church where the 43rd had their battle is still there.

Notes

1 Aylmer, Bradford and Campbell.
2 Both are still standing and in good repair, though the scars of the battle can still be seen.
3 Where the main road passes between the Lac de Mouriscot and the rounded hill – now a flyover on the N.10.
4 They had just heard news of Napoleon's defeat at Leipzig on 10 October.

Order of Battle: Nive – 12 December, 1813

ALLIES					FRENCH	
Division	*Commander*	*Strength*	*Brigades*		*Division*	*Strength*
	Hill (*Right*)				Foy	5,608
2nd	Stewart	8,480			Darmagnac	5,914
Portuguese	Le Cor	4,949			Abbé	6,372
Spanish	Morillo	5,129			Taupin	6,098
					Maransin	5,216
	Beresford (*Centre*)				Daricau	5,519
3rd	Colville	7,334			Leval	4,704
4th	Cole	6,585			Boyer	5,423
6th	Clinton	6,718			Villatte (Reserve)	5,397
7th		6,068			Paris (Brigade)	3,881
	Hope (*Left*)					
1st	Howard	6,898				
5th	Hay	4,553				
Light	Alten	4,970				
	Indep. Brigades					
	Aylmer	1,930				
	Bradford (Port)	2,185				
	Wilson (Port)	1,614				

Commander	Wellington		Soult
Strength	63,500		66,500
Cavalry	8,000		600
Guns	—		—
Casualties	1,500		1,400

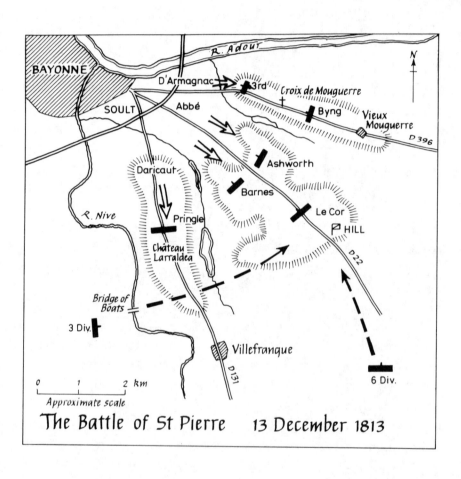

BAYONNE

R. Adour

D'Armagnac ⇒ 3rd ‖‖‖ Croix de Mouguerre ✝

SOULT   Abbé   Byng   Vieux Mouguerre   D 396

Daricaut

Ashworth

Barnes

R. Nive

Pringle

Le Cor ⚑ HILL

Château Larraldea   D 22

Bridge of Boats

3 Div.

Villefranque   D 131

6 Div.

0   1   2 km
Approximate scale

The Battle of St Pierre   13 December 1813

CHAPTER THIRTY-THREE

The Battle of St Pierre

Allied Positions

A problem for Wellington investing Bayonne in December, 1813, was the dispersion of his forces which forced him to delegate more than he liked. He had already seen Hope getting into trouble, and now he foresaw that Hill, isolated on the east side of the Nive, might be attacked and overrun before reinforcements could reach him.

Hill commanded a force of 14,000 men and 14 guns between the Nive and the Adour along high ground some three miles east of Bayonne, near St Pierre d'Irube. It was a strong position, about three miles wide, with both flanks protected by rivers, and there were only three possible lines of approach for the enemy. It would be secure, provided that he could hold out for at least four hours until reinforcements reached him across one of the two pontoon bridges over the Nive at Ustaritz and Villefranque.

But on the night of 12 December the river rose suddenly, due to storms further upstream, and the new bridge at Villefranque was swept away. The one at Ustaritz fortunately just held.

The country consisted of three distinct ridges, all running east from Bayonne, with ponds of swampy ground between them, so that any French attack had to be a frontal one and be split into three separate columns.

The main road from Bayonne to St-Jean-Pied-de-Port ran along the middle ridge. A secondary road ran parallel to it to the east through Mouguerre, while there was a third one to the west past the impressive Château Larraldea.

Hill sited his force to defend each of the three ridges, which were, from left to right, about 400, 900 and 500 yards wide.

On the left he put Pringle's Brigade[1] centred on the Château Larraldea. On the right he had Byng's Brigade;[2] the 3rd (the Buffs) were placed 800 yards forward on a ridge at Partouhirie, while the remainder of the brigade were in front of Vieux Mouguerre, from where they could most easily support the Allied centre.

In the centre, which was the likeliest enemy approach, Hill placed Barnes's Brigade,[3] together with Ashworth's Portuguese Brigade and 10 of his 14 guns.

In reserve he had Le Cor's Portuguese Division and two guns near his headquarters.

The Battle

At 0800 on 13 **December, 1813**, Hill could see dense columns of French infantry with artillery advancing confidently along all three approaches to his positions. There were seven infantry divisions altogether (35,000 men), with 22 guns, while an eighth division with cavalry support threatened the Allied rear. It was an impressive sight, but also a very worrying one, for Hill realized that he would have to face odds of 3 to 1 for at least four hours before any help could reach him via the bridge at Ustaritz.

On the left Pringle's Brigade of 1,800 was attacked by 5,000 French, but the enemy columns were broken up by the heavily wooded country and made little progress.

On the right things went less well. The Buffs were in a very exposed position, and were soon driven back to beyond Mouguerre, thus exposing the rear of Ashworth's line in the centre.

The main French attack was launched against the Allied centre, where Abbé's division, 6,000 strong, attacked with great vigour and, after three hours of fierce fighting, began to push Stewart's force steadily back.

"Dead or alive, we must hold our ground," declared Colonel Brown of the Gloucesters. General Barnes led the 92nd in a counter-charge, but the pressure continued

At a crucial moment there came a severe setback, when the 71st (Glasgow Highlanders) abandoned their positions on the orders of their commanding officer, Colonel Sir Nathaniel Peacock. He had only just arrived from England, to replace the gallant Colonel Cadogan who had died at Vitoria, and he did not fancy the front line. He fled to the rear, where Hill found him, pretending to drive forward some Portuguese ammunition carriers; the incident is said to have provoked Hill into swearing for only the second time in the whole Peninsular Campaign.[4]

Now came the crisis of the battle. The Allied centre was giving way and the guns were threatened. Hill summoned some troops from the right, and brought up his last reserve, a brigade from Le Cor's Division. Stewart personally re-formed the 71st and led them forward again. Ashworth and Barnes were both wounded, and Soult, sensing victory, reinforced the attack on the centre.

It was now 1200, four hours since the battle had begun.

Collecting every available man together into one body, Hill personally led them forward in a desperate last counter-attack. The Gordons charged, as they had at Maya, behind a solitary piper, who despite a broken leg, played them on with "Cogag na shee".

General Stewart, of Albuera fame, had every member of his staff struck down, but remained in the thick of the fighting. "A shell, Sir, very animating," he remarked, as one fell at his feet.

Hill's desperate action restored the situation. The French were checked and the Allied guns were saved. It was enough, for 6th Division, headed by Wellington, were now in sight, approaching Horlope, having marched since dawn, and crossed the river at Ustaritz. Close behind them were 3rd, 4th and 7th Divisions, who had used the bridge at Villefranque, which had been repaired.

Hill offered to hand over control of the battle to Wellington, but the Duke declined with the generous comment, "My dear Hill, the day's your own."

Hill gladly accepted, and went over to the offensive as soon as he could. He sent orders to Byng's Brigade to advance, but it had so few senior officers surviving that the ADC carrying the orders found himself leading the attack.

By about 1400 the Allies were in a position to undertake a general advance, and by 1500 the French were withdrawing.

Both sides later agreed that this battle "was one of the most desperate of the whole war", with some 5,000 casualties being incurred in three hours in one square mile. (The Allies lost 1,775 and the French over 3,000.)

It had been another "close-run thing", for it is doubtful how much longer Hill could have held on had the reinforcements not arrived when they did.

Summary

The battle of St Pierre was a rare example of Wellington trusting one of his subordinates in an independent command, and in this instance, with the ever-reliable Hill, it was fully justified.

How did it happen that 14,000 Allied troops with 12 guns managed to defeat 35,000 French with 22 guns? There are several reasons:

a. Soult could not deploy his superior strength because of the lie of the land, and only 16,000 French troops were actually engaged.

b. Hill had spotted the enemy moving forward on the evening of the 12th, and was thus able to get Barnes's Brigade into position, which was a decisive factor.

c. Hill made masterly use of his reserves.

THE BATTLEFIELD OF ST PIERRE

Where To Go

Take the D.52 east from Bayonne along the south bank of the Adour River. After passing under the motorway, take the next turning right and follow the signs to Croix de Mouguerre. After about a mile, at the top of the hill, there is a sharp turn left, and the Monument is 200 yards further on.

One can also drive along the road on the southern ridge, past the Château Larraldea.

What To See.

The Monument is itself of interest, having been erected by the French to honour Soult, who, "with inferior forces, foot by foot, defended this country for seven months against the army of Wellington".

There is a panoramic view of the countryside all round Bayonne and of the city itself, which lies to the west. The Adour is obvious, and the line of the Nive can be picked out. It is possible on a clear day to see the Pyrenees and the Greater Rhune.

The Mouguerre ridge is the northern or right-hand one held by Hill, and the other two can be identified to the south. Château Larraldea is a landmark.

Notes

1   28th, 38th and 39th.
2   3rd, 31st, 57th and 66th.
3   50th, 71st and 92nd.
4   The other ocasion was at Talavera (see page 95). Wellington's comment when told of the incident was, "Well. If Hill is starting to swear, we must all mind what we are about."

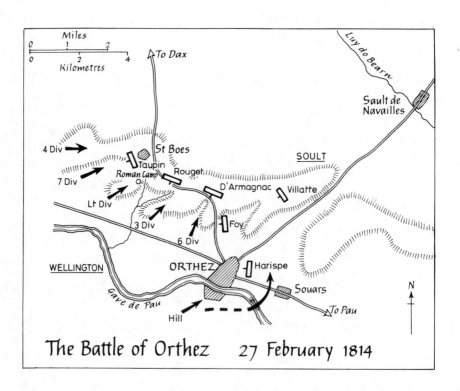

Miles

0   1   2

0   2   4

Kilometres

To Dax

Luy de Bearn

Sault de Navailles

4 Div

St Boes

SOULT

Taupin

Roman Camp

7 Div

Rouget

D'Armagnac

Villatte

Lt Div

3 Div

Foy

6 Div

WELLINGTON

ORTHEZ

Harispe

Gave de Pau

Souars

Hill

To Pau

N

The Battle of Orthez   27 February 1814

CHAPTER THIRTY-FOUR

The Battle of Orthez

The French Positions

On **24 February, 1814,** the Allied armies began their advance eastwards from Bayonne and crossed the Gave d'Oloron on a 15-mile front; Soult fell back and concentrated at Orthez, in order to defend the line of the Gave de Pau, which runs east and west through the town.

He had 36,000 men, and 48 guns, and he deployed them along a 500-foot ridge that runs for three miles to the west of the town parallel to the river. There were three spurs protruding towards the Gave with marshy, impassable valleys between them, and to the west of them a fourth spur ran parallel, with a Roman camp on it. At the west end of the main ridge was the village of St Boes; the main Bayonne-Pau road ran betwen the ridge and the river, as it still does today.

It was a strong position, but Soult was thinking of a further withdrawal. He had one division in reserve, but that was more to cover any retreat rather than to counter-attack.

Wellington's Plan[1]

By the morning of **27 February** Wellington had closed in on Orthez, and had moved five divisions and two cavalry brigades (31,000) north of the river, leaving Hill with 13,000 on the south bank opposite Orthez.

Hill was ordered to make demonstrations against Orthez from the south, while the main attack came in from the west along the Pau road. 4th Division was to attack St Boes from the west, supported by 7th Division. The Light Division was to seize the Roman Camp, from where Wellington planned to direct the battle. 3rd Division was to assault the westernmost point, and 6th Division the centre spur.

The Battle

At 0830 on **27 February** Ross's Brigade of 4th Division attacked St Boes from the west and captured the church, but were held up short of the village, which lay further east.

Picton's attack on the French centre was also checked, and there was then a pause of almost two hours while Wellington reorganized and made a new plan.

At 1130 the attack was renewed, with 7th Division replacing 4th Division. The 52nd were ordered to push north from the Roman Camp and take Taupin's Division opposite 7th Division in the flank. 6th Division were sent up the centre spur, and the French were thus under attack from three directions.

This fresh, coordinated attack was successful and, after two hours of hard fighting, the French gave way.

Hill had meantime maintained the pressure south of Orthez, and then sent a force of 12,000 to Souars, two miles upstream, where they seized a ford and so threatened Orthez from the east. This move also threatened Soult's line of retreat, and he now withdrew his whole force north-eastwards. He had lost over 4,000 men and 6 guns against 2,164 Allied casualties.

This time Wellington pursued the French vigorously and their retreat did not end till they reached Sault de Navailles, 10 miles to the north-east.

During the pursuit, Wellington received his third slight wound of the war, being struck by a spent bullet which drove his sword hilt into his side.[2] It could have been serious, but in fact only prevented him from riding for a week.

THE BATTLEFIELD OF ORTHEZ

Where To Go and What To See

Take the N.117 east out of Bayonne towards Pau, and Orthez is 35 miles east. When you reach the village of Baights de Bearn, you have arrived at the left of the Allied positions.

Turn north into Baights and at the crossroads turn east (right) through Castlebarbe to Orthez. The ridge occupied by Soult lies all the way to the north (left) and the four spurs can be identified.

The Battle of Orthez

In Orthez take the D.947 to St Boes, where the main fighting took place. The original buildings were so badly damaged in the battle that the village was re-built on a new site, which makes identification difficult.

From Orthez, drive east along the river to Souars, the scene of Hill's crossing of the Gave.

Notes

1   Wellington was sitting on a stone, writing his orders, wearing a white winter cloak, and one officer remarked to Colborne, "Did you see that old White Friar sitting there? I wonder how many men he is marking off to be sent into the next world." (*Colborne*, by Moore Smith, p.199.)

2   There are two versions of this incident. One is that Wellington and his Spanish aide, General Alava, were both laughing at a Portuguese soldier for saying that he had been "*offendido*", meaning "wounded". The next moment, Wellington was exclaiming that he too had been "*offendido*". The other account is that General Alava called out that he had had "a knock on the bottom". Wellington laughed, but was then "knocked" himself, and Alava said it was a punishment for laughing at him. (*Life of Arthur, Duke of Wellington*, Gleig, 1899, p.449. *Private Journal*, Larpent, 1853, II, p.187).

Order of Battle: Orthez – 12 December, 1813

ALLIES

Division	Commander	Strength	Brigades
	Hill		
2nd	Stewart	7,780	Byng
			Barnes
			O'Callaghan
			Harding (Port)
Portuguese	Le Cor	4,465	Da Costa
			Buchan
	Wellington		
3rd	Picton	6,626	Keane
			Brisbane
			Power (Port)
4th	Cole	5,952	Anson
			Ross
			Vasconcello (Port)
6th	Clinton	5,571	Pack
			Lambert
			Douglas (Port)
7th	Walker	5,643	Inglis
			Gardiner
			Doyle (Port)
Light	Alten	3,480	
	Hope (Bayonne)		
1st	Howard		
5th	Hay		
	Three Indep.		
	Brigades		Aylmer
			Wilson
		18,000	Bradford
Spanish	Freire, de Espana	16,000	

FRENCH

Division	Strength
D'Erlon	
Foy	4,600
Darmagnac	5,500
Reille	
Rouget	5,000
Taupin	5,600
Clausel	
Villatte	5,200
Harispe	6,600
Bayonne Garrison	17,000

	ALLIES	FRENCH
Commander	Wellington	Soult
Strength	44,400	37,000
Cavalry	3,373	3,200
Guns	54	48
Casualties	2,164	Over 4000

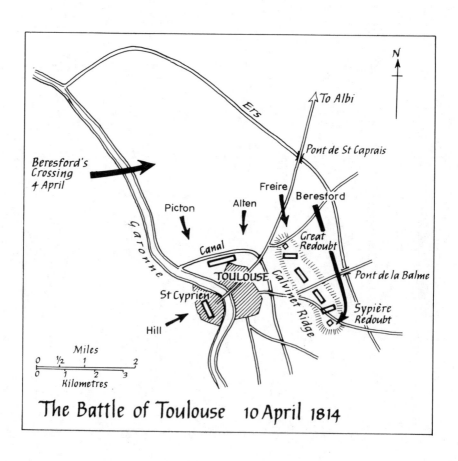

N

To Albi

Ers

Pont de St Caprais

Beresford's
Crossing
4 April

Freire

Beresford

Picton

Alten

Great
Redoubt

Canal

Garonne

TOULOUSE

Calvinet Ridge

Pont de la Balme

St Cyprien

Sypière
Redoubt

Hill

Miles

0   ½   1   2

0   1   2   3

Kilometres

The Battle of Toulouse   10 April 1814

CHAPTER THIRTY-FIVE

The Battle of Toulouse

French Positions

Following his defeat at Orthez on **27 February**, Soult withdrew to Toulouse on **24 March, 1814,** and prepared to defend it. He had 42,000 men and plenty of artillery, and the town was well fortified, protected by the Garonne to the west and the River Ers to the east. Its weak point was the 600-foot Calvinet Ridge, which dominated the town from the east. Soult concentrated nearly half his force here on a two-and-a-half-mile front, strengthened by earthworks and artillery positions.

Wellington's Plan

Wellington closed in on Toulouse on **26 March**, but he faced considerable difficulties and did not attack until 10 April. He had only 49,000 men, and 50 guns to Soult's 100, and the city was virtually inaccessible on three sides, due to water. The best approach was from the north and east, but this was the side furthest from his lines of communication, and he would have the 500-foot wide Garonne dividing his army. He also had to cross the Garonne before he could even launch his assault, and it was the largest river he had faced yet, except the Douro. His lines of communication stretched 150 miles to the Atlantic and he had only one battalion guarding them.

His first plan was to attack from the south, and on **27 March** a pontoon bridge was laid to the south of Toulouse, just below the junction with the Ariege, but it proved to be 80 foot too short and had to be dismantled.

On the **30th** a bridge was successfully built a mile further south, and Hill crossed with 13,000 men. But the roads on the other side proved to be so bad that Wellington decided that a major assault from that direction was not feasible and the force was recalled.

Wellington now planned to attack from the north, and on **4th April** his engineers managed to get a bridge across 15 miles north of the town. Beresford crossed with 19,000 men, but the river then flooded and the bridge was swept away. Beresford was now cut off and very vulnerable, but fortunately Soult did not attack, and by the **7th** the bridge was in operation again.

Wellington now moved his whole army across, except for Hill's corps, who were to demonstrate against the suburb of St Cyprien on the west bank of the Garonne. Picton's 3rd Division and Alten's Light Division were to do the same against the north edge of Toulouse between the Garonne and the Albi road.

The main attack was to be by Beresford with 4th and 6th Divisions against the south-east end of Calvinet Ridge, even though this meant that they had first to march south for nearly three miles under fire between the ridge and the River Ers to get into position. As soon as Beresford launched his attack, two Spanish divisions under Freire were to attack the north end of Calvinet Ridge.

It was a bold and complicated plan, and soon ran into trouble.

The Battle

At 0500 on Sunday, **10 April, 1814,** the Battle of Toulouse began. As at Badajoz, it happened to be Easter Day.

Hill manoeuvred skilfully, but Soult was not deceived. Picton, instead of feinting, disobeyed orders and launched a full-scale attack, which was duly repulsed with heavy loss.

Beresford set out on his long approach march, but was badly slowed down by mud and the swampy ground along the Ers. After about a mile he ordered his gunners to open fire on the French in order to protect his troops.

Unfortunately, when Freire heard the guns, he thought it was Beresford making his attack, and so launched his two Spanish divisions into their assault. They advanced gallantly, but met the French in full strength and were thrown back in disarray, whereupon Wellington remarked rather unkindly that he "had never before seen 10,000 men running a race".[1]

Beresford meanwhile pushed on and was finally in position to attack the Sypière Redoubt from the south-east. 4th and 6th Divisions advanced in line, and the French commander, General Taupin, unwisely launched a counter-attack against them with two brigades in column. As always in the Peninsular War, the line won; General Taupin was killed and his attack was repulsed. Beresford's force pushed on northwards, but against stiff resistance.

Around 1400 there was a lull in the fighting, whereupon the belligerent Picton attacked once again, supported by the Spaniards, who lost 1,000 men, including four generals, but made little progress. Their gallant efforts did, however, relieve the pressure on Beresford, who renewed his advance. In fierce fighting, the Redoubt of the Augustins changed hands five times.

Finally, at about 1700 the French began to withdraw, and by 1800 the battle had petered out, with Soult abandoning Calvinet Ridge except for a small bridgehead across the Canal.

Welington had won the day, but he was in a difficult position. He had lost 4,568 men[2] against 3,236 French, and his troops were exhausted. He expected Soult to counter-attack, he was short of ammunition, his army was divided, and all supplies had to come across the Garonne. But, to his relief, Soult abandoned Toulouse on the night of the 11th and retreated to Carcassone, leaving behind 1,600 wounded and most of his guns.

On **12th April 1814,** Wellington entered Toulouse in triumph, and at 1700 that evening Colonel Frederick Ponsonby of the 12th Light Dragoons rode in from Paris with the first news of Napoleon's abdication.

THE BATTLEFIELD OF TOULOUSE

Where To Go

The city has expanded vastly since 1814, and the area of the battlefield is completely built over. It is still possible, however, among all the buildings, to identify the main features of the battle.

The River Garonne flows to the west of the city, and the Ers to the east, crossed by the Pont de Balme.

The crossing places over the Garonne can be worked out, and the Canal still encircles the old town; it is now called the Canal du Midi.

Approaching Toulouse from the west, as Wellington did, one drives through the suburb of St Cyprien.

Driving east along the wide Allèe Jean Jaures, one crosses the Canal just south of the railway station. Straight ahead is some obvious high ground, which is the northern end of the Calvinet Ridge, also known as Mont Rave. On it, close to the Observatory, can be seen an obelisk, which is a memorial to the French soldiers who fell on 10 April, 1814, and to the people of Toulouse.

The road leading north-east out of Toulouse is still called Route d'Albi. The streets in the Calvinet district are named after the French commanders of 1814 e.g. Rue Soult, Rue D'Erlon, Rue Reille, etc.

Notes

1   It was before the days of the London Marathon!
2   1,900 were Spanish and 400 were the result of Picton's attacks.

28. **San Sebastian.** The fortress as it was in 1813, viewed from the British positions to the east. "A small compact town, only some 400 yards square, and dominated by the Castle on the height of La Mota". (p.181) (*National Army Museum, London*)

29. **The Bidassoa.** Cadoux's Bridge over the Bidassoa at Vera, looking north to the Great Rhune in the background. "The crossing of the Bidassoa was a masterpiece of both planning and execution". (p.207)

30. **The Bidassoa.** The river at Vera with Cadoux's Bridge and the village.

31. **St Pierre.** The memorial at Mouguerre on the battlefield of St Pierre, to Marshal Soult, who "with inferior forces, foot by foot, defended this country for seven months against Wellington's Army." The Great Rhune is just visible in the background. (p.226)

Order of Battle: Toulouse – 10 April, 1814

ALLIES				FRENCH	
Division	*Commander*	*Strength*		*Division*	*Strength*
	Wellington				
3rd	Picton	4,566		Daricau	3,839
Light	Alten	4,275		Darmagnac	5,022
Spanish	Freire	7,916		Taupin	5,455
Spanish	Morillo	2,001		Maransin	3,717
				Villatte	4,609
	Beresford			Harispe	5,084
4th	Cole	5,363		Travot	
6th	Clinton	5,693		(conscripts)	7,267
	Hill				
2nd	Stewart	6,940			
Portuguese	Le Cor	3,952			

Commander	Wellington	Soult
Strength	49,000	42,000
Cavalry	3,617	2,700
Guns	48	100
Casualties	4,568	3,236

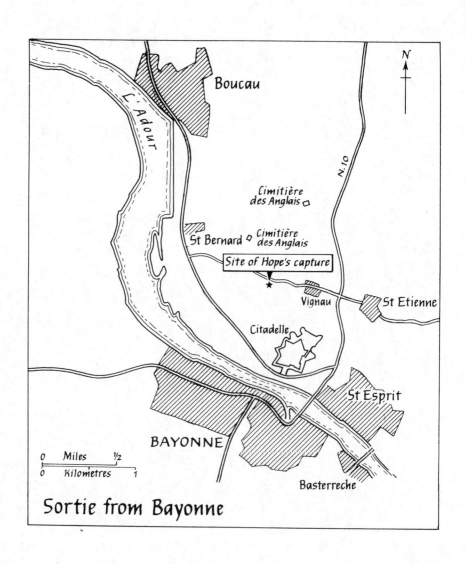

Sortie from Bayonne

CHAPTER THIRTY-SIX

The Sortie from Bayonne

Background

When the dramatic news of Napoleon's abdication reached Wellington at Toulouse on **12 April, 1814,** he promptly informed Soult, who in turn sent a message at once to the Governor of the besieged garrison of Bayonne, General Thouvenot.

The French garrison numbered about 14,000 and held positions on both the north and south banks of the River Adour.

The besieging force was under the command of Lieutenant-General Sir John Hope, and consisted of 1st Division north of the Adour, and 5th Division south of the river. There were a further three infantry brigades and also one cavalry brigade, and the two divisions were linked by a pontoon bridge across the Adour west of Bayonne.

The Allied line encircling Bayonne to the north consisted of a line of outposts, supported by picquets, and extended from the Adour east of Bayonne through St Etienne to the Adour at St Bernard. The left was held by 5th Brigade of 5th Division. The centre was the responsibility of 2nd Guards Brigade,[1] while the 1st Guards Brigade[2] held the right of the line. Hinuber's German Brigade was in support on the left, with the remainder of 1st Division encamped around Boucau.

Rumours of Napoleon's abdication and an armistice had reached the Allied troops, and there seems to have been a distinct relaxation in their vigilance. Indeed, one commander is said to have gone round on the evening of the **13th** telling his men that they would soon be home with their wives and sweethearts.

But the French had other ideas, and were busy planning one final sortie. They considered attacking from their positions south of the river, capturing the pontoon bridge, and then assaulting 1st Division from both east and west, but decided that that was too risky. Instead, they settled for a strong sortie northwards from the Citadel at dawn on 14 April against the Allied picquets around St Etienne.

The Sortie

At about 0200 on **14 April, 1814,** the relaxed calm in the Allied lines round Bayonne was disturbed by the arrival of two deserters from the French garrison. They were brought to Major-General Hay, who was the General Officer of the Night, but he could not speak French, and so sent them to Major-General Hinuber of the King's German Legion who discovered from them that a sortie was due to be made at dawn.

Hay apparently did not believe the men's story, for he did not order any additional precautions to be taken. Hinuber, on the other hand, put his men under arms and passed the information on to General Hope.

Thouvenot meanwhile, hearing about the deserters, brought the time of his sortie forward from dawn to 0300, and at that time, the assault was duly launched.

A feint attack was made by Lieutenant-General Baron Abbé against Anglet and Bellevue, while the main assault, 3,000 strong, under General Maucomble, was launched northwards from the Citadel. The Allied picquets were taken by surprise and soon overwhelmed.

The right-hand column (95th Regiment) captured St Etienne, and the only house retained by the Allies was one occupied by a picquet of the 38th, under Captain Forster, who held out.

Major-General Hay was killed in St Etienne, just after he had belatedly ordered it to be held "to the last extremity".

Both the other two French columns broke through, and considerable confusion reigned for a while; Major-General Stopford, commanding 2nd Guards Brigade, was wounded and was replaced by Colonel Guise. The left-hand French column (82nd Regiment), supported by gunboats on the river, attacked Basterreche.

As the fighting developed, General Hope rode forwards towards St Etienne to see what was happening. He had two officers with him, Lieutenant Moore, a nephew of Sir John Moore who was his ADC, and Captain Herries of the Quartermaster General's Department.

He came up in the darkness "by a hollow road which led close behind the line of picquets, one of which had been improperly withdrawn by an officer of the Guards, and the French thus lined both banks". For some strange reason, he seems to have been in plain clothes.

The party was ambushed by 20 men of the 82nd Regiment, and to quote General Thouvenot's despatches, "were taken by Mr Pigeon, Adjutant-Sergeant-Major of the 70th, by Sergeant Beregeot and

Voltigeur Bonencia, of the 82nd. I named Mr Pigeon Sub-Lieutenant on the field of battle."

Napier's account of the incident paints the scene well: "A shot struck him [the General] in the arm, and his horse, a large one, as was necessary to sustain the gigantic warrior, received 8 bullets and fell upon his leg; his followers had by this time escaped from the defile, yet two of them, Captain Herries and Mr Moore, a nephew of Sir John Moore, seeing his helpless state, turned back and endeavoured amidst the heavy fire of the enemy, to draw him from beneath his horse. While thus engaged, they were struck down with dangerous wounds; the French carried him off, and Hope was again severely hurt in the foot by an English bullet before they gained the Citadel."

The serious situation for the Allies was largely saved by the efforts of Major-General Hinuber, who rallied the troops round St Etienne, launched a counter-attack from St Esprit, and drove the French out.

The left French column was meanwhile repulsed by 1st Guards Brigade under Colonel Maitland.

The French bridgehead north of the Citadel was now under attack from both east and west, and Thouvenot ordered his troops to withdraw. Dawn had broken and the Allies had recovered from the confusion of the night.

The Allies had come close to defeat, and had lost 826 men, 231 of whom were prisoners, though the French claimed that the figure was three times higher. They themselves lost 910, all a tragic waste, when peace had been declared.

The siege continued for almost another two weeks and did not end until **26 April,** when Thouvenot accepted news of the armistice at Toulouse, and surrendered the same day, nearly three weeks after Napoleon had abdicated.

THE SORTIE FROM BAYONNE

Where to go

Head northwards across the Adour by the N.10 road bridge, and the Citadel can be seen on the north bank, to the west of the bridge.

Continue north along the N.10 for half a mile to a crossroads just beyond a water tower. St Bernard is then to the west, along the Rue de Laharie, which leads to the scene of General Hope's capture, and also to the Coldstream Guards Cemetery. St Etienne is to the right (east).

Return to the N.10 and go north from the water tower just over a mile, and the Third Guards Cemetery is on the left of the road.

What to see

The Citadel

This can be seen well from the south bank of the river, and is little changed from 1814.

St Etienne

Now completely built up, but the area of the fighting can be identified.

Lord Hope's Capture

About half a mile west down the Rue de Laharie, at the junction with the Chemin de Hausses, is a small copse, and it must have been close to here that General Hope was wounded and captured.

Coldstream Guards Cemetery

This is further west along the Rue de Laharie, just east of St Bernard, and is marked on the maps as 'Cimetière des Anglais'; it dates back to 1814, with some interesting graves. It also marks the site of the Coldstream Guards Camp.

Scots Guards Cemetery

A similar cemetery for the Third Guards is also marked on the map just west of the N.10.

The Crossing of the Adour

It is intriguing to drive to the estuary of the Adour west of Bayonne, and try to work out where the bridge of boats was built on 23 February, 1814.

Notes

1   *2nd Guards Brigade* (Stopford)
    1st Battalion Coldstream Guards
    1st Battalion Third Guards
2   *1st Guards Brigade* (Maitland)
    1st Battalion First Guards
    3rd Battalion First Guards

A Short Reading List

Since this is but a guide to the Peninsular War, it does not warrant a comprehensive Bibliography of every source and every possible reference book. Instead I have made two very short selections of books which those interested in the subject might enjoy reading and also be able to obtain without undue difficulty.

The 'First XI' are 'easy to read' books that give a general picture of the campaign and those involved, while the 'Second XI' are more specialized; they elaborate on the information in the 'First XI', but without becoming involved in delving into despatches, diaries and other primary sources.

For those who want to research further, there are four classic historic accounts of the campaign, which are:

> *Wellington's Despatches*, edited by Colonel Gurwood, 1834–39 and 1844.
> Fortescue's *History of the British Army*, 1899–1930.
> Napier's *History of the War in the Peninsula*, 1850.
> Oman's *A History of the Peninsular War*, 1903–30.

The First XI

ALDINGTON, Richard, 'The Duke', 1943
BRYANT, Arthur, 'Years of Victory. 1802–1812.' 1944
BRYANT, Arthur, 'The Age of Elegance. 1812–1822.' 1950
BRETT-JAMES, A, 'Wellington at War. 1794–1815'. 1961
BRETT-JAMES, A, 'Life in Wellington's Army'. 1972
GATES, David, 'The Spanish Ulcer'. 1986
GLOVER, Michael, 'The Peninsular War'. 1974
GLOVER, Michael, 'Wellington's Army'. 1977
GRIFFITHS, Paddy, 'Wellington Commander'. 1985

LONGFORD, Elizabeth, 'Wellington. The Years of the Sword'. 1985
WELLER, Jac, 'Wellington in the Peninsula'. 1973

The Second XI

GLOVER, Michael, 'Wellington as Military Commander.' 1973
GUEDALLA, Philip, 'The Duke'. 1931
HARRIS, Rifleman, 'Recollections of Rifleman Harris'. 1848
HUMBLE, R, 'Napoleon's Peninsular Marshals'. 1973
KINCAID, J, ' Adventures in the Rifle Brigade and Random
    Shots from a Rifleman'. 1981
LACHOUQUE, H, 'Napoleon's War in Spain'. 1982
OMAN, Carola, 'Sir John Moore'. 1953
ROGERS, H.C.B, 'Wellington's Army'. 1979
WARD, S.G.P, 'Wellington's Headquarters'. 1957
WARD. S.G.P, 'Wellington'. 1963
WHEELER, W, 'The Letters of Private Wheeler'. 1951

Wellington

Wellington so dominates the Peninsular War that the reasons why need to be studied. It would be easy to write reams, but this is an attempt at a two-page analysis.

Certain characteristics emerge:

a. *Toughness*

He was mentally and physically very tough, leading a spartan life, working from 0600 to midnight, riding 30–50 miles a day, always on the go and in control, an "Iron Duke" indeed.

b. *Self-Confidence*

He had tremendous confidence in himself, his capabilities and his decisions. He was bold too, as was proved at Oporto and Salamanca. But no decisions were taken without careful long-sighted calculations, a thorough reconnaissance and a full grasp of the problem.

c. *A Clear, Sharp Mind*

He had a tremendous grasp of detail, be it in brilliant strategic thinking or planning the supply of bullets and biscuits.

He grasped points quickly, and was particularly good at anticipating events and so being at the right place at the right time. He himself observed that he knew more than most people of what was going on the other side of the hill.

His practical approach shows in his laconic speech, and his simple, brief style of writing.

d. *Close Personal Control*

He controlled everything and everyone all the time. He gave clear, concise orders, expected them to be obeyed exactly, and would check that they were.

On the debit side, he seldom delegated (till the very end of the campaign).

On the plus side, he won many battles (and above all, Waterloo) by his close control of events, seeing what needed to be done and seeing that it was done (which Beresford failed to do at Albuera).

He led from the front and was amazingly lucky not to become a casualty.

e. *Care of his Troops*

He took great pride in his army, and great care in looking after it. "I know of no point more important," he declared, "than closely to attend to the comfort of the soldiers." He never asked too much of his men, and could claim as a result that they never failed him.

What were his weaknesses? He was certainly aloof and severe, though he could be remarkably human at moments.

His main failure was his inability to delegate, and it is interesting to think what would have happened if he had been a casualty in the first three or four years of the war.

Why Did He Win?

He consistently defeated skilled and experienced French commanders, and some of the reasons were:

a. His battles were nearly all well and carefully planned, so that he fought, as far as possible, on his own terms.

b. His close control of the battle at all times, and effective reaction when crises occurred.

c. His reading of his opponents' minds – and so his ability to be one move ahead.

d. He organized and trained a very high-class army.

Verdict

As he said himself the morning after Waterloo, "I don't think it would have done if I had not been there."

The Peninsular Army

We tend to think of the Peninsular Army as being primarily British, but by 1810 it was almost half Portuguese. Wellington set out from the start to train the Portuguese as soldiers, and gave this task to General William Beresford, who did it most successfully. He was helped by British officers who received two ranks' promotion on being seconded to the Portuguese Army.

Wellington also had under command the *King's German Legion* (K.G.L.) who had been formed in 1803 from Hanoverian refugees to England. They were highly professional and their cavalry were outstanding. One of the K.G.L. officers, General Alten, took over command of the Light Division from 1812.

Organization

Divisions
The Peninsular Army eventually consisted of eight infantry divisions (numbered 1 to 7, plus the Light Division.) Each was 5–6,000 strong and was commanded by a general to whom Wellington gave orders direct.[1] They were all self-contained, except for cavalry.

The *Light Division* was smaller (4,000) and contained the "Light Infantry" regiments[2] who had been specially trained (initially by Sir John Moore) as mobile troops and skirmishers. The Division had its own artillery (Ross's Battery) and its own cavalry (1st Hussars, K.G.L.).

Brigades
Each division contained two or three Brigades, each 1,500 to 2,000 strong and named after their commander, e.g. Anstruther's Brigade, Kempt's Brigade.

Wellington put one Portuguese brigade into some divisions, and also had two independent Portuguese brigades.

Battalions

Each Brigade contained two or three "battalions", each of 550–1,000 infantrymen, who were organized into ten Companies of up to 100 men. The largest men usually joined the "grenadier" company, who held the right flank, while the nimblest men went into the "light" company, who acted as skirmishers.[3] The battalion was, and still is, the basic unit of the British Army.

The system of numbering battalions was complex. Each battalion belonged to a "Regiment", which might consist of one or more battalions.[4] The Regiment had a number (dating back to 1751) and also a territorial or other title (dating back to 1782). Thus, for example, you had the 29th (Worcestershire Regiment) or the 71st (The Gordon Highlanders).

As today, there was intense Regimental pride and loyalty, and, although soldiers were not necessarily recruited from their regimental area, they soon acquired and were prepared to die for its spirit and traditions.

There were over 100 regiments in the British Army at this time as well as three Guards regiments; more than 50 different Line regiments served in the Peninsular War. (see *Appendix G*)

The British Soldier

Unlike the French troops, who were conscripted, the British soldiers were all volunteers (some less willing than others perhaps!). They were mostly men from the lowest level of society, and they were commanded by officers who were not usually from the aristocracy (except perhaps in the cavalry and the Guards), but were gentlemen, whose main virtues were their natural leadership and their courage. It was a combination that worked remarkably well; the men followed their officers, and both fought gallantly and effectively. Officers from generals downwards led from the front, and at Albuera, for example, 2nd Brigade had 1,054 casualties out of 1,651, and the senior surviving officer was a Captain; but they did not retreat.

There was a small element of rogues and ruffians, perhaps ten per cent, and it was them that Wellington described as "the scum of the earth", not the majority of his army, of whom he was extremely proud. It is a pity that the second half of this quotation is all too often ignored, for he went on to add, "It is really wonderful that we should have made them the fine fellows they are."

Life was tough for all the lower classes in those days, and punishments were severe in civilian life as much as in the Army, where discipline had to be even tougher. The standard punishment was flogging, and a man might receive 100 lashes and carry on with his duties; some might get 1,000. But, as Private Wheeler commented when two men were flogged for dropping out on the Retreat to Corunna, and the rest were made to watch by General Craufurd, "If he flogged two, he saved hundreds."

The British soldier was a rough, tough fellow, but he was the equal of any in Europe, particularly when properly led. The deciding factor was the pride he felt in his Regiment, which was his family and his life. "Come what may, in brawls or battles, he would defend the honour of the Regiment. There was never a court martial charge of cowardice against a man in the ranks."[5]

It was a tough life, but most of them were used to hardship. They were paid a shilling a day (5p),[6] but half of it was deducted for food. They also had to pay 2p a week for washing and about 1p a week for cleaning materials, plus one day's pay a year for the Chelsea Pensioners. So there was not much left to spend or save.

The daily food ration was 1 lb of meat, 1 lb of biscuit (or 1½ lbs of bread) and 1 quart of beer (or 1 pint of wine or one third of a pint of spirit.) The women got half rations, (which would hardly be acceptable today!)

A soldier was issued with two pairs of shoes, which were the same for both feet (a practice which continued till 1847). When campaigning he slept in the open until 1813 when tents were issued, but it was 20 to a small tent, and as one soldier commented, "none could turn without general consent, and the word 'Turn' given." He carried some 60 lbs of equipment, including a large cooking pot, for the men did all their own cooking in groups of six; the weight he carried was one of the reasons why the French generally marched slightly faster than the British.

Army wives were authorized on campaigns on a scale of 4–6 per company of 100 men, and they were drawn by ballot. They accompanied the Regiment everywhere, even into battle, where they tended the wounded; they were proud, tough and intensely loyal – and also skilled and incorrigible pilferers! They cooked, mended and looked after the sick; they sometimes gave birth on the line of march, and would catch up the same day. If their husband died, they usually married again with 48 hours.

In addition to the "official" wives, there were thousands of local girls (4,500 in 1813) who were picked up during the campaign and "followed the drum". But in 1814 they were all sent home unless they were married.

Training

There were two basic infantry weapons – the musket and the rifle.

The Brown Bess musket had been the standard weapon for the Army since the 1720s. It was a smooth-bore flintlock, 39 inches long and weighed 9 lbs 1 oz. It took 20 drill movements to load and 7 to reload; it could fire only 3 rounds a minute, and each man carried 60 rounds in a waterproof pouch. It had a 17-inch detachable bayonet.

The bore was 0.75 inches and the ball was 0.681 inches, which did not encourage accuracy, and you were unlikely to hit the man you aimed at over 30 paces. Misfires occurred perhaps twice in 13 shots, and it was useless in the rain (as at Albuera). It fouled up badly after 25–30 rounds.

The aim was to produce the maximum fire-power, and the British Army developed controlled "rolling fire", whereby sections fired in disciplined sequence to produce almost continuous volleys; they carried out "live firing" on training, which the French did not.

In addition to musketry, the infantry soldier had to learn how to manoeuvre rapidly under fire, and a battalion was trained to carry out the "Nineteen Movements" – Line into Column, Column into Line, Line into Square, and so on. The standard formation was "the Line", normally two-deep, which meant that every man could fire his weapon; but it also meant that he must stand still, shoulder to shoulder, and not duck even if he saw a cannon ball coming straight at him!

The answer to a cavalry attack was to "Form Square", which took a battalion about 40 seconds. The front rank knelt down and presented a wall of bayonets which no horse would face; three ranks stood behind them, firing controlled volleys over their heads. The officers commanded from the centre of the square, and the gunners, having fired till the last possible moment, then took refuge inside the square.

Marching was normally in columns, protected by cavalry, and a normal day's march might be around 20 miles.

The Baker Rifle

The Baker Rifle was issued in 1800 to just two regiments, the 60th

(The American Rifles) and the 95th (The Rifle Regiment). Being rifled, it was more accurate than the musket, but slower to load; it was used to good effect by these two regiments for sniping and skirmishing, and a company of the 60th was usually allotted to each brigade for this role.

Cavalry

Until 1811 Wellington was very short of cavalry and had only six regiments, though the number then rose to 15 by 1813. They were mostly inexperienced in war and lacked training, and, as a result, tended to get out of control in battle, which made them unpopular with Wellington.

They consisted of heavy cavalry (Dragoons and the Household Cavalry) whose role was set-piece attacks, and light cavalry (Light Dragoons and Hussars), who were used for scouting, screening and patrolling, as well as mobile actions.

Their organization was four squadrons each of 200 men, forming a Regiment.

Artillery

The artillery were either field or horse and the normal unit was a battery of 6 guns (5×6 pounders and 1×5.5" howitzer). There were also 3 and 9 pounders, and heavier siege guns. Shrapnel was just coming into use, and was extremely effective against French columns.

Gunners were usually big, strong men, able to manhandle their guns.

Wellington was almost always short of artillery and usually had only 2 guns per 1,000 men, whereas the French had 5 per 1,000.

Wellington's Headquarters

Wellington was C-in-C of the Peninsular Army and refused to have a Deputy or a Second-in-Command. He had a remarkably small headquarters and depended on three key figures.

The first was his *Quartermaster General*, who handled all administration, and also much of the operational side. Except for one year (1812), the post was held by the brilliant Major-General George Murray.[7] The second was the *Adjutant General*, who ran the personnel aspect, discipline and statistics. From 1809–13, this post was held by

Major-General Charles Stewart (later Lord Londonderry). The third post was the *Military Secretary*, who ran all Wellington's correspondence, and was held from 1810 to 1814 by Major Lord Fitzroy Somerset (later Lord Raglan).

There were nine Departments within the headquarters; they were: Quartermaster General; Adjutant General; Military Secretary; Commissariat; Chief of Artillery; Chief Engineer; Surgeon General; Apothecary General; Paymaster General.

Supplies were the responsibility of the *Commissariat*, who had a thankless task, but became extremely efficient in the end.

Wellington kept tight control of his headquarters and the administration of his Army, and insisted on knowing exactly what everyone was doing.

There were remarkably few full-time staff officers in the headquarters. There were only 10 in the whole British Army, and in 1813 Wellington had 4 of them for 60,000 men. The remainder were untrained Regimental officers reluctantly seconded from their units to work on the staff. It worked, largely because each division was almost entirely self-supporting.

Communications

Communications were extremely slow and always a problem. All letters and despatches had to be copied out in longhand.[8] Routine letters were carried by "letter parties" of the Corps of Guides, who covered 120 miles in 48 hours, by organizing staging posts.

Important messages, in or out of battle, were delivered by ADCs. They took pride in being well-mounted, and if Wellington said "Quick", they would cover 4 miles in 18 minutes or 12 miles in an hour.

ADC's

ADC's were an important element of the headquarters, and Wellington once commented that he would be as careful over recommending an ADC to a general as "in recommending a girl for a man to marry".

The scale of ADC's was 1 for a Major-General, 2 for a Lieutenant-General and 3 for a C-in-C, but Wellington usually had up to 7, on whom he placed great reliance.[9]

Wellington's Routine

Wellington's capacity for work was astonishing, and a typical day might be:

0600–0700	Write letters and despatches. Breakfast.
1000–1400	See Heads of Departments.
1400–1800	Ride.
1800	Supper.
2100–2400	More correspondence.

His great relaxation was riding, and he much enjoyed his hunting; his staff soon learned not to bother him with unimportant matters on days when there was a meet.

Intelligence

Much of Wellington's success was due to his outstanding intelligence system. He nearly always knew more about the French strengths, plans, moves and operations than did their own commanders.[10]

Above all, he had the support of the Portuguese and Spanish people, and the guerrillas, who constantly provided valuable information, for which they were paid. He also employed *Observing Officers*, such as Major Colquhoun Grant and Lieutenant Andrew Leith Hay, who operated most skilfully up to 150 miles behind the enemy lines and reported back.

He organized a network of *Correspondents* throughout Spain, who collected and passed back information. They were from all walks of life, and included Dr Patrick Curtis, Rector of the Irish College in Salamanca, and the painter Goya, who used to glean news from French generals he painted, and pass it on.

Finally, he had *Captain George Scovell* of the 57th, who was a brilliant cryptographer and regularly broke the French cyphers, particularly the Great Paris Cypher, so that Wellington knew the contents of messages from Napoleon as well as local plans. The similarity to the 'Ultra' story in World War Two is striking!

The Supply System

Wellington had to build up his supply system from scratch, and it was one of his greatest achievements that he did it so successfully. It was also one of his greatest advantages over the French, in that he was always able to keep his army supplied with food and ammunition, which the enemy could not do without plundering. Approximately 80% of the Peninsula was too infertile to provide food for an army, but Wellington overcame this by using his sea power to bring supplies.[11] He then organized depots 50 miles behind the lines, while in front of them were "forward supply depots", from where regimental mule trains collected their rations.

The task of supplying the army fell on the Commissariat, who were in 1808 described by an angry Wellesley as "very incompetent and . . . incapable of managing anything outside a counting house". But by 1813 they were providing 100,000 lbs of biscuits every day, as well as 200,000 lbs of forage, and 300 head of cattle to be slaughtered for meat. They used some 12,000 mules, and by 1813 seldom failed to look after the needs of an army of 81,000 men and 20,000 animals, even when it advanced from Portugal to France.

Wellington's final verdict was that "much of the sucess of this army has been owing to its being well supplied with provisions".

Body and Soul
Medical

Medical resources were extremely limited. Each infantry battalion had one surgeon and two assistant surgeons, who dealt with the wounded on the spot, often by amputation. The other normal treatment was bleeding, which can hardly have helped. One wounded officer had 36 leeches applied to his head; another, more lucky, was treated by a Portuguese Army doctor who prescribed "at least two bottles of Madeira a day". He survived and lived to be 75!

The wounded were usually left in local houses or hospitals, but Major-General James McGrigor, who came out in 1812 as Chief Medical Officer, established portable hospitals which moved with the army and saved many lives.

Sickness was a constant and considerable problem, particularly from 1812 when reinforcements brought with them an epidemic of malaria or Walcheren Fever. The sick rate was at times up to 33%, and in 1812 9,000 men died in action, but 25,000 died in hospitals from sickness.

Spiritual

There was a Chaplain on the strength of every regiment, thanks to the Duke of York who in 1796 set up the Army Chaplain's Department.

Chaplains were scarce in the Peninsular Army, but there were five during the Retreat to Corunna, and the Reverend H. J. Symons, Chaplain to the Guards Brigade, read the prayers at Moore's burial.

Wellington had an excellent chaplain, Samuel Briscall, at his headquarters, and "was very regular in attending Divine Service". He was constantly trying to obtain more Chaplains for his army.

The Verdict

The final verdict on the Peninsular Army is covered by three quotations.

Michael Glover comments: "Wellington created one of the finest armies of any country at any time in history. It was essentially a personal achievement."[12]

Wellington himself remarked in 1813: "It is probably the most complete machine for its number in Europe."[13]

He also said later: "I have the satisfaction of reflecting that, having tried them frequently, they have never failed me."[14]

Notes

1 From 1813 he formed 'corps', consisting of two or more divisions under an independent commander, such as Hill, Hope or Beresford.

2 Initially they were 43rd, 52nd and 95th, and by 1814 had been joined by 51st, 68th and 71st.

3 At other times the "light" company was on the left flank.

4 Some regiments had more than one battalion, in which case the number of the battalion preceded the regimental number in the title, e.g. 5/60th, would be the 5th Battalion of the 60th Regiment. If the regiment had only one battalion, the figure '1' was usually omitted, as being unnecessary.

5 *Wellington's Army*, Michael Glover, p 73.

6 The Guards got 5½p and the cavalry 6½p.

7 Among other achievements he had by 1810 initiated the first accurate maps of Portugal (¼inch to the mile), and this gave Wellington a distinct advantage over the French, who had no good maps.

8 One must here record Wellington's famous, masterly comments on excessive paperwork: "If I attempted to answer the futile mass of correspondence that surrounds me, I would be debarred from all serious business of campaigning. As long as I hold an independent position I shall use my utmost endeavour to ensure that my officers are not prevented by the scribbling of mere quill drivers from attending to their first duty which is the training and care of the private men under their command."

9   Compare this with Monty's all-important Liaison Officers.

10 It is interesting to compare this happy situation with the Waterloo campaign, when the situation was very much reversed, and it was Wellington who exclaimed, "Humbugged, by God".

11 He remarked, "One must follow the history of a biscuit from its leaving Lisbon until it reaches a soldier's mouth on the frontier."

12 *Wellington's Army*, M. Glover, p. 183.

13 Wellington, 21 November, 1813.

14 Glover, op. cit, p. 183.

The French Army

The French armies in the Peninsula were organized along very similar lines to Wellington's, except that the soldiers were conscripts, not volunteers.

The basic formation was the "division", which were on occasions formed into "corps" of two or more divisions. Each division had a number and was also named after its commander e.g. 3rd. Ney's Division; they were usually about 4,000 strong.

Each division consisted of two to three "Brigades", containing a number of "Battalions".[1] Battalions were 8-900 strong and had six companies, one of which was a "grenadier" company and one was a "voltigeur" (light) company.

The French had plenty of excellent cavalry, but seldom had scope to use them effectively, the main occasions being Albuera and Fuentes de Onoro.

They also had considerably more artillery than Wellington, but were prevented from using it by the terrain and a lack of horses. Their commanders tended to concentrate their artillery, whereas Wellington preferred using his guns in small groups fighting with each division.

The French had troops of many nationalities fighting for them, including Poles, Swiss, Germans, Irish and Italians. There were also some units of disaffected Spaniards called *"Juramentado"*, but they were unreliable.

Towards the end of the war, when the fighting was in or near France, French "National Guard" units were formed, organized into "cohorts" (battalions). They fought bravely, but were poorly equipped and not very effective.

There were three main differences between the French and Allied armies.

First, the French believed in the attack, and advanced with great élan in column, a technique that had proved extremely successful over the previous 16 years. But they failed to realize that such tactics were not suited to the situation in Portugal and Spain, and also that Wellington's new tactics would prevent them from succeeding.

Second, the French armies were trained to "live off the land", and were very expert at it. But again, this did not work in the impoverished conditions of the Peninsula, which severely restricted their manoeuvrability.

Finally, and probably most important of all, their command and control system was as inadequate as Wellington's was efficient. They had no overall commander and therefore no coordinated policy; their communications were poor and constantly harassed by the guerrillas, and their intelligence system was non-existent.

The French soldiers fought gallantly and well throughout the campaign until the last few months, but they were very seldom given a real chance of getting the better of the Peninsular Army.

Notes

1   Confusingly, two or three battalions were on occasions grouped together and called a "Regiment".

Allied Commanders

Wellington never showed great confidence in his subordinate commanders, and was reluctant to give them much independence until the last year of the campaign.

As late as 1811 he wrote, "I am obliged to be everywhere, and if absent from any operation, something goes wrong."

They did improve markedly with experience under his command, and some of them commanded "corps" successfully during 1813 and 1814, but there was never any obvious successor to Wellington among them.

Notes on some of the leading Allied commanders may be of interest.

ALTEN, Major General Charles, (1764–1840)
A Hanoverian who served with the King's German Legion. Took over command of the Light Division on the death of Craufurd in 1812. Commanded a division at Waterloo.

BERESFORD, Major General William, (1764–1854)
A large, strong man, honest, inflexible and tough. Irish. A fine administrator, his great achievement was the organization and training of the Portuguese Army. He did not do so well in independent command at Albuera, but was trusted with independent commands in 1813 and 1814, and was largely responsible for victory at Toulouse.

BALLESTEROS, General Francisco, (1770–1832)
An Asturian who was prominent in the war in southern Spain. He objected to Wellington as Generalissimo in 1812 and was dismissed by the Cortes.

BLAKE, General Joachim, (1759–1827)
Of Irish descent. Commanded the Army of Galicia in 1808. Was replaced by La Romana. Fought in the south and east of Spain 1809–11. Captured at Valencia 1812.

CASTANOS, General Francisco, Duke of Baylen, (1756–1852)
Won the Battle of Baylen 1808, but was defeated at Tudela the same year. Held administrative posts 1809–13. Was dismissed by the Cortes in 1813.

COLE, Lieutenant General Lowry, (1772–1842)
Commanded 4th Division 1810–14. A brave, capable subordinate commander. Saved the day at Albuera, but failed in an independent role at Roncesvalles. Wounded at Albuera and Salamanca.

CLINTON, Lieutenant General Henry, (1771–1829)
Was Adjutant General to Moore 1808–9. Commanded 6th Division from 1811 till 1814.

COTTON, Lieutenant General Stapleton, (1773–1865)
A fine cavalry general who commanded the Allied cavalry in 1809. Returned home in 1810, but returned to command the 1st Division and then the cavalry again, when they became a separate division in 1811. Was C-in-C at Horse Guards 1822–25. Became Lord Combermere in 1829.

CRAUFURD, Major General Robert, (1764–1812).
A brilliant infantry commander and an inspiring leader. Commanded the Light Brigade from 1809 and the Light Division in 1810 until he died of wounds at Ciudad Rodrigo in 1812. A thinking scientific soldier. He made enemies due to his quick temper and caustic tongue. Known as "Black Bob." But he was loved and admired by his men. "I do not think I ever admired any man who wore the British uniform more than I did General Craufurd," wrote Rifleman Harris.

DALHOUSIE, Lieutenant General George, 9th Earl, (1770–1838).
Joined the Peninsular Army in 1812 and commanded the 7th Division till 1814. A rather slow commander.

FREIRE, General Manuel, (1765–1834).
Commanded in Murcia and Granada 1810–12, and took over the Army of Galicia 1813. Won the Battle of San Marcial 1813.

GRAHAM, Lieutenant General Thomas, (1748–1843).
Joined the Army in 1794 at the age of 46. Was ADC to Moore at Corunna. Commanded the British garrison in Cadiz and won the fine victory at Barrosa in 1811. Commanded the left wing in the advance of 1813. Besieged San Sebastian in 1813. Had to return home with eye trouble after Bidassoa. A fine, fighting soldier. Later became Lord Lynedoch.

HILL, Lieutenant General Rowland, (1772–1842).
A exceptionally generous and humane commander, who was universally liked and respected, and widely known as "Daddy" Hill. Also a fine, bold commander, who could always be relied upon. He was one of the few to whom Wellington would entrust independent tasks with confidence. He commanded a brigade under Moore and served throughout the campaign. He commanded the right wing in 1813–14, and won a fine victory at St Pierre in 1813. Created a Baron in 1814. Was C-in-C at Horse Guards 1825–39.

HOPE, Lieutenant General John, 4th Earl of Hopetoun, (1785–1823).
A divisional commander at Corunna. Returned to the Peninsular Army 1813 to replace Graham. Commanded a division at Salamanca and the left wing at the Nivelle and Nive. Was captured during the Sortie from Bayonne in 1814.

LA ROMANA, General Pedro, Marquis of, (1761–1811).
Commanded Spanish "hostage" corps in Denmark 1807–8. Commanded Spanish forces in Galicia and supported Moore in 1809. Took over the "Army of the Left" in November 1809. Failed to save Seville in January 1810, but fought effectively in Portugal and Estramadura. Died of a heart attack while trying to relieve Badajoz in 1811.

LONGA, General Francisco, (1770–1831).
Began as a successful guerrilla leader and rose to command a division in the Spanish regular forces. Did well at San Marcial.

MOORE, Lieutenant General John, (1761–1809).
A fine soldier of the highest character. A Major General in 1798 and a Lieutenant General in 1805. Knighted 1804. An outstanding trainer of men, encouraging individuality and initiative for the first time, which led to the concept of the Light Division. Was mortally wounded at Corunna.

PAGET, Lieutenant General Edward, (1775–1849)
Fourth son of Lord Uxbridge. Served under Moore and commanded the Rearguard during the Retreat to Corunna and in final battle. Lost his right arm at Crossing of the Douro 1809. Returned to the Peninsula 1812. Was captured after Burgos.

PAGET, Major General Lord Henry, (1768–1854).
Eldest son of Lord Uxbridge. Commanded 7th Light Dragoons. An outstanding cavalry commander, who distinguished himself at Sahagun in 1808 and at the Retreat to Corunna. Became unpopular with Wellington in 1809 by eloping with his sister-in-law, but was accepted as Allied cavalry commander at Waterloo, where he lost a leg. Became Marquis of Anglesey in 1815.

PAKENHAM, Major General Edward, (1778–1815).
Was a brigade commander in 1810 and a Major General in 1811. Distinguished himself with 3rd Division at Salamanca and led 6th Division in 1813. Described by Wellington as "one of the best we have." Was sent to North America and was killed at New Orleans in 1815. Wellington married his sister Catherine in 1806.

PALAFOX, General Jose, Duke of Saragossa, (1780–1847)
The inspiring leader of the defence of Saragossa in 1808–9. Captured and remained a prisoner till 1814, after which he had a good military career.

PICTON, Lieutenant General Thomas. (1758–1815).
A tough, impetuous, unconventional Welshman. Wellington called him "... a rough, foul-mouthed devil ... with an astounding power of malediction." But he was a magnificent, front-line fighting commander, intrepid and extremely brave. Took command of 3rd Division in

1810. Was wounded at Badajoz, where he opened the way to success. Headstrong, but one of Wellington's best generals. Commanded 3rd Division again 1813–14, and was killed at Waterloo.

SANCHEZ, General Don Julian.
A fine Spanish guerrilla leader, whose mounted force later became regular cavalry in 1813. There is a memorial to him at Ciudad Rodrigo.

STEWART, Lieutenant General William, (1774–1827)
Commanded 2nd Division 1811–14. Always in trouble and Wellington said of him that "with the utmost zeal and good intentions and abilities, he cannot obey an order."

WELLESLEY, Sir Arthur, Duke of Wellington, (1769–1852).
Commissioned 1787. India 1797–1805. Copenhagen 1807. Lieutenant General and Commander in Portugal 1808. Commander in Peninsular War 1809–14. Waterloo 1815. C-in-C at Horse Guards 1827 and 1842–52. Prime Minister 1828–30.

French Commanders

BONAPARTE, Joseph, (1768–1844)
Brother of Napoleon. King of Naples 1806. King of Spain 1808–13. Sacked as C-in-C after Vitoria 1813. Benevolent ruler in Spain.

BONAPARTE, Napoleon, (1769–1821)
First Consul 1799. Emperor 1804–14. Exiled to Elba. Returned to France for Hundred Days, March–June 1815. Exiled to St Helena 1815–21.

CLAUSEL, General Bertrand, Count, (1772–1842)
Commanded "Army of Portugal" at Salamanca 1812. Commanded "Army of the North" under Soult 1813–14. Marshal 1831.

D'ERLON, General Jean-Baptiste, Count, (1765–1844)
Divisional general, 1803. Commanded IX Corps in Spain 1810. In Andalusia 1810–12. Commanded "Army of Portugal" in recapture of Madrid 1812, and "Army of the Centre" at Vitoria 1813. Corps Commander under Soult 1813–14 and at Waterloo. Marshal 1843.

JOURDAN, Marshal Jean Baptiste, Count, (1762–1833)
A private in the Royal army. Marshal 1804. Chief of Staff to King Joseph, 1809 and 1812–13. Sacked after Vitoria 1813.

JUNOT, General Jean, Duke of Abrantes, (1771–1813)
Led invasion of Portugal 1807. Signed Convention of Cintra. Commanded VIII, then III Corps in Spain, fighting at Saragossa. Commanded VIII Corps under Massena 1810–11. Left Peninsula after Fuentes de Onoro 1811, and served in Russia. Went insane and committed suicide 1813. Very brave, but irrational.

MARMONT, Marshal Auguste, Duke of Ragusa,(1774–1852)
A gunner. Divisional general 1800. Marshal 1809. Replaced Massena as Commander of "Army of Portugal" May 1811. Gravely wounded at Salamanca 1812. Served in Germany and France 1813–14. Went over to Bourbons 1814, thus originating the word *"raguser"* – to betray.

Better educated than most of Napoleon's Marshals, and resented Emperor's patronising attitude. Excellent administrator, but uncertain in battle.

MASSENA, Marshal Andre, Prince of Essling, (1758–1817)
Marshal 1804. Commanded 'Army of Portugal' 1810–11. One of Napoleon's most talented commanders, wily, bold and tenacious. Wellington said of him, "When Massena was opposed to me, I never slept comfortably'. But he failed at Busaco, in front of the lines of Torres Vedras and at Fuentas de Onoro, and was not given a key command again.

MURAT, Marshal Joachim, Prince and King of Naples, (1767–1815)
Fired the "whiff of grapeshot" on 13 Vendemiaire. Married Napoleon's sister, Caroline, in 1800.

Divisional general 1799. Marshal 1804. Prince 1805. An outstanding cavalry commander, extremely brave, with great tactical skill, but no strategic sense. Occupied Madrid 1808 and suppressed uprising on 2 May, 1808. Then retired on health grounds and replaced Joseph Bonaparte as King of Naples. Commanded the cavalry in Russia. Changed to Bourbons in 1814, and back to Napoleon in 1815, and was executed by the Bourbons.

NEY, Marshal Michel, Prince of the Moskowa, Duke of Elchingen, (1769–1815)
Divisional general 1799. Marshal 1804. Commanded VI Corps in Spain and Portugal 1805–11. Dismissed by Massena for insubordination 1811. Served in Russia (where he earned the title of "the bravest of the brave"), Germany, France and at Waterloo. Was shot by the Bourbons for treason in 1815.

An outstandingly brave soldier and inspiring leader. Extremely professional.

REILLE General Honoré Charles, Count, (1775–1860)
Divisional general 1806. To Spain 1808. Fought at Wagram 1809.

Commanded "Army of Portugal" October, 1812–July, 1813. Corps Commander under Soult 1813–14, and at Waterloo. Marshal 1847.

SOULT, Marshal Nicholas Jean de Dieu, Duke of Dalmatia, (1769–1851)
Enlisted 1785 as a private. Commissioned under Napoleon. Marshal 1804. Distinguished himself at Austerlitz 1805. Led pursuit of Moore to Corunna 1809. Defeated by Wellesley at Oporto in May, 1809, and at Albuera. Chief of Staff to King Joseph, then commanded in South Spain and re-occupied Madrid in 1812.

Appointed C-in-C in Spain and France after Vitoria 1813–14. Chief of Staff to Napoleon during the Hundred Days, and was banished by Bourbons till 1820. Minister of War 1830–34.

A brilliant strategist and organizer, but lacked the ability to win a battle. Wellington said of him, "He gets his troops to the battlefield, but then is not sure what to do with them."

SUCHET, Marshal Louis Gabriel, Duke of Albufera, (1720–1826)
Divisional general 1799. Served in Austria, Prussia, Poland and Spain 1805–9. In Spain 1808–14. Series of victories against Spaniards. Marshal 1811. In command in Catalonia 1813.

A rare combination of exceptional administrative and battlefield ability. It was said that "if Napoleon had had two Suchets, he would have captured and kept Spain."

VICTOR, Marshal Claude Victor-Perrin, Duke of Bellune, (1764–1841)
Divisional general 1797. Marshal 1807. Commanded I Corps in Spain 1808–11. Won at Espinosa (1808) and Medellin (1809) but defeated at Talavera and Barrosa. Served in Russia, Germany and France 1812–14.

A courageous commander, but did not get on with Napoleon. Supported Bourbons from 1814 and was Minister of War 1821–23.

British Regiments in the Peninsular War

CAVALRY   *Household Cavalry*

The Life Guards
The Royal Horse Guards

Dragoon Guards

3rd Prince of Wales's
4th Royal Irish
7th Princess Royal's

Dragoons

1st Royal
3rd King's Own
4th Queen's Own
7th Queen's Own Light Dragoons (Hussars)
9th Light Dragoons
10th Prince of Wales's Own Light Dragoons (Hussars)
11th Light Dragoons
12th Prince of Wales's Light Dragoons
13th Light Dragoons
14th Duchess of York's Own Light Dragoons
15th The King's Light Dragoons (Hussars)
16th The Queen's Light Dragoons
18th Light Dragoons (Hussars)
20th Light Dragoons
21st Light Dragoons
23rd Light Dragoons

Note: Titles are as at the time of the Peninsular War.

INFANTRY   *Foot Guards*

1st Bn. First Guards
3rd Bn. First Guards
1st Bn. Coldstream Guards
1st Bn. Third Guards

Regiments of the Line

3/1st Royal (Royal Scots in 1812)
1/2nd Queen's Royal
1/3rd East Kent (The Buffs)
1/4th King's Own
1/5th Northumberland
2/5th Northumberland
1/6th 1st Warwickshire
1/7th Royal Fusiliers
2/7th Royal Fusiliers
1/9th East Norfolk
2/9th East Norfolk
1/11th North Devon
1/14th Bedfordshire (Buckinghamshire in 1809)
1/20th East Devonshire
1/23rd Royal Welch Fusiliers
2/24th 2nd Warwickshire
1/26th Cameronian
3/27th Inniskilling
2/28th North Gloucestershire
1/29th Worcestershire
2/30th 1st Cambridgeshire
2/31st Huntingdonshire
1/32nd Cornwall
2/34th Cumberland
1/36th Herefordshire
1/38th 1st Staffordshire
2/38th 1st Staffordshire
2/39th Dorsetshire
1/40th 2nd Somersetshire
2/42nd Royal Highland (later The Black Watch)
1/43rd Monmouthshire (Light Infantry)
2/44th East Essex

1/45th Nottinghamshire
2/47th Lancashire
1/48th Northamptonshire
2/48th Northamptonshire
1/50th West Kent
1/51st 2nd Yorkshire West Riding (Light Infantry)
1/52nd Oxfordshire (Light Infantry)
2/53rd Shropshire
2/57th West Middlesex
2/58th Rutlandshire
2/59th 2nd Nottinghamshire
5/60th Royal American
1/61st South Gloucestershire
2/62nd Wiltshire
2/66th Berkshire
1/67th South Hampshire
1/68th Durham (Light Infantry)
1/71st Glasgow Highland (Light Infantry)
1/74th Highlanders
1/76th Foot
1/77th East Middlesex
1/79th Cameron Highlanders
1/81st Foot
1/82nd Prince of Wales's Volunteers
2/83rd Foot
2/84th York and Lancaster
1/85th Bucks Volunteers (Light Infantry)
2/87th Prince of Wales's Irish
1/88th Connaught Rangers
1/91st Foot (later Gordon Highlanders)
1/92nd Gordon Highlanders
1/95th Foot (Rifles)
2/95th Foot (Rifles)
3/95th Foot (Rifles)

Note: The first number is that of the Battalion and the second that of the Regiment; eg: 3/1st is the third Battalion of the First Regiment of Foot.

Index

Notes

This Index is intended as a guide to the text rather than as a source of references in itself. It therefore only includes names of places, individuals, units and events that not only appear in the text, but are important enough to warrant a mention.

All the 'Divisions' of the Peninsular Army and their commanders are listed, but not necessarily all 'Brigades' and 'Regiments'. The various Orders of Battle give details of all the major elements on both sides involved in the major battles.

Where units or individuals were involved in a battle, the reference in the index covers the whole battle, e.g. '154–63', even though they are not necessarily mentioned on every page.

'n' after a page number refers to a Note.

Index

Index

Index

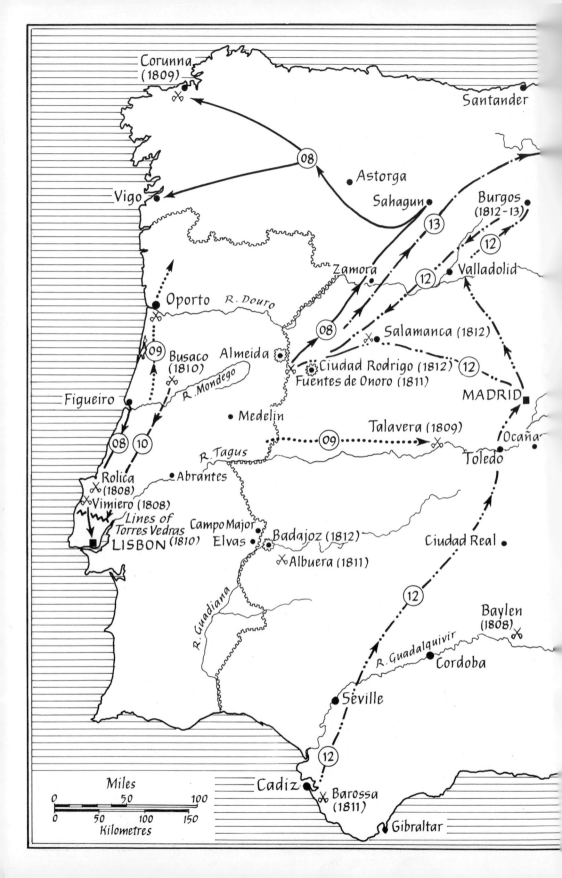

Corunna
(1809)

Santander

08

Astorga

Sahagun

Burgos
(1812–13)

13

12

Vigo

Zamora

12

Valladolid

Oporto   *R. Douro*

08

Busaco
(1810)

Almeida

Salamanca (1812)

12

Ciudad Rodrigo (1812)

Fuentes de Onoro (1811)

12

MADRID

Figueiro

R. Mondego

09

Medelin

Ocaña

08 10

R. Tagus

09

Talavera (1809)

Toledo

Rolica
(1808)

Abrantes

Vimiero (1808)

Lines of
Torres Vedras

Campo Major

Badajoz (1812)

Ciudad Real

LISBON (1810)

Elvas

Albuera (1811)

R. Guadiana

Baylen
(1808)

12

R. Guadalquivir

Cordoba

Seville

12

Miles

0   50   100

0   50   100   150

Kilometres

Cadiz

Barossa
(1811)

Gibraltar